REPRODUCTIVE POLITICS AND
THE MAKING OF MODERN INDIA

REPRODUCTIVE POLITICS AND THE MAKING OF MODERN INDIA

MYTHELI SREENIVAS

UNIVERSITY OF WASHINGTON PRESS

Seattle

Reproductive Politics and the Making of Modern India is freely available in an open access edition thanks to TOME (Toward an Open Monograph Ecosystem)—a collaboration of the Association of American Universities, the Association of University Presses, and the Association of Research Libraries— and the generous support of Ohio State University Libraries. Learn more at the TOME website, available at: openmonographs.org.

Composed in Minion Pro, typeface designed by Robert Slimbach

25 24 23 22 21   5 4 3 2 1

Printed and bound in the United States of America

UNIVERSITY OF WASHINGTON PRESS
uwapress.uw.edu

In South Asia, print copies of this book are available from Women Unlimited, 7/10, First Floor, Sarvapriya Vihar, New Delhi 110016.

LIBRARY OF CONGRESS CATALOGING-IN-PUBLICATION DATA
Names: Sreenivas, Mytheli, author.
Title: Reproductive politics and the making of modern India / Mytheli Sreenivas.
Description: Seattle : University of Washington Press, [2021] | Includes bibliographical
    references and index.
Identifiers: LCCN 2020053120 (print) | LCCN 2020053121 (ebook) | ISBN 9780295748832
    (hardcover) | ISBN 9780295748849 (paperback) | ISBN 9780295748856 (ebook)
Subjects: LCSH: Reproductive rights—India—History—19th century. | Families—
    India—History—19th century. | Marriage—India—History—19th century. | Birth
    control—India—History. | Economic development—India—History—19th century.
Classification: LCC HQ766.5.I4 S74 2021 (print) | LCC HQ766.5.I4 (ebook) |
    DDC 363.9/60954—dc23
LC record available at https://lccn.loc.gov/2020053120
LC ebook record available at https://lccn.loc.gov/2020053121

The paper used in this publication is acid free and meets the minimum requirements of American National Standard for Information Sciences—Permanence of Paper for Printed Library Materials, ANSI z39.48–1984.∞

CONTENTS

ACKNOWLEDGMENTS

During the years I spent writing this book, I have accrued many debts. Grants from the American Institute of Indian Studies, the National Endowment for the Humanities, and the Rockefeller Archive Center funded the research for this book. Support from Ohio State University, including in the form of research leaves and funding from the Departments of History and Women's, Gender, and Sexuality Studies helped to make research and writing possible. I have relied on the generosity of librarians and archivists in India, the US, and the UK. I especially want to thank G. Sundar at the Roja Muthiah Research Library for enabling me to work with material I never expected to find, and Bethany Antos at the Rockefeller Archive Center for her patience and diligence in securing images. I am grateful, as well, to all those who shared their oral histories as part of this project, and I thank Archana Venkatesh for conducting these interviews with such care and commitment. Research assistance from Adriane Brown and Haley Swenson was invaluable in the early stages of this project.

My research in India would have been impossible without the kindness and support of friends. I especially thank Jyoti Thottam for so generously welcoming our family to Delhi. I am grateful to Padmini and S. P. Venkateshan, and to Sharada and M. Ganeshan, for, as always, making Chennai home. Support from Naazneen (Munni) and Vishal helped to make work possible.

To write this book, I relied upon the intellectual generosity of many colleagues. As I began my research in Delhi, advice and support from Janaki Abraham, Charu Gupta, Janaki Nair, and Mohan Rao proved to be invaluable. I am also grateful to everyone who was willing to listen to me talk about the project, who commented on rough drafts and conference presentations, and who encouraged me to believe that this was, indeed, a book. My gratitude goes to Sanjam Ahluwalia, Srimati Basu, Indrani Chatterjee, Geraldine Forbes, Douglas Haynes, Pranav Jani, Robin Judd, Guisela Latorre, Thomas (Dodie) McDow, Durba Mitra, Rahul Nair, Shailaja Paik, Sumathi Ramaswamy, Barbara Ramusack, Haimanti Roy, Jennifer Siegel, Mrinalini Sinha, Birgitte Soland, Renae Sullivan, Ashwini Tambe, Mary

Thomas, Archana Venkatesh, and Judy Tzu-Chun Wu. I am grateful to the participants in the seminar "Women, Nation-Building, and Feminism in India," whose comments on my work helped me think through the 1950s, and postindependence historiography more generally. I especially thank Anjali Bhardwaj Datta and Uditi Sen for their insightful feedback. Susan Hartmann and Katherine Marino were kind enough to read the entire manuscript and provide their detailed feedback. I thank you so much for your insights, support, and generosity. Sarah Grey gave careful attention to my writing, for which I am deeply grateful. And finally, what a pleasure it has been to complete this book alongside my writing group friends and colleagues: Elizabeth Bond, Theodora Dragostinova, Tina Sessa, and Ying Zhang. Your work and commitments inspire my own.

In preparing the manuscript, I appreciate the support I have received from everyone at the University of Washington Press. Special thanks to Hanni Jalil for her patience in working through my questions, to Elizabeth Mathews for the careful copyediting, to Eileen Allen for the index, and to Larin McLaughlin for her editorial acumen and enduring interest in this book. I also thank the two anonymous readers of the manuscript for their generous and helpful advice. And closer to home, I thank Savita Jani and Meenakshi Jani for their invaluable bibliographic assistance.

This book would have looked different without my students at Ohio State. During the years I spent writing, my students, especially in courses on reproductive justice, South Asian history, and transnational feminisms, have pushed me to think in new directions, and to bring my research into dialogue with the here and now. I am truly grateful to each of them. My colleagues at OSU have fostered the spaces where this kind of thinking can happen. For creating such an energizing and hopeful workplace, my gratitude goes to current and former WGSS colleagues, especially Jill Bystydzienski, Lynaya Elliott, Elysse Jones, Jackson Stotlar, and Shannon Winnubst. My work has been sustained, as well, by the fierce feminist board and staff of Women Have Options. Thank you for pushing me to keep asking questions, even when they are not comfortable, and for continuing to expand the boundaries of reproductive justice in our community.

This book is, ultimately, about life—how it is measured and valued, and how this calculus shapes our society and politics. I write these acknowledgments in the midst of a global pandemic that has made these calculations even more explicit, in a push to reopen "the economy" regardless of its human cost. At this moment, when the lives of those most marginalized and vulnerable are made expendable in the pursuit of profit, the brave insistence that Black Lives Matter, both in the US and globally, is all the more inspiring in its call for a different world.

In closing, I wish to thank all those friends and family who remind me of the joy, hope, and possibility of life outside of a grim economic calculus. In the last stages of writing the book, I am full of gratitude for the friends who shared walks and socially distanced chats in parks and yards, for all those on the cousins Zoom calls, the support and solidarity chats, and the virtual family get-togethers that enlivened the days of quarantine. I thank family near and far, especially Vandana and Mahendra Jani, for their affection and support these many years. My parents, Nagarathna and Venkatachala Sreenivas, make all things possible, and I am deeply grateful for all they have given me. I am not sure that Meenakshi and Savita remember a time when I was *not* working on this book, and in the many years it has taken me to write it, they have grown into the kind of inquisitive and thoughtful readers I would be grateful to have. Your optimism, kindness, and commitments to justice give me hope even in the darkest of times, because they remind me to turn on the light. Finally, my enduring gratitude to Pranav, whose companionship and love has sustained this book, as it has my life.

REPRODUCTIVE POLITICS AND
THE MAKING OF MODERN INDIA

INTRODUCTION

ON NOVEMBER 24, 1952, HUNDREDS OF DELEGATES AND OBSERV-
ers gathered at the Sir Cowasji Jehangir Hall in Bombay to inaugurate a
conference of the International Committee for Planned Parenthood (ICPP).
The crowd exceeded the expectations of the organizers, who had been
unsure of the interest that the event—the first of its kind in independent
India—might generate. The main auditorium was soon overflowing, attendees jostled for space in the standing-room-only balcony, and late arrivals
were turned away.[1] The first person to address this assembled Indian and
foreign audience was the venerable Kamaladevi Chattopadhyay. A founding member of the All India Women's Conference, a stalwart nationalist,
and former leader of the Congress Socialists, Chattopadhyay was a longtime
advocate for birth control. In her capacity as the chair of the conference
reception committee, she reiterated her support for contraception within a
broadly internationalist and anti-imperialist framework while calling upon
her audience to support the "sanctity attached to human life."[2] She then
introduced the main speaker of the day, Sarvepalli Radhakrishnan, a scholar
of comparative religion and philosophy who had become India's first vice
president earlier that year.

In a wide-ranging address, Radhakrishnan quoted Sanskrit texts to demonstrate that controlling birth was in line with indigenous Hindu-Indian
ideas and called for family planning as a vital national need to combat poverty. "The poorer we are," Radhakrishnan argued, "the more ill-nourished
we are. Sex is the only indoor sport open to us, and large families are produced." Since the country could no longer sustain such large families, he
concluded, "our need is desperate" to find methods of controlling reproduction.[3] With these words, Radhakrishnan inaugurated the conference and
was met by a standing ovation from the audience.[4] Several days later, at the
conclusion of conference proceedings, delegates reassembled and voted to
create the International Planned Parenthood Federation (IPPF), a group that
would soon become one of the largest and most influential organizations

in the fields of contraceptive advocacy, family planning, and population control anywhere in the world.[5]

The achievements of the Bombay conference may have come as some surprise to the leadership of the Family Planning Association of India (FPAI), which had hosted the event. The president of the organization, Dhanvanthi Rama Rau, had been excited to receive an invitation from the American birth control advocate Margaret Sanger to hold the conference in India.[6] While welcoming the opportunity to forge transnational connections, Rama Rau and other FPAI leaders were concerned that the organization was too new—and the issue itself too novel—to raise sufficient support for an international conference. It was difficult to bring family planning to public attention, Rama Rau later recalled, because people were hesitant to discuss issues of reproduction and sexuality. The Indian government had not yet committed its support to family planning, and Health Minister Rajkumari Amrit Kaur, a Gandhian and veteran nationalist, was opposed to "artificial" modes of contraception. Nevertheless, Rama Rau saw in the early 1950s a new opening. "Family planning was a new and controversial subject for the general public," she acknowledged, "but the close relationship of population to the development of the country's economic resources had been so emphasized" that the question of reproductive regulation could no longer be ignored.[7] In other words, Rama Rau aimed to make reproduction a question of public discussion as part of a broader discourse on population and economy. The growing population of India and its supposed national economic impact could bring reproduction to the forefront of debate and policy-making.

Rama Rau understood the Bombay conference, which brought together Indian and foreign birth control advocates to develop a global population agenda, to be a pivotal moment in this process. The year 1952 was monumental for another reason as well. In its First Five Year Plan, which began that year, the Indian government allocated funds for family planning in order to "stabilize population at a level consistent with the requirements of national economy," thus making the country the first in the world to launch a program of state-sponsored population control.[8] However, while the plan marked a notable realignment of reproduction, population, and economy with the goals of the postcolonial Indian state, there was a much longer history to these connections as well. Despite Rama Rau's concern that reproduction was too sensitive a topic for public discussion in the 1950s, people had in fact engaged in public debate about a variety of reproductive norms and practices for decades. Over the course of the nineteenth and twentieth centuries, colonial administrators alongside Indian nationalists, eugenicists alongside feminists, and demographers alongside family planners had all questioned reproduction in a variety of ways. They asked, for instance, how individuals' ages at marriage might affect their health and the vitality of the population. They debated about how many children married couples ought to have and how to raise them. They interrogated existing sexual practices and asked what might constitute a modern and Indian (hetero)sexuality. They challenged social norms about remarriage, monogamy, and celibacy and examined the impact of these practices on individual bodies, families, and wider communities. The result was the wide-ranging, complex, and sometimes contradictory reproductive politics that forms the subject of this book.

The question of reproduction in modern India was thus not limited solely to biological processes but became a place to work out the relationships that linked biological life to historical change. To trace this history, I focus on two key concepts that animated reproductive politics at the Bombay conference but also reverberated across the decades: population and economy. As we shall see, reproduction became a public question—that is, it acquired a politics—beginning in the late nineteenth century, in relation to anxieties about the size of India's population. Reforming individual reproduction, via changing marriage practices or introducing birth control, became a means to shape the life of the population as a whole. In other words, reformers promised to curb the growth of the population and to improve its health and eugenic "quality" through intervening in reproductive sexualities. As concerns grew about Indian "overpopulation" in the mid-twentieth century, these reproductive interventions intensified in state-led campaigns for population control. However, while the state's campaigns may represent the most obvious and well-known example of the intersections between reproduction and population, this book documents a much longer genealogy of their connections. By historicizing population control more deeply in time, I suggest that the ideologies and institutions that encouraged the Indian government to intervene in the reproductive lives of its subjects were not mid-twentieth-century inventions but arose from a nexus of population and reproduction that first took shape in colonial India.

These anxieties about population, in turn, led many to argue that reproductive reform was a vital economic question. Radhakrishnan's inaugural address in Bombay amplified this long-standing argument, suggesting that curbing Indian reproduction would enable the population to align with the country's economic needs. As reproduction was rendered into a category whose value and meaning were thus understood in economic terms, reproductive practices became suffused with claims about their macroeconomic benefits and costs. Within a wide range of public discourse, suggested reforms to sexuality, marriage, and childbearing were explained and justified within economic frameworks. Reproductive reformers began to represent individual reproductive practices as either an economic opportunity or a threat to progress, prosperity, and development. When reproduction was thus situated on an economic grid, life itself was calibrated against the costs of its subsistence; the value of lives born or "births averted" was measured in terms of their impact on "the economy." Borrowing from Michelle Murphy's conceptualization of the economization of life, I term this dense entanglement of reproduction and economy a process of *economizing reproduction*, whereby economic calculations saturated processes of biological reproduction, in the process transforming bodies and lives, sexualities and sentiments.[9]

The book traces these histories from the 1870s to the 1970s, asking how biological reproduction—as a process of reproducing human life—became central to reproducing a modern India. My analysis brings together three histories that have often remained distinct within existing scholarship: histories of marriage and birth control, of ideas of "population" and "economy" as abstractions, and of famine and crises of subsistence. The book begins its narrative during a period of British imperial consolidation in India, when I locate the emergence of new ideas linking reproduction, population, and economy in the context of massive famines that devastated lives across the subcontinent. Although the existing historiography of reproduction has paid little attention to these nineteenth-century developments, focusing instead on the interwar period, pushing the chronology back to the 1870s makes clear the enduring relationship between the politics of reproduction and the political economy of empire.[10] In other words, I argue, the contours of Indian reproductive politics took shape alongside processes of imperial consolidation. The book then turns to new forms of nationalist reproductive politics, which engaged questions of land and migration alongside anxieties about gender and bodies during the last decades of colonial rule. These national politics of reproduction took new shape in the aftermath of independence and partition, with the emergence of state-led population planning and increasingly intensive regulation of reproduction to meet the needs of national economic development. The historical narrative concludes with the massive expansion of population control during the 1960s and with the years of Emergency rule under Indira Gandhi from 1975

to 1977. The draconian policies of the Emergency years have been represented, and rightfully so, as a watershed moment in postcolonial Indian
history. However, as a longer view makes clear, Emergency-era population
policy was also deeply embedded in the reproductive politics of earlier
decades, and its ideologies and assumptions have carried on well beyond
1977.

The book demonstrates that, across a century, historical actors of varying political stripes used a flawed narrative about population and economy
to justify interventions into people's reproductive bodies and lives. This narrative emerges in both expected and unexpected places. I find it, for
instance, in the words of Malthusian colonial administrators explaining
why it was important to limit aid for famine relief, or among postcolonial
bureaucrats aiming to meet state-assigned targets for controlling population. However, I also locate this narrative in less expected places, including
in the words and actions of activists in the women's movement, who claimed
that family planning was a critical part of national planning. Women like
Dhanvanthi Rama Rau and Kamaladevi Chattopadhyay, alongside numerous others who implemented family planning programs, positioned their
work as a service both to women, whose contraceptive use would improve
their health and well-being, and to the nation, which could meet its economic development goals by curbing population growth. They thus insisted
that controlling population was a key component of their activism on behalf
of women. This early alignment of feminism and family planning might
seem surprising, since the Indian government's family planning programs
would eventually sacrifice women's bodies and reproductive autonomy in
favor of a relentless drive to meet population targets. In fact, contemporary
feminist activists have documented these programs' violations of women's
rights.[11] However, across the middle decades of the twentieth century,
middle-class and upper-caste activists in the women's movement were
among India's most committed family planners, and they positioned reproductive control as an important part of their political commitments. The
book traces the historical conjunctures and complicities that prompted feminists to connect reproduction to population and economy in this way, and
its implications for regimes of population control and development.

While focused on colonial and postcolonial India, the book also demonstrates that India was central to a global history of reproduction. Beginning with a set of imperial circulations between India and Britain, I consider
India's presence within a wider transnational network of feminists, Malthusians, eugenicists, and family planners, which, as in the case of the Bombay

conference, extended across many parts of the world. My focus on India within these networks complicates existing historical scholarship on global or transnational population control, which, although including India and Indians in important ways, tends to recenter Europe and the United States as the drivers of historical change.[12] My point here is not simply that "India" was a national space upon which "global" forces operated. Rather, I demonstrate how Indian developments transformed the "global," and helped to produce the very grounds over which reproduction was called into question in the modern world.

This India-in-the-world approach draws upon recent feminist scholarship, which traces historical change across transnational encounters, suggesting that "Indian" history is not easily separable from the broader world of which it is a part.[13] Moreover, "India" as a national space was reimagined during this time, and claims about population and economy shaped this imagination. Political boundaries in the subcontinent shifted during the decades examined here, most notably with the partitions in 1947 and 1971, and remain contested. Although I begin in colonial India, which included the territories that now constitute India, Pakistan, and Bangladesh, subsequent chapters focus only on Indian reproductive politics after independence. I hope the book may invite further research on reproductive histories in South Asia more broadly.[14]

Before turning to this history in the following chapters, I focus in the remainder of this introduction on the three key concepts that animate my analysis: reproduction, population, and economy. Of course, these terms are in wide popular use, and their meanings may seem to be obvious or self-evident. However, each concept also carries with it a history and, as I suggest here, these histories are deeply interconnected. In the sections that follow, I trace the meanings of these concepts as they took shape across the nineteenth and twentieth centuries and ask how—and with what implications—these meanings continue to shape popular understanding and academic scholarship. These sections on reproduction, population, and economy thus develop the conceptual framework of the book and suggest the theoretical interventions that a feminist history of reproduction may make to the historiography of India in the modern world.

Reproduction

Reproduction, as Sarah Hodges reminds us, is "always simultaneously a physiological as well as social act," and its meanings rely on this "slippage between society and biology."[15] We may trace the history of reproduction by investigating the social meanings that adhere to biological acts, even as we consider how social norms and practices construct reproduction as a biological category. In developing this historical perspective, the book draws inspiration from Linda Gordon's insistence that reproduction is not transhistorical but is embedded in, and contributes to, historical change. She argues that "in different historical periods there are specifiable hegemonic and resistant meanings and purposes to reproduction control; that these meanings are socially and politically, not individually, constituted; and that they express the (unstable) balances of political power between different social groups."[16] While people have aimed to control their own reproduction across time, in other words, their reasons and means for doing so have not remained static. The values associated with reproductive behaviors, the assumptions about which bodies and lives may be "appropriate" to reproduce, and the laws and norms governing reproductive practices have all changed over time—responding to and shaping a wide array of social, political, and economic relations.[17] Historians of reproduction have aimed to document these shifts, while asking how these changes might illuminate broader histories.

My work takes this historical approach to reproduction. The book investigates the wide implications of the politics of reproduction across the colonial/postcolonial divide and demonstrates that these politics shaped fundamental aspects of Indian life. This includes areas we might conventionally associate with reproduction, namely histories of gender, sexuality, and the body. However, investigating histories of reproduction can also take us in less expected directions. As I argue here, from the late nineteenth century onward, reproductive politics engaged claims about colonial poverty and scarcity, about the nation and its sovereignty, and about modern progress and development.[18] In short, Indians negotiated their present and imagined their futures through debates about reproductive norms and practices. Indeed, as we shall see in the pages to follow, attention to these histories makes clear the connections between the supposedly "private" domains of reproductive sexualities or reproducing bodies and the "public" arenas of nations and states. Therefore, through its investigation of reproduction, the book offers a reassessment of histories of gender, sexuality, and the body as they intersect with the trajectories of colonialism, nationalism, and development.

Specifically, I trace how these intersections rendered reproduction into an economic question—asking how reproductive discourses and practices were calibrated within a calculus that rendered life itself an economic cost. This process of economizing reproduction profoundly transformed how Indians understood their own reproductive practices, including marriage, childbearing, and contraceptive use. It also transformed how they understood "the economy": that is, how they measured poverty and wealth, inequality and hierarchy, sovereignty and national status. In short, as reproduction was figured as a point of intervention into the economy, both "reproduction" and "economy" shifted in complex, sometimes unexpected ways. To understand these changes, the book locates reproductive politics in a variety of places: some that addressed specific reproductive practices, others that brought reproduction to bear on a wider discourse. This includes the history of contraceptive advocacy and the rise of population control programs. It also includes moments and events that were less obviously connected to reproduction, such as the colonial administration of famine, the intersection of feminist activism with state-led development, and the representation of small families as a site of desire. Locating contests over reproduction in these disparate spaces, my work outlines the wide-ranging scope and impact of reproductive politics across a century of Indian history.

My arguments join with an emerging feminist historiography that tracks how reproduction has been a site to uphold, and also challenge, inequality and hierarchy and implicates the gendered politics of reproduction in the politics of race, class, caste, and sexuality. To take just a few examples, feminist historians have shown how control over women's reproduction has helped to maintain racist regimes of power, to underwrite colonial policies, to mark national boundaries, to regulate migration, to shape social welfare policies, and to influence international diplomacy.[19] Reproductive relations have thus also been relationships of power. Consequently, as Aiko Takeuchi-Demirci argues, "the knowledge and discourses regarding female reproduction have been socially constructed to justify hierarchical power relations: between men and women, Westerners and non-Westerners, whites and nonwhites, and the elites and the masses."[20] The centrality of reproduction to relationships of power is also made clear by scholarship in queer studies, which scrutinizes the production of heterosexuality and its marginalization of queer subjects. Reproduction, as scholars such as Judith Butler, Penelope Deutscher, and Lee Edelman suggest, was central to the creation and normalization of heterosexual identities; the queer was marked, by definition, as a nonreproductive subject who was not committed to the future, represented by the figure of the child.[21]

Historicizing reproduction thus requires attention to the multiple inter-sections that link individual reproducing bodies to the reproduction of a wider body politic, and that connect systems of reproduction to wider systems of power. A rich scholarship has documented these connections across varying times and places, tracing the contours of reproductive oppression alongside struggles for reproductive autonomy, freedom, and justice. Much of this work uncovers how the regulation and control of reproduction sustains hierarchies whereby some people's reproduction is valued and that of others is devalued. The sociologist Shellee Colen, in a study of West Indian childcare workers in New York City, terms this a process of "stratified repro-duction" or "the power relations by which some categories of people are empowered to nurture and reproduce, while others are disempowered."[22] This selective valuing of certain people and bodies as reproducers has been the crux of reproductive oppressions of various kinds. For example, in the Indian case, the reproduction of lower-caste, poor, and non-Hindu women was marked as the source of colonial poverty and blamed for the failures of postcolonial economic development. Within transnational population con-trol movements, the childbearing of black and brown women—both in the "Third World" and among racial minorities in the "First World"—was held responsible for putting the very planet at risk through a population explo-sion. These are just a few examples, among many, that suggest how repro-duction intersects with sites of inequality and oppression, differentiating among people as appropriate or inappropriate reproducers.

This approach to reproduction necessarily challenges the liberal femi-nist assumption, common in public discourse, that the trajectory of repro-ductive history can be encapsulated as a "simple passage from subjection to freedom."[23] That is, there was no straightforward path from a lack of reproductive control in the past toward greater autonomy in the present due to changing sexual norms or more effective reproductive technologies. The history of reproduction is simply too complex for such a trajectory. The ideas and practices that shape people's reproductive lives cannot be abstracted out from their wider histories, and reproductive politics can just as easily main-tain inequalities and injustices as challenge them. Moreover, even while the narratives of greater freedom may hold true for some people—especially elite women in the "First World" or Global North—a wealth of scholarship on both the past and the present shows that gains for some people have often occurred at the expense of others and that technological developments do not automatically expand reproductive freedoms.

Scholars of South Asian reproduction history make this point abundantly clear. Perhaps this is because, following Hodges, "unlike the American or European historiography of birth control, the uneasy legacy of population control is not part of any emancipatory narrative."[24] The measures undertaken by the postcolonial state to control women's reproduction offer a cautionary tale against assumptions that contraceptive technologies or reproductive reforms are necessarily liberating. The grim history of Emergency rule connects reproductive regulation to antidemocratic and authoritarian politics while challenging any simplistic narrative about progress over time. Historians of colonial India also testify to this complexity, pointing out that support for reproductive technologies did not necessarily signify support for reproductive freedoms. For instance, as Sanjam Ahluwalia maintains in her study of birth control in the early twentieth century, "within the dominant feminist understanding, birth control and contraceptive technologies are largely represented as necessarily empowering for all women at all times. The history of birth control in colonial India, however, did not empower all women to control their bodies and determine their fertility."[25] Moreover, as Asha Nadkarni notes, even movements claiming to support "reproductive rights" have "been aligned with far less emancipatory discourses" of racism and imperialism, and have sometimes deepened caste, race, gender, and class inequalities rather than challenging them.[26] These are difficult and disturbing histories that feminist scholars must grapple with if we are to imagine more just reproductive futures.

Despite these grim histories, however, not all reproductive politics prior to the 1960s was a prehistory of population control, a term that references top-down policies and programs to limit the growth of population. In the Indian case, this term was often used interchangeably with *family planning*, which, at least ostensibly, refers to the policies that support individual people in determining their own fertility. The collapse of these two terms—including at the Bombay conference that created the IPPF—should not obscure the fact that not all programs to support individual decision-making about fertility were necessarily a means to regulate population.[27] Indeed, scholarship on colonial India documents a history that was at once more complex and multilayered, offering multiple possibilities for change. Not all campaigns promoting reproductive reform centered on controlling population, and not all reproductive politics centered only on changing marriage or implementing birth control. The book thus understands reproduction broadly, and not only as a history of contraceptive technologies or population regulation.

To build this analysis, I draw upon an existing historiography, which, although it does not necessarily name reproduction as a category of analysis, has touched on reproductive questions. For instance, scholars have documented how colonial-era reproductive reforms—to the practices of sati, widow remarriage, child marriage—were critical to fashioning a modern gendered and sexual politics in the nineteenth century.[28] By the 1920s and 1930s, moreover, reproduction became discursively central both to Indian nationalism and to the Indian women's movement, as practices of birth control, childbirth, and reproductive healthcare were newly politicized. During the same period, as I discuss in more detail in chapter 2, reproductive politics also became entangled in a politics of land, migration, and sovereignty as a global "color line" made reproduction a key rationale in the separation of white and nonwhite races. Meanwhile, across the twentieth century, the reform of reproductive practices surrounding marriage, family life, and patrilineality was critical to the construction of modern subjectivities.[29] These are just a few examples of topics that might be included in histories of reproduction in modern India; they point toward a narrative that acknowledges, but cannot be collapsed into, a history of postcolonial population control. While space limitations prevent my addressing all of these topics, the book aims to make this expansive history more visible.

Finally, in developing this perspective on reproductive history, I draw inspiration from scholarly and activist understandings of reproductive justice as a politics of liberation. Concepts of reproductive justice, as first developed by women of color activists in a US context, aim to expand the terrain of political struggle beyond the dominating framework of abortion and to contest a range of hierarchies and forms of oppression that curtailed reproductive freedom. As articulated by Loretta Ross and Rickie Solinger, reproductive justice rests on three principles: "(1) the right *not* to have a child; (2) the right to *have* a child; and (3) the right to *parent* children in safe and healthy environments. In addition, reproductive justice demands sexual autonomy and gender freedom for every human being."[30] By such a measure, much of the history recounted in this book may read as a dispiriting account of reproductive *injustice*, whereby people's reproductive lives were subjected to ever-more-intimate forms of oppression as reproduction was economized and population control became a dominant mode of reproductive politics. Nevertheless, I highlight a reproductive justice frame for its consistent reminder that reproduction is always about gender (and gendered forms of oppression and liberation) but is never only limited to a gendered politics. Reproductive justice compels an investigation of intersecting axes of difference but, equally importantly, calls attention to how reproductive oppression and liberation are deeply implicated in wider histories. Finally, I suggest that reproductive justice cannot be envisioned solely in relation to a single intervention—be it birth control, abortion, or population control—but must situate the impact and possibilities of these interventions within a deep analysis of inequality and oppression.

Population

Population, according to its *Merriam-Webster* dictionary definition, refers to the "whole number of people or inhabitants in a country or region," as well as "the organisms inhabiting a particular locality." Bringing in reproduction, the definition also names the "group of interbreeding organisms" as constituting a population.[31] It links aggregate life (numbers of people or organisms) to identifiable place (country, locality) and to reproductive process ("interbreeding"). In this sense, "population" is a measurable, concrete, and bounded thing; we observe populations of bacteria in a petri dish, fish in a lake, or people on the planet. We measure population densities—how many organisms exist in relation to their bounded space—and its increase or decrease. However, while population thus has concrete manifestations, it is also an idea, a categorization, and a way of imagining and understanding the world. In this sense, "the population" is an abstraction, produced through identifiable modes of thought and habits of classification. This concept of the population as an entity whose life can be measured, regulated, and compared with other populations underpins what Michel Foucault identifies as a "biopolitics of the population." The reproductive politics I examine in this book were an aspect of this biopolitics—this management of the life of populations.

Foucault traces the history of biopolitics to seventeenth- and eighteenth-century Europe, when new forms of biopower challenged older notions of sovereign power. Within mercantilist regimes of sovereign power, the population was imagined as a group of juridical subjects who held an individual and collective relationship with the sovereign. A large population might indicate the power of the ruler, since many people might allow for the mobilization of a large army or signal a thriving marketplace.[32] By contrast, *biopower*, which Foucault links to the rise of a capitalist modernity, understood the population not as a group of individuals but as a species body, or the "body imbued with the mechanics of life, and serving as the basis of the biological process."[33] Population became a set of processes to be managed—processes of birth and death, of health and disease, of life itself.

This politics of life, or *biopolitics*, as Asha Nadkarni suggests, prompted the "birth of population as a political actor in its own right."[34] Reproduction became a key point of entry to manage this newly constituted population. By regulating the "anatamo-politics of the human body," in Foucault's terms, reproductive reform became a site to intervene in the "species body" of the population.[35] This centrality of reproduction shaped how biopolitics was gendered. As Ruth Miller argues through a case study of abortion and adultery in the Ottoman Empire and Turkey, biopolitical power was founded on "the right to make live rather than the right to take life." It rooted women's political subjectivities in their presumed capacity to reproduce life—to make live—and thus create the population. Consequently, biopolitical regimes aimed to include in the space of politics not only the public square, but also the womb, justifying their reproductive interventions in terms of "the common good."[36] Twentieth-century programs of population control, as several scholars suggest, were quintessential examples of this gendered Foucaultdian biopolitics.[37] Targeting individual bodies at the most intimate level—through surgical sterilization, intrauterine device (IUD) insertion, or menstrual cycle monitoring, for instance—these programs invoked as their rationale the "species body" of the population as a whole.

This notion of the population depended upon a process of disindividuation: that is, it de-emphasized the individual characteristics of people in favor of norms and processes that shaped the life of the population as a whole. However, the biopolitics of population also differentiated among people, marked out social margins, and valued some lives and bodies over others. Within an imperial world, race became a central axis of difference that distinguished the life processes of one "population" from that of another and enabled a "politics of life" in which some bodies were devalued and rendered suitable for death.[38] Moreover, whereas all biopolitics pathologized the social margins, scholars suggest that "colonial biopolitics" pathologized entire populations, rendering the "native" outside the boundaries of the normative "population."[39] In the aftermath of colonial rule, indigenous elites countered these racist underpinnings of population discourse while repositioning themselves as the appropriate regulators of their "own" lower-class, lower-caste, or subaltern populations. Their drives for economic development depended upon a biopolitics of the population in which life processes became the site of state intervention.

The eighteenth-century English political economist Thomas Malthus must loom large in any historical account of these biopolitics of population. Malthus, perhaps more than any other thinker of his time, gave life to the concept of "the population" and articulated its relationship to place, reproduction, and economy. In his enormously influential *Essay on the Principle of Population* (1798), Malthus argued that human population would always overrun its means of subsistence. This was because human reproduction proceeded "geometrically" (as in 2, 4, 8, 16), whereas food production increased only "arithmetically" (as in 1, 2, 3, 4). The result of this imbalance was a continual struggle for land, a finite and limited resource. The rapid growth of human population thus always threatened to exceed the available land. For Malthus, the reason the population had not already overrun the land was due to both "positive" and "preventive" checks on its growth. "Positive" checks increased death rates; they included war, disease, infanticide, pestilence, and famine. "Preventive" checks, on the other hand, controlled reproduction to reduce birth rates. Late marriage or sexual abstinence were the principal preventive checks Malthus outlined; he disapproved of contraception.[40]

Malthusian ideas proved to be remarkably enduring both in India and globally and have formed the common sense of modern thinking about the relationship between population and reproduction. In late nineteenth-century India, as I discuss in chapter 1, Malthusian theories seemed to explain famine, which some commentators understood as a "positive check" on an Indian population whose "overreproduction" had caused widespread poverty and hunger. This prompted fears that India was overpopulated well before there was any demonstrable increase in population size. Malthusian claims about population continued into the twentieth century, when they joined with eugenic thinking, which was widely accepted as the "science" of improving the genetic and racial characteristics of populations. Malthusianism and eugenics enjoyed a particularly close relationship in India, where, as Rahul Nair suggests, they shaped a growing "population anxiety" during the interwar decades.[41] This period also witnessed the emergence of communal discourses on population, whereby "Hindu" and "Muslim" populations were imagined as distinct entities and compared with each other. Indeed, claims about population came to underpin a growing communalization of Indian politics overall, especially in the Hindi-speaking north and in Bengal, where proponents of communal discourse aimed to mobilize "Hindus" or "Muslims" in census counts and claimed that the "opposing" community was reproducing more rapidly than their own.[42] The partition of the subcontinent in 1947, which depended upon Hindu and Muslim population counts, both drew upon and reshaped this kind of communal demography.

In the aftermath of Indian independence and World War II, Malthusian thinking reemerged through social-scientific research about the population. In particular, the science of demography, a discipline devoted to the study of populations, arguably has Malthusian roots.[43] However, whereas Malthus had understood population growth as a grim inevitability, periodically checked by famine and disease, mid-twentieth-century demographic models insisted that population growth could be managed through targeted interventions. Far exceeding the *Essay*'s suggestions about forgoing sexual intercourse and postponing marriage, demographers imagined a range of policies and tactics that might encourage populations to limit their reproduction. Their models, in turn, gave shape to population control programs that began in India, and elsewhere in Asia, Africa, and Latin America during the 1950s, 1960s, and 1970s. As Mohan Rao documents in devastating detail, Malthusian assumptions underpinned Indian campaigns to manage population, and regimes of population control adhered to these theories despite mounting evidence about their damaging impact on individual lives, especially the lives of women.[44] In a brutal biopolitical calculation, as I discuss in chapter 4, some individual lives were curtailed or sacrificed in pursuit of benefit to the "species body" of the population. As individual life was valued differentially—along lines of caste, race, nationality, gender, class, and religion—population control programs became increasingly draconian in meeting their goals and targets.

Of course, Malthusian ideas have also been challenged by critics, who suggest that Malthus's theory of population simply blames poor people's reproduction for their poverty. This way of thinking, they argue, serves to obscure the true causes of inequality and misunderstands the reasons for population growth. One of Malthus's early and influential critics along these lines was Karl Marx; since the mid-nineteenth century, Marxist critiques of Malthus have argued that poverty is not caused by poor people having "too many" children but by an inequitable distribution of wealth due to the exploitation of labor within systems of capitalist production. Building from this critique, more recent challenges to Malthusianism have documented its empirical inadequacies. As they note, Malthus never foresaw the massive increases of agrarian production that could support much larger populations than he imagined.[45] Consequently, the balance between resources and population was not quite as fragile as Malthus suggested. Moreover,

human beings do not simply reproduce ad infinitum but make childbearing decisions in relation to the circumstances around them. Far from exacerbating poverty, bearing many children may actually *increase* economic
security for some rural families and communities by providing necessary
labor and support in old age.[46] Further, as Betsy Hartmann suggests, Malthusian thinking has historically carried with it a racist and sexist disregard for variously "othered" populations—such as poor people in formerly
colonized countries and racial and ethnic minorities in the former imperialist nations.[47] Here again, the issue is of inequality and stratification rather
than numerical growth in population. All this is not to say that population
size is immaterial. Rapid growth or decline in population can have important impacts on individuals, communities, and environments. Numbers *do*
matter, in other words, but we can draw no straight Malthusian line from
population to poverty. Numbers alone can be only part of the story.

Despite these critiques, the legacy of Malthus continues to shape thinking about population today. Although the sustained activism of feminist
groups has successfully eliminated the term *population control* in favor of
a focus on "reproductive health," Hartmann notes that "the belief that over-
population is a root cause of poverty, environmental degradation, resource
scarcity, migration, violent conflict, and even climate change is pervasive."[48]
Indeed, Malthusian fears about the unmanaged growth of population have
gained new life in contemporary climate change debates, as some environmental activists call for reducing fertility as a means to reduce carbon emissions globally. As I discuss in the epilogue, environmentalist critics of
Malthusianism have questioned this connection between reproduction and
climate through documenting that unequal patterns of consumption, driven
by a fossil fuel economy, are far more responsible for climate change than is
population increase in the Global South. Despite this evidence, the notion
that reproduction is a central driver of planetary catastrophe—an idea that
motivated so many population control campaigns in the mid-twentieth
century—remains powerful many decades later. In India in recent years,
moreover, these discourses have combined with an ongoing communalization of population to fuel a majoritarian Hindu nationalist politics, thus
recentering population in a wide range of claims about contemporary
India.[49]

My work is indebted to these scholarly and activist critiques of Malthusian population politics and to the analysis of modern biopolitics more
broadly. From Foucauldian investigation of population as a target of governance, to empirical critiques of Malthusian theory, to historical research

on the communalization of population, to feminists' emphasis on the real and devastating consequences of population control for ordinary people, this body of work makes visible the ways in which "population" is never just a number that exists independent of a wider history. In other words, colonial and postcolonial anxieties about population in India were not simply a result of population growth. Rather, various historical conjunctures— from ideas about population size to the material impact of scarcity and hunger—rendered "population" into a problem and made it the target of control, management, and intervention. This historicized understanding of population underpins my analysis of reproduction. Without assuming that reproductive anxieties were an automatic outcome of population numbers, I approach them as a particular set of political questions that engaged specific relationships of power within colonial and postcolonial society. The book traces these political questions—these biopolitics of population management—across landscapes of famine and scarcity, of imperial economies and national development, and of bodily and sexual politics.

Economy

In India during the nineteenth and twentieth centuries, biopolitical concerns about reproduction and population hinged on claims about the economy, and the reproductive practices of ordinary Indians were blamed for population growth and consequent economic failures. However, even though contemporary commentators insisted that reproduction thus affected the economy, historical research shows that "the economy" is not a transhistorical object "out there" that exists prior to its analysis. Whether in colonial India or in our contemporary moment, "the economy" has been brought into being through a set of identifiable historical practices, discursive representations, and theoretical claims. This requires a delineation of "the economy" as distinct from an implied noneconomy of relationships and interactions that are then rendered outside of economic rationality or calculation. In broad terms, it has meant a separation of certain market-based transactions from other social, political, moral, or material relationships. Moreover, "the economy" is constructed through techniques of measurement and calculation, such that the generation and organization of data helps to produce "the economy" as a knowable entity—indeed, as a way of knowing the modern world itself.

As a category of the imagination—and buttressed by ever-growing reams of data—the economy, of course, has real material effects. How we measure "the economy" shapes who and what gets counted, what policies exist and can be imagined, and how we understand life and well-being. Among these myriad effects of constructing the economy as a category of life in modern India was the rearticulation of reproduction to align with goals of economic progress and development. This process, as I outline in more detail below, was twofold. First, the creation of "the economy" in the eighteenth and nineteenth centuries excluded reproduction, gendering it private rather than public, particular rather than universal, and cultural rather than political. However, with the rise of anxieties about population in the late nineteenth century, reproduction reentered public and political debate. But this time, it was legible only as an economic cost, its "public" meanings limited to an economic calibration about reproducing the life of the population. In this sense, the process of economizing reproduction did not imply that reproductive practices were measured against an already existing economy; rather, reproduction and economy were co-constituted in a measurement of human life.

Historians trace the elaboration of "the economy" to the eighteenth-century Enlightenment, arguing that the creation of the concept was inseparable from the development of capitalism.[50] This notion of the economy, as Manu Goswami suggests, was a "concrete abstraction" that classical political economists imagined as "an autonomous, self-contained, and objective realm."[51] During the nineteenth century, the relatively deterritorialized conception of the classical political economists gave way to more specific spatial references. That is, as the "economy" became bound up with colonial and national space, both in Europe and in its empires, colonial administrators and Indian nationalists came to speak of an "Indian economy" as a distinct set of relations that circulated within a bounded territorial space.[52] However, the economy so imagined did not simply exist but was actively distinguished from other social relations. In colonial India, as Ritu Birla demonstrates, this act of delineation depended upon the colonial law, which distinguished between "legitimate" forms of capitalist economic activity it imagined to be universal and rooted in markets and "illegitimate ones," imagined as local, particular, and rooted in kinship. Birla argues that the category of "the economy" was demarcated against a separate arena of "culture" to produce "economy and culture as exclusive, a priori ethico-political arenas."[53]

Moreover, "the economy" was assumed to be public and thus a legitimate site of state governance; it was also universal, insofar as all countries "had" economies that could be compared with each other. Not coincidentally, this place-making function of the economy helped to make economic progress a centerpiece of the colonial civilizing mission. Colonial administrators thus claimed to be contributing to what they termed India's "moral and material" progress through British rule.[54] The economy simultaneously became an arena of nationalist contention, as thinkers like M. G. Ranade, R. C. Dutt, and Dadabhai Naoroji aimed to document that colonial rule had stifled India's path on a universalizing course of economic development. Their economic critique, exemplified by Naoroji's calculation of Indian per capita income and his comparison with British figures, would eventually become the ideological foundation of Indian nationalism's challenge to colonial rule. For nationalism as for colonialism, reference to the economy shaped what could be counted as public—and thus a legitimate terrain of nationalist contention with the colonial state—and what were rendered private cultural and social relations that were ostensibly separate from the public domain. Nationalist discourses depended and built upon these distinctions, such that a private sphere incorporating reproduction became a national counterpoint to a public sphere governed by the imperial state.[55]

The idea that "the economy" was a separate and distinct arena of life gathered force during the early decades of the twentieth century.[56] The new discipline of econometrics, alongside the conceptual invention of the "macroeconomy," helped to make the economy a target of state calculation and regulation.[57] Much of the data for these new calculations came from colonial contexts, notably from British India. For instance, John Maynard Keynes—the preeminent theorist of the macroeconomy—worked in the India Office and began his career by trying to measure the circulation of money and its effects on the Indian colonial economy, which he published as *Indian Currency and Finance* (1913). Keynes's articulation of the macroeconomy, as Suzanne Bergeron notes, "provides an early encounter with the idea that the nation is a manageable economic unit represented in terms of aggregate data."[58] Econometric measurements like the gross domestic product (GDP), first calculated in the US in 1937 and widely adopted by other countries after the Bretton Woods conference in 1944, came to encapsulate the idea that the nation and its economy could be represented by a single numeric figure.

In the aftermath of Indian independence, this relationship between nation and economy took new shape through the intervention of the postcolonial state. Jawaharlal Nehru and other Congress leaders staked the state's legitimacy upon its ability to foster economic growth and development, and state-led planning became the means to achieve this goal. The

National Planning Commission (NPC), a state agency responsible for creating the country's Five Year Plans, relied upon econometric measurement and such measures as GDP to mark the successes or failures of national development. In its First Five Year Plan in 1952, as noted above, the NPC included population as a key variable, arguing that it had to be aligned with the economic needs of the nation. Economic planning, in this sense, required and depended upon population planning, paving the way for state-directed programs to regulate reproduction in the service of population goals. The biopolitics of population management were thus part of the very architecture of the postcolonial economic planning regime.

Across this shifting discursive history of "the economy"—and its relationship to nation, state, and development planning—there was a foundational continuity: the separation of "the economy" from social relations that were then termed "noneconomic." In other words, identifying something called "the economy," measuring it, and intervening in it required a set of principles and assumptions about what exactly ought to be counted and who might do the counting. On the surface at least, reproduction appeared to be quintessentially "private" and outside these conceptualizations of the economy. After all, biological reproduction has long been gendered feminine and connected with sexuality, another intimate and ostensibly private domain. Moreover, although it was arguably central to capitalist economic growth, the labor associated with reproducing life—which Marxist feminists have since termed *social reproduction*—was not figured into the calculus of economic activity in its eighteenth-century origins, its nineteenth-century nationalist configurations, or its twentieth-century econometric elaboration.[59] The work of childcare, cooking, cleaning—typically unwaged work and generally performed by women—was not considered an "economic" activity and was thus excluded from such critical calculations as the GDP. Moreover, women's labor in agrarian production was similarly discounted in the calculations of mid-twentieth-century development economics and was left out of analysis of the costs and benefits of economic planning across the Global South.[60] As a result, the very concept of "the economy" was built upon the exclusion of reproductive labor, which remained unmeasured and unmarked, imagined as separate from economic life. A major task of feminist research has thus been to make this labor "count," whether it be the tasks of social reproduction, the work of subsistence agrarian production, or the gendered "care labor" that makes contemporary neoliberal globalization possible.

Historical analysis can contribute to this feminist project by investigating the co-constitution of "reproduction" with "the economy" over time. As I argue, once reproduction was rendered not part of the economy, it reentered economic discourse from the outside, as a set of practices and social relations that had the power to impinge upon the economy so constituted. By increasing (or decreasing) the population, reproduction could now foster or threaten economic development, raise or lower the GDP, and mark the distinction between poverty and prosperity. Reproduction, in short, would eventually become one point of intervention into an economy always marked as external to it. One of the clearest examples of this logic that I have encountered in the historical archive comes from Behramji Malabari's appeal in 1884 to the British colonial government to legislate on "infant and widow remarriage." As I discuss in more detail in chapter 1, Malabari acknowledged that a "foreign government" might hesitate to intervene in Indians' marriage practices, an arena already constituted as "private" and outside the ordinary domain of public debate and contestation. However, Malabari urged the colonial regime to reconsider this assumption, arguing that marriage in fact had a public aspect: its connection to the economy. The early age of marriage in India, he claimed, had promoted the increase of the country's population and the poverty of its inhabitants. As this was undoubtedly an "economic phase of the evil," Malabari suggested that this was a legitimate terrain of colonial lawmaking.[61] The public face of marriage and reproduction, in short, was at its point of intersection with the economy.

As we now live in a neoliberal age when the economization of everything is alternately deplored and celebrated, Malabari's comments may not seem so startling. Moreover, we have witnessed decades of population control programs that have rested on precisely this assumption that state intervention in processes of biological reproduction is justified in the name of economic growth and development. The book traces the long historical processes that have brought together reproduction, population, and economy in this way. In the pages that follow, I investigate a range of historical conjunctures and contingencies that shaped how reproduction came to be articulated in economic terms, as a force simultaneously outside the economy and integral to it. There was nothing inevitable about this process. Rather than documenting the slow unfolding of a hegemonic conception, the book studies contests over the meaning of reproduction, its connection to "population" and "economy," and its relationship to life itself.

Plan of the Book

The book traces these intertwined histories of reproduction and economy, population and development, bodies and sexualities, across a century. To tell this story, I rely on archival texts from a wide variety of sources ranged across three continents. Within colonial and postcolonial state archives, I ask how "reproduction" became defined and targeted for regulation. I locate the state's reproductive politics not only in its reports about marriage practices or birth control use, but also in dispatches about famine, inquiries about food production, and plans for agricultural and industrial development. By the mid-twentieth century, transnational donors and foundations aimed to shape, and sometimes implement, government policies. Their grant programs, scientific conferences, and propaganda are all part of the reproductive politics I consider here. The book also looks to a range of organizations, both large and small, that debated, reimagined, and reformed reproduction. Some focused explicitly on population and family planning, such as the Madras Neo-Malthusian League, or the Family Planning Association of India; others made reproduction part of other agendas, such as the All India Women's Conference, or the Self Respect movement. Beyond these organizational spaces, reproduction was also called into question within a wider public sphere of contraceptive manuals, self-help books, scholarly works, and newspaper editorials. With the institutionalization of population control after independence, the public sphere was saturated with state propaganda—film and radio broadcasts, alongside posters, billboards, and pamphlets—that constitutes part of the archive of reproductive politics.

Many of these sources come from the perspective of elite actors, and I do not assume that the nexus linking reproduction, population, and economy was a shared concern that cut across hierarchies of class, caste, religion, or gender. While reproductive politics as articulated by elites had outsize effects in the form of laws, policies, and programs, their targets of intervention did not necessarily share a common understanding of reproduction as a social question. Wherever possible, I aim to make visible alternative and competing perspectives. I find these alternatives in some unlikely places, such as in the actions of people in famine relief camps, in radical anticaste arguments for birth control, in debates about racialized migration laws, and in the questions that ordinary women raised when confronted by feminist family planners. Although these interventions tend to appear only as fragments in the archive, they also point toward different

frameworks for understanding the connections between biological reproduction and its social meanings—between bodies and the body politic—that
I examine in the book. I revisit questions of alternatives in the epilogue, in
dialogue with oral history interviews collected for this project in rural Tamil
Nadu, in which women shared accounts of their own reproductive lives.

The remaining chapters document this history. The narrative begins in
the late nineteenth century, when colonial administrators and Indian commentators began to frame Indian reproduction as an economic question.
They forged these connections in the crucible of the massive famines that
rocked India from the 1870s to the 1890s. Although the population was not
increasing at the time, the specter of widespread starvation fostered Malthusian fears that the land could no longer sustain the people who depended
upon it and prompted a new calibration of life that measured the survival
of the population against the cost of its sustenance. In this new measurement of life, I suggest in chapter 1, we may find the origins of a new reproductive politics, which turned to reproduction as a point of intervention in
the economic life of the population. For some colonial administrators,
Indian reproductive practices seemed to explain poverty in the colony. They
blamed "native" marriage and sexuality for creating the conditions that kept
so many Indians living on the edge of starvation. Reproductive reformers—
both Indian and British—also seized upon this moment of economic crisis
and food scarcity. They called upon Indians to transform their marriage
practices and utilize birth control, with the goal of realigning reproduction
to meet the economic constraints of colonial rule.

Connections between reproduction and economy persisted across subsequent decades, taking new shape in the context of anticolonial nationalism, global economic depression, and the rise of eugenic thinking. While
the massive famines that shaped late nineteenth-century life did not recur
during the 1920s and 1930s, population continued to be a source of anxiety
across a wide spectrum of public opinion. Malthusian fears that India's population was too large joined eugenic concerns about its health, vitality, and
genetic fitness. Many reformers wondered how India, with a population that
was both economically impoverished and eugenically "unfit," might take
its rightful place in an emergent "comity of nations."[62] Chapter 2 traces the
entanglement of reproduction with two distinct but related sets of debates
about the nation and its future sovereignty during the late colonial decades.
The first, sparked by the publication of Katherine Mayo's incendiary *Mother
India* in 1927, grappled with the relationship between the biopolitics of
Indian reproduction and the geopolitics of race, migration, and rights to

land. The second, encapsulated in a series of reforms that centered on birth control and the age of marriage and were promoted by the Indian women's movement, aimed to solve the supposed problems of Indian reproduction within the territorial framework of the Indian nation and, more specifically, within the constraints of an Indian national economy. Yet, even as the question of reproduction was increasingly asked and answered through the prism of the nation, I argue, alternative frameworks also developed. Radical critiques of patriarchy found a place alongside challenges to class and caste oppression, albeit at the margins of interwar reproductive politics.

As independence neared, the nationalist politics of reproduction began to focus more narrowly on national development; that is, on the role of the state in promoting economic and social progress. By 1952, India's First Five Year Plan formally charted out the national state's development vision and, as mentioned above, included a program of "family planning." As I argue in chapter 3, the Indian women's movement played a critical role in this process, helping to position reproductive reform as a vehicle for economic development in independent India. The chapter traces the activities of a range of women's movement leaders, such as Dhanvanthi Rama Rau, Avabai Wadia, and Lakshmibai Rajwade, during the transitional decade from the early 1940s, when they incorporated family planning into their development vision, to the early 1950s, when the ideological and institutional foundations of Indian family planning were put into place. These women mobilized their connections within the Indian women's movement while simultaneously intervening in transnational population control networks to argue that family planning represented a form of development for and by women. Their approach centered the postcolonial nation-state as an agent of women's emancipation, linking the women's movement to the agenda of state-led development.

However, women leaders' ostensibly feminist commitments to family planning advanced a population control agenda that ultimately had little interest in challenging the structures of women's oppression. Rather, with the promise of alleviating poverty without tackling class, caste, or gender inequalities, family planners targeted the reproduction of poor women as the cause of the nation's economic problems. As I discuss in chapter 4, this targeting intensified during the 1960s and 1970s, when family planning programs gained urgency amid growing fears about India's rate of population growth and global anxieties about a "population bomb" that threatened the planet. Meanwhile, new reproductive technologies enabled more intensive scrutiny of sexualities and bodies, notably in campaigns to insert IUDs and to promote surgical sterilization. Within this context, poor women were represented as dangerous bodies—sometimes just as dangerous uteruses—whose reproductive capacities posed national and global threats. As a result, their bodies became the very ground over which key debates about Indian population and economic development played out. These gendered politics of population control shifted briefly during the Emergency period, when men emerged as targets of reproductive regulation. However, as the chapter demonstrates, the Emergency also deepened the long-standing connections that linked reproduction to population and economy in modern India and, in its aftermath, again placed women's bodies at the center of debate.

Even while feminists and activists, nationalists and bureaucrats, and eugenicists and Malthusians all aimed to control reproduction to align with "the economy," they also envisioned an alternative model of family life. Specifically, they imagined a "small family"—composed of a husband, wife, and their two or three children—as the exemplar of rational reproductive planning, responsible citizenship, and economic foresight. Chapter 5 traces these discourses of the small family as they came to saturate public space across the mid-twentieth century. I examine representations of the small family from the 1920s, when they first began to appear in print media, to the height of population control campaigns in the 1960s and 1970s, when spreading a "small family norm" became the explicit goal of communications experts devoted to family planning. Exhorting audiences to remember that "A Small Family Is a Happy Family," these discourses situated the small family as a site of desire and aspiration, suggesting that controlling one's reproduction would promote both individual and national prosperity. Considering a variety of texts and images depicting small families—including cartoons, drawings, advertisements, and films—the chapter examines how the institutions and structures of heterosexuality came to underpin development planning, merging marriage with population control and marshaling affect in service of economy. Finally, the epilogue considers the enduring impact of the reproductive histories examined in the book. Drawing upon oral history interviews with women in rural Tamil Nadu who rely on the state for access to reproductive health care, I ask how discourses of population and economy both enter into and are challenged by women's representations of their reproductive bodies and lives. By historicizing the nexus of reproduction, population, and economy—and demonstrating how and why these connections took shape as they did—the book questions some of the fundamental assumptions that continue to underpin the politics of reproduction today. I hope, as well, that it contributes to visions of more just reproductive futures.

A Note on Terms

My use of terms draws inspiration from Loretta Ross and Rickie Solinger, whose book "recognizes the limits of traditional, biologically based binary definitions of gender at the same time as it chronicles and analyzes histories that these definitions have produced."[63] In writing about the past, I use the term *women* when discussing discourses, policies, and programs that claimed to target cisgender women. In hopes of not echoing the historical erasure of transgender lives and experience, however, I also aim to use more inclusive, context-sensitive language, recognizing that gender identity cannot be assumed to flow simply from a bodily capacity to menstruate, become pregnant, or give birth.

CHAPTER 1

ECONOMIES OF REPRODUCTION
IN AN AGE OF EMPIRE

AFTER TRAVELING FOR SEVERAL WEEKS THROUGH THE PARCHED and famine-stricken districts of Madras Presidency in early 1877, Sir Richard Temple arrived at the seacoast town of Mahabalipuram, south of the city of Madras, on the eleventh of March. He immediately felt refreshed by the weather, and rejoiced that "in the midst of this drought-stricken district . . . the breeze is so fresh and cool that we are wearing flannel."[1] Temple seated himself upon a granite slab beside the ruins of a Pallava-era temple, and there, in the shadows of another bygone empire, he composed a letter to Sir John Strachey, the finance member of the viceroy's Executive Council. Temple had been appointed by the viceroy to inquire into the Madras and Bombay governments' administration of famine relief. As the famine raged and many thousands perished from hunger and disease, Temple had visited famine-relief camps and conferred with local administrators. When he finally reached Mahabalipuram, removed from proximity to the starving and gazing outward to the sea, he was apparently at leisure to reflect on broader questions about the finances of the British Empire and the life and death of its Indian subjects. Writing of the condition of the hungry with equanimity, he noted that there was "distress" in the famine districts. What concerned him more, however, was that Madras administrators were supposedly giving indiscriminate relief, in the form of food and wages, to hungry people. Invoking Adam Smith's theories about the role of free markets in supplying grain, alongside Thomas Malthus's strictures about limiting poor relief to control overpopulation, Temple argued that the government must rein in its famine expenditures immediately.[2] Leaving Mahabalipuram, Temple launched a campaign to do precisely this, by reducing the number of people receiving state support and limiting the amount of relief they received. The government of India seemed to approve of Temple's efforts, and he was soon promoted to become governor of Bombay Presidency. Meanwhile, by the government's own estimate, at least five million people died from starvation and disease during the famine of 1876–78.[3]

While Temple was advocating his cost-cutting measures across the Deccan plateau and peninsular India, the activist Annie Besant, who would later become known for her Indian nationalist leadership, was formulating a campaign for birth control in London. In March 1877—coincidentally just days after Temple's Mahabalipuram letter—Besant and her associate Charles Bradlaugh were arrested for publishing a book by the American physician Charles Knowlton that outlined methods to prevent conception. Accused of spreading obscenity, Besant and Bradlaugh defended their actions on Malthusian grounds, arguing that birth control was necessary to prevent overpopulation and reduce poverty in Britain. After a sensational trial, they were acquitted on a legal technicality, and Besant immediately continued her contraceptive campaign. As summer turned to fall in London, British newspapers were filled with accounts of the Indian famine, and the tragedy soon came to occupy a central place in Besant's rationale for birth control. In October of that year, she authored a best-selling pamphlet on contraception, *The Law of Population: Its Consequences, and Its Bearing upon Human Conduct and Morals*. For Besant, the famine seemed to offer proof that "our Indian empire" was beset by overpopulation and that birth control was the best solution. As she asked her readers, "Is it possible to sit down with folded hands and calmly contemplate the recurrence at regular intervals of such a famine as lately slew its tens of thousands?"[4] Resolving that the answer was no, Besant offered contraception as a solution to poverty, overpopulation, and famine in Britain's Indian empire.

At first glance, Temple's letter from Mahabalipuram may seem an odd juxtaposition with Besant's birth control pamphlet. The letter was intended for limited circulation to the highest levels of the colonial administration, documented bureaucratic details about famine relief, and made an economic case to rein in state expenditures. The pamphlet, by contrast, aimed for a massive public audience, offered detailed information about bodily and reproductive processes, and made an impassioned argument that contraception was a remedy for the economic problems of empire. Yet taken together, the two texts suggest the contours of a distinct moment in the history of reproductive politics. This was a moment, during the late nineteenth century, when food scarcity and economic crisis called Indian reproduction into question and provoked demands for reproductive reform. As we shall see in this chapter, these calls for reform encompassed everything from the universality of marriage to the structures of Hindu conjugality to the advocacy of contraception. Remedies differed in their specifics but were held together by a common set of assumptions about poverty and population that was indebted to Malthusian ideas and gained strength in the context of the famines that recurred across India during this period. As the texts from Temple and Besant suggest, further, this new reproductive politics developed through a series of imperial circulations—of food, of finance, and of frameworks of ideas between the British metropole and the Indian colony. We cannot understand the history of reproduction, therefore, without attention to the politics and economies of empire.

To trace this history, the chapter follows two lines of inquiry, each of which was critical to a new politics of reproduction during the "high noon" of the British Empire in India. The first was an emerging concern that India was overpopulated. This population anxiety was not due to any demonstrable increase in numbers. In fact, and in contrast to Western Europe at the time, population in most parts of India stagnated between 1870 and 1920.[5] Concern about Indian overpopulation was provoked less by population growth than by famine. The scale and massive mortality rates of late nineteenth-century famines prompted claims that the land held more people than it could reasonably support and that the food available was inadequate to the needs of the inhabitants. These concerns were indebted to the thinking of Thomas Malthus; for many contemporary observers, both British and Indian, the fact of famine seemed to indicate that India had already reached a Malthusian limit of population. These claims about the population also depended upon practices of enumeration and, more generally, upon the role of numbers in the colonial administration; this represents a second line of inquiry. The late nineteenth century marked the beginning of the all-India census, first attempted in 1872, then established more comprehensively in 1881. Alongside these counts, the colonial state increasingly relied on numbers to rationalize its administration, leading to a "quantificatory episteme" that shaped colonial policy and rule.[6] Famine administration was one important site for this turn toward quantification.

Together, these anxieties about population and focus on numbers as a mode of governance produced a new reproductive politics that linked conjugality to economy. Some colonial administrators developed these links to argue that Indian marital, sexual, and familial practices were responsible for Indian impoverishment. Among some Indian intellectuals and reformers, these concerns about reproduction provoked demands to change Indian conjugality in order to avert economic disaster. This included a reform of marriage and, in some cases, birth control. Such connections between marriage and famine, and between childbearing and impoverishment, created the terms by which reproduction became a question of public debate. To investigate these connections, the chapter begins with the discourses of quantification and population that shaped nineteenth-century colonial administration, in particular the administration of famine. As I argue, the logics of colonial famine administration provoked a new calibration of life that measured the survival of the population against the cost of its sustenance. The chapter then turns to the famine of 1876–78, an event that helped to crystallize and make visible these new calculations about the cost of life. In the context of this crisis and its aftermath, anxieties about the life and death of the population helped to make reproduction into a target of scrutiny and a site for reform in ways that would have lasting impact in colonial India. It would also place India at the center of an emerging global politics of population, whose implications would reverberate into the twentieth century.

Counting and Quantifying Population

Practices of enumeration and quantification were critical to emergent discourses about population in the nineteenth century. Although the fact of counting itself was not new to this period, colonial modes of generating and recording numerical data helped to connect population to reproduction in novel ways. Specifically, the task of managing population became intimately linked to gathering quantitative and statistical data about reproduction. In a shift that began with the all-India censuses, the process of enumerating population would eventually situate such measures as fertility and nuptiality on a quantitative grid, paving the way for reproduction to be connected to economy in new ways.

To trace this history, I begin with early colonial modes of counting, which relied heavily on precolonial enumeration practices. The Mughal Empire and its successor states counted as a way to determine taxes and land revenue. What they counted, and how, depended upon the structure of revenue demands. For instance, if the state taxed each household, then censuses of households ensued; if household taxes were differentiated by caste or occupation, then revenue administrators counted and recorded these categories. If the state collected a portion of the crop, then assessing the area of land planted or the number of cattle became ways to determine land revenue.[7] The East India Company drew upon these earlier exercises in counting, and their debts to indigenous systems were multiple. Company officials found census enumerators among village-level accountants who had engaged in administrative counting in precolonial regimes. They decided what to count, in part, based on interaction with these indigenous enumerators, and their purposes for counting held much in common with earlier rulers.[8] During the eighteenth and early nineteenth centuries, the Company counted as part of taxation and land revenue assessment. Its great projects of "settling" the land revenue, as in the case of the Bengal Permanent Settlement of 1793, depended upon a massive cadastral exercise of surveying, counting, and measuring. Such projects helped to develop the expertise for later human censuses.[9]

The Company's interest in counting also developed vis-à-vis a British and European milieu in which statistics were increasingly a mode of governance. Through the course of the seventeenth and eighteenth centuries, developments in numeracy, literacy, state fiscalism, and actuarial thinking made numbers part of the British political imagination.[10] This emphasis on enumeration produced the country's first national census in 1801. It also found expression in new institutions, most notably the Statistical Society of London, founded in 1834. The turn to numbers, as Arjun Appadurai suggests, was part of a growing sense that a powerful state could not survive without making "enumeration a central technique of social control."[11] This resulted in interconnections among developments in statistical science, the generation of statistical knowledge for purposes of governance, and the policies of the state. These changes occurred within a broader imperial network that encompassed both metropole and colony.

The Indian census of 1872 marks an important moment within this longer history of quantifying population across the British Empire. The idea for such a census had been floated in the final years of Company rule. The rebellion of 1857 put a temporary halt to these plans, but they were resumed after the establishment of Crown rule to produce the first count of population in British Indian territories in 1872. This was followed by the more comprehensive census of 1881, ushering in a series of decennial counts that continued unbroken through independence. While drawing upon earlier enumerations, the new censuses also marked a significant departure from their predecessors. Unlike prior efforts, which had been localized and did not aim to generate data commensurate with other local counts, here the goal was to conduct a national census. This was not quite achieved in 1872, since the enumeration did not include all areas under Crown rule and did not count the princely states at all. Beginning in 1881, however, the census became more truly national and was forced to generate nationally commensurate categories of caste, religion, and occupation. The 1881 census was also synchronous; that is, it counted everyone on the same day.[12] This required employing an army of census enumerators and producing an ever-growing library of census reports to present the data collected. In this sense, the census became a major administrative undertaking of the colonial regime. At the same time, it produced vastly more statistical data than could be used for directly utilitarian purposes like revenue or taxation, unlike earlier enumerations that privileged information collection for clearly defined ends. After 1872, the census became at once justificatory, disciplinary, and pedagogical, far exceeding the more specific purposes for which numbers had been generated before.[13]

Significantly, the new mode of national census-taking enumerated individuals. While previous counts had sometimes hazarded population estimates based on numbers of households, the census of 1872 and its successors aimed to count each person by age, sex, and social identity. The novelty of this practice is suggested by the Madras census commissioner, W. R. Cornish, who noted with some frustration that the "female population" was likely undercounted in the presidency. He attributed this failure to the local census enumerators, who had "been singularly obtuse in comprehending the fact that the counting of females was a matter of any importance in census work. To understand how this is, we must take into account the low estimation in which females are held in this country, and also the reticence of the people on all matters connected with their female relatives."[14] Perhaps census enumerators—accustomed to earlier regimes of counting that emphasized the household—did not see the purpose of inquiring into the details of household inhabitants. However, the administrators of the 1872 census and its successors were far more ambitious in their goals and eventually built the kind of population profile that we associate with census data in our own time.

When census enumerators were pressed to uncover how many people lived in the household, alongside their age, gender, and marital status, they began to generate new kinds of data that situated reproduction within a quantitative grid. To understand the significance of this shift, we might compare this moment with earlier eras, when such data was not collected.

As Sumit Guha argues, seventeenth- and eighteenth-century accounts explained population growth primarily through migration and movement. Administrative benevolence or tax concessions might induce people to migrate into a kingdom and thus increase population. In precolonial India, "the West European concern with fecundity was therefore absent" and "it was not necessary for such an administration to penetrate into the household to ascertain its demographic contents."[15] But once the 1872 census enumerators had, so to speak, "penetrated the household," their data began to quantify population in new ways. As Foucault argues for modern Europe, states began to understand the "population" less as people and more as a phenomenon to be managed to maximize wealth or labor capacity; this was a population "balanced between its own growth and the resources it commanded."[16] Increasingly, managing this population seemed to depend on generating statistical data about reproduction, which of course was intimately connected to sex and sexuality. Through collecting information about individuals within households, statisticians could surmise how many children women had, on average, and could correlate this with markers of social identity, such as caste or religion. They could generate new information about mothers' average ages when their children were born and could document the children's rates of survival through infancy. In short, aspects of population size and rate of growth could now be measured in relation to quantified markers of reproductive behavior. Fertility, nuptiality, and age of marriage thus became foundational to collecting data about and managing the population as a whole. These figures existed "at the boundary line of the biological and the economic domains," merging a set of claims about reproductive sexuality with assertions about the economic prosperity of the population.[17]

Historicizing Famine

Even as new methods of enumeration provoked a new way of understanding the "population" in the late nineteenth century, the frequency and severity of famines during these decades prompted a concern that this population was, in fact, an "overpopulation," an excess of people in relation to the land. To explain why famine, rather than actual population growth, led colonial administrators to claim that India was overpopulated, this section turns to the history of late nineteenth-century famine, and to the wider political and economic relations that made famines so devastating wherever they occurred across the subcontinent. Considering this history, which takes us through the causes and consequences of famine events, helps to clarify how the "population"—and its reproduction—emerged as a target of governance in the late nineteenth century. Claims about the population that first developed in the context of famine, I argue, would become foundational to the new reproductive politics that I examine later in the chapter.

Famine had been a feature of South Asian life even before colonial rule, but it occurred with depressing regularity during the nineteenth century.[18] Some of the major instances included famines in Guntur District in Madras Presidency from 1832 to 1833; in the North West Provinces, Punjab, Rajasthan, and Kutch from 1860 to 1861; in Orissa and Bihar from 1866 to 1867; in the Central Provinces and Rajasthan from 1868 to 1870; and in Bihar from 1873 to 1874. But even these massive calamities were relatively limited in their geographical range, in comparison with the more widespread disasters to follow in the last quarter of the nineteenth century. The famine of 1876–78 affected much of Madras and parts of Bombay Presidencies, alongside the North West Provinces and the princely states of Mysore and Hyderabad. Even more severe famines closed the century: in 1896 and 1897 across most of India, and again in 1899 and 1900, when large parts of western, northwestern, and central India were impacted.[19] Colonial administrators tended to blame famines on the failure of monsoon rains; indeed, each of these crises was accompanied by adverse weather conditions. But while climate was crucial in the timing of famines, the extreme "social vulnerability to climate variability" still needs to be explained.[20] That is, as many contemporaries recognized and as scholars have since confirmed, famines were not necessarily provoked by an absolute lack of food but by people's inability either to buy food or to secure the means of subsistence in any other way. This collapse of people's means to access subsistence—their "exchange entitlements," in Amartya Sen's terms—requires explanation.[21] In other words, what made people so vulnerable that a failure of monsoon rains could bring many millions to the brink of starvation?

The short answer to this question is colonialism. The conditions of colonial rule produced or exacerbated a slow erosion of food security among landless laborers and smallholding peasants, the two groups most likely to face starvation during periods of famine. Over the course of the nineteenth century, a decline in other sources of employment, including weaving and other industries, rendered agriculture the only source of livelihood for an increasing percentage of the population. At the same time, farming became an increasingly precarious source of employment. Growing commercialization of agriculture exposed peasants to the risks of market fluctuation with few of its rewards, and in consequence, landowners had little incentive to invest in the land, and agriculture was undercapitalized.[22] Shifts away from food crops to commercial production also reduced food security in times of crisis. Meanwhile, the burdens of colonial taxation fell especially hard on the agrarian economy.[23] These taxes raised funds not only for Indian administration but also for British expansion in Asia and Africa, thus welding the Indian agriculturist to the finances of the British Empire.[24] Increases in land revenue rates sometimes coincided with and prompted the onset of famine conditions; more broadly, the demand for land revenue and its mode of collection squeezed the most marginal occupants of the land during both "ordinary" and famine years.[25] When the monsoon rains failed, therefore, people were left with few resources to fall back upon.

Landless laborers and smallholding peasants thus constituted an impoverished population that lived on the edge of subsistence even in ordinary years and risked starvation during periods of famine. Moreover, as Mike Davis reminds us, the financial precarity of Indian peasants in the late nineteenth century did not develop outside of an emergent capitalist and imperialist world system. Rather, millions died "in the very process of being forcibly incorporated into its economic and political structures."[26] More specifically, European governments' continuing capacity to feed their own populations, as David Arnold suggests, was "achieved at the expense of hardship and hunger in the colonial world."[27] Famines in late nineteenth-century India were thus both a consequence of a global transfer of wealth and resources to the Western imperialist powers and a further engine to accelerate inequalities on a world scale.[28] However, they were not, as colonial administrators often assumed, a consequence of population growth; population size was, in fact, mostly stagnant at this time. The connection administrators made between famine and population depended upon Malthusian theories, as I discuss in more detail below.

The devastating impact of famine was magnified by the limitations of state support for affected populations; in most cases, the colonial administration failed to prevent large-scale mortality during periods of famine.[29] During the late eighteenth and early nineteenth centuries, state assistance was constrained by limited technologies of communication and transport; in addition, East India Company administrators had limited knowledge of Indian agriculture and rural conditions. As the century wore on, however, and modes of transport and communication improved, limited state funding continued to constrain famine relief efforts. The same logic that mandated a high rate of land revenue—which required the Indian taxpayer to bankroll both colonial administration and imperial expansion—also severely reduced funds for supporting starving populations. Free charitable relief was therefore always limited. Punitive regimes required famine-affected populations to labor on public works distant from their homes, and these conditions dissuaded many from even applying to the state for help. Private charity, though locally effective at times, could never exist on the scale that was required. Consequently, many famines resulted in massive mortality. In the Guntur famine, for instance, historians estimate that one-third of the population died; in Orissa, one-quarter of the population may have perished.[30] Not coincidentally, the only famine in which state efforts substantially limited mortality was in Bihar in 1873 and 1874, when the government expended significantly more per capita on the affected population than in other relief efforts.[31]

The colonial regime's limited funding for famine relief rested upon a broader ideology that limited state intervention in market operations—a laissez-faire economic policy indebted in particular to Adam Smith. Classical political economy, as developed by Smith and his followers, began from the premise that individuals' unconstrained pursuit of their own interests would necessarily produce the greatest social good. As Smith's *Wealth of Nations* (1776) notes, the state's role was therefore to avoid regulation of markets, leaving an "invisible hand" to effect both individual good and social benefit. The principle of state nonintervention extended to a "free trade" in food supplies. Smith rejected previous political theory that made securing food a state responsibility, arguing that state actions to fix prices, punish hoarding, or purchase grain risked exacerbating the problem they were intended to solve.[32] Such action would only turn "dearth," which Smith termed an "unavoidable misfortune," into a full-scale famine. As a case in point, Smith wrote about the East India Company's market interventions in Bengal in 1770, claiming that "famine has never arisen from any other cause but the violence of government attempting, by improper means, to remedy the inconvenience of a dearth."[33] State intervention in food markets was thus not only futile but also harmful. These doctrines became increasingly important to how colonial administrators approached famine in India, as they had in Ireland. Although Smith's ideas did not provide a detailed blueprint for each specific case of famine, a devotion to free-market ideologies built the foundation of nineteenth-century famine policy in colonial India.[34]

Within this longer history of colonial famine and its administration, the famine of 1876–78 marked a watershed moment. Like its predecessors, the famine was prompted most immediately by a disruption in the monsoon rains. This disruption—likely caused by an El Niño southern oscillation pattern—was exceptionally severe, of the sort to occur only once in two hundred or even five hundred years.[35] The crisis was unprecedented in its geographic scale and impacted districts previously considered immune to famine. Still, as in other famines, affected districts did not suffer from an absolute lack of food; with a sharp rise in food prices in late 1876, however, many people found themselves unable to buy food or to access it in other ways.[36] Contemporaries recognized this distinction. Thus, writing in December 1876, one correspondent for the Marathi newspaper *Dnyan Prakash* argued that "the present distress cannot, in strict truth, be called a scarcity of food. . . . The real fact is that, the suffering people have no power of purchasing food, and therefore, they are experiencing all the horrors of a famine."[37]

In piecemeal fashion, local and provincial governments began to institute relief measures. As the crisis worsened in the early months of 1877, the Indian government grew concerned about the growing cost of these efforts and attempted to rein in expenditures by appointing Richard Temple as its famine delegate. Within months, Temple followed his mandate to curtail the number of people receiving state support, increase labor requirements on relief works, and reduce the food and cash wages offered in exchange for this labor. The goal, on some level, was to make relief as unpleasant as possible, so as to minimize the number of people who sought assistance. Men, women, and children over ages seven or eight were required to pass a "distance test" for relief, which meant they had to travel at least ten miles away from their homes to be eligible for support.[38] Once arrived at the relief camps, applicants were tested for their physical fitness, sometimes via blows to the chest. If deemed capable of work, they would labor in gangs to complete assigned tasks; partial completion would mean only a partial wage. Those determined to be unfit for manual labor were eligible for charitable relief, which was distributed under punitive conditions that could include forced residence in camps.

Famine-affected populations resisted these measures in multiple ways, such as refusing to seek state relief and even going on strike to protest wages and conditions on the relief works.[39] In the meantime, the crisis continued its grim course. By 1878, newspapers reported that people were reduced to eating inedible foods, and even the carcasses of dead animals.[40] Families were being destroyed, lamented the *Paschima Taraka and Kerala Pataka* in October 1878, as "parental and other natural affections and sympathies are losing their force."[41] Eager to end its relief administration as soon as possible, the government declared the famine over with the onset of some seasonal rains in 1878. For people who had lost their cattle, seed, and tools, however, there was no clear end to the crisis, whose effects were long-standing even after the government declaration.

The scope of the disaster provoked an administrative reckoning in its aftermath. The British government appointed a Famine Commission to investigate the causes and consequences of the crisis and, in 1880, instituted its first official Famine Code. This document, which David Arnold terms "one of the most significant administrative measures devised during the entire period of British rule in India," would set state policy for decades to come.[42] It helped to enshrine Smith's ideas about the primacy of the market in grappling with famines, while regularizing systems of relief administration. In retrospect, then, the famine of 1876–78 was the last to occur before the development of more fixed policies. It afforded officials "their last chance to dispute the adequacy of cost-cutting relief, or to challenge presuppositions about the famine process and the population" before official positions on these issues limited the scope of debate.[43] Therefore, although famine policy was not unchanging in later decades, this crisis prompted the articulation of principles and practices that would have a long life in colonial India.

Calibrating the Cost of Life

Among the effects of the famine was a new quantification of life and life processes. Linking famine administration to enumeration as a mode of state power, colonial officials counted the famine in multiple ways. They documented the number of people affected; noted how many had applied for relief; divided this population by sex, age, and bodily capacities; and finally accounted for the number who had died from starvation. Administrators marked increases and decreases in these numbers, calculated the percentage of the population receiving state support, and compared these figures across villages and districts.[44] In short, numbers were the language with which colonial officials told the story of famine, and numbers shaped how they responded to the crisis. In the process, the lives of famine-affected people became newly quantifiable, and colonial administrators calibrated the cost of saving life against the finances of the imperial government.

On one level, numbers served to document the extent and severity of the famine. A telegram from the viceroy, Lord Lytton, to the secretary of state for India in January 1877 exemplifies this use of numbers. In a few terse sentences, the text notes that the situation was especially grave in Madras Presidency, "where 13 districts out of 21, containing a population of 20 millions," were affected. The number on relief works was over 840,000, which the author compares with only 250,000 in Bombay. The result was an estimated loss of five million rupees to the Madras revenue, though Bombay was unaltered. The author concludes that through all this there were perhaps "one or two isolated" cases of starvation, but that the government had endeavored to prevent any mortality due to famine.[45]

Numbers also structured the narrative of famine at the level of the individual body. Famine administrators debated the exact amount of food required to sustain the life of famine-affected people. For instance, during his cost-cutting tour of Madras Presidency, Temple pushed to reduce the wages on famine-relief works to just sixteen ounces of grain per day for adult men, with lower amounts for women and children. This shocked observers, who noted that it was less than what the government provided for prisoners in jails, or for laborers sent on ships overseas, neither of whom performed hard manual labor.[46] Temple's opponents, most notably the former Madras census commissioner W. R. Cornish, insisted that this wage was insufficient "for the physiological requirements of the body" and it "cannot be said to preserve life, although it may postpone death."[47] Cornish drew upon scientific studies and personal observation to argue for anywhere from twenty-four to forty-eight ounces, with precisely calibrated ratios of "carboniferous" and "nitrogenous principles" in the food.[48] Another medical officer documented the insufficiency of food by weighing the inhabitants of famine-relief camps, then compared this data with information obtained from jailed prisoners in the district.[49]

Even as the government thus assigned meaning to the famine through numbers, quantification also offered a language with which to contest the government's narrative about the famine administration. For instance, the Poona Sarvajanik Sabha, a civic association supported by some of the Deccan's largest landholders, conducted its own village-level censuses to counter the state's claims. Working with village accountants, postmasters, schoolteachers, and retired civil servants, the Sabha gathered data about rainfall, food prices and availability, the condition of cattle, and the numbers of migrant populations. In a series of published "famine narratives," it documented "disproportionate" rates of birth and death and enumerated starvation deaths to counter the state's claims that the famine had not resulted in significant mortality.[50] In response to the sixteen-ounce "Temple wage,"

the Sabha generated its own data about the food needs of affected populations and concluded that, with only sixteen ounces, "people starve or are
half famished."[51] Numbers thus became the grounds to evaluate the success
or failures of the state's famine administration.

Most significantly, numbers in the famine administration enabled a precise calculation of the cost of life itself, and a calibration of this cost against
the finances of the imperial government. This calculus of life unfolded in
debates about famine mortality due to starvation. On the one hand, the government claimed responsibility for preserving the lives of famine-affected
populations; in Temple's terse summation, "Every effort is to be made for
the prevention of deaths by famine."[52] On the other hand, famine administrators were urged to balance their mandate to save lives with the costs
entailed in doing so. In the words of one government missive, "While the
necessity of preventing, as far as practicable, death by starvation is para-
mount, the financial embarrassment which must in any case arise will be
most difficult to overcome."[53] Indeed, as Temple added, this "embarrassment
of debt" through relief expenditures would be "more fatal to the country
than famine itself."[54] Administrators sought to manage these contradictions
by assuring each other and the public at large that saving all lives was the
primary goal of relief efforts, and they claimed success in their implementation. When faced—as they inevitably were—with the deaths of their subjects, they tended to blame epidemic disease rather than starvation. Often,
they critiqued individuals' "obstinacy" in refusing to seek relief, rather than
acknowledging that the state's limited and punitive relief regime contributed to the deaths.[55] In other words, the finances of the imperial administration would limit the parameters by which lives could be saved or deaths
prevented, even as colonial rhetoric insisted that there was only negligible
mortality due to famine.

These competing principles—of saving lives or saving imperial finances—
resulted in tense negotiations among the upper administration, the lower-
level officials who organized famine relief, and famine-affected populations
themselves, who demanded a subsistence that exceeded the limited food and
wages provided by the state. After much internal discussion, the government
of India finally outlined its competing priorities in a careful calibration that
measured the state's financial responsibilities against the lives of its subjects:
"Considering that the revenues are barely sufficient to meet the ordinary
expenditure of the empire, and that heavy additional taxation is both finan-
cially and politically impracticable we must plainly admit that *the task of*

saving life, irrespective of the cost, is one which is beyond our power to undertake."[56]

This weighing of life against cost produced a kind of economization of life, in which the financial resources required to sustain a population were compared with the value of its life. This calculation was perhaps implicit in ordinary years, but it became especially fraught in the context of famine, as millions of people left their homes, sought relief elsewhere, and succumbed to disease and death. In this moment of crisis, it became necessary for the government of India to make explicit that imperial finances would not allow the sustenance of life under any and all conditions. Critics of the famine administration, notably the Poona Sarvajanik Sabha, offered an alternative calculus. Just as they provided numerical data to contest the government's representation of the famine itself, the Sabha also outlined a different rationale of relief, arguing that it was not an inadequacy of resources but a failure of policy and political will that prevented the state from saving life.[57]

Ultimately, however, even as deaths mounted, the state remained unwilling to embrace the full implications of its own calibration of life, death, and finance. The same memo that announced lives would not be saved "irrespective of cost" concluded that the government could still apply "rules of action" that would allow "efficient assistance" and prevention of mortality.[58] Though the government had limits to its expenditures, in other words, these expenditures could still save all lives if properly managed. Despite this resolution of the problem on paper, famine mortality was in fact immense, as was recognized by many people at the time and as is perfectly clear in hindsight. Indeed, as the Madras census commissioner acknowledged in the first census conducted after the famine, in 1881, "The mark which that calamity made upon the population was so deep that it stains every column of these [census] returns."[59]

In sum, the state's famine administration developed at the particular intersection of new rationales for counting, the consequent emergence of a new idea of the "population," and the material conditions of crisis and scarcity. My point here is not that counting leads to starvation, or that enumeration practices led directly to famine policies, which is of course not the case. Rather, the new regimes of counting that developed during the late nineteenth century, and the accompanying importance of numbers in the colonial administration, prompted a new economization of life, whereby the benefit of lives saved was calibrated against the cost. Thus, as the "population" became a target of governance, it was also measured against other imperatives of imperial rule. In the specific context of famine in 1876–78, this calibration forced a question about the lives and deaths of people in the Deccan and peninsular India.

Famine and Colonial Malthusianism

Colonial administrators calibrating life in the context of famine found in Malthusian theories of population and reproduction an explanation for the crisis that surrounded them. They were likely familiar with these ideas since Thomas Malthus himself, who served as the first chair of political economy at the East India Company's training college, had introduced several generations of the Company's servants to his own theories and to the principles of classical political economy more generally. Even after the closure of the Haileybury College in 1855, political economy remained a required subject in the Indian Civil Service Examinations, thus ensuring that aspiring British administrators in India were educated in the doctrines of Malthus alongside those of Adam Smith.[60]

Like colonial famine administrators, Malthus, in his *Essay on the Principle of Population*, engaged in a calculus of life that weighed the growth of a population against the costs of its sustenance. This calibration was prompted, for Malthus, by the extension of the English Poor Laws. He argued that systems of poor relief in England subsidized "paupers" regardless of whether they worked, thus acting as a stimulus to their unfettered reproduction. He noted that ordinarily, the poorest classes were most likely to die in a subsistence crisis like a famine; however, poor laws would prevent these deaths while allowing the poor to marry earlier and bear more children. This growing population of the poor would strain the food supply, and under free-market conditions, this would result in rising grain prices. These higher prices, in turn, would make it more difficult for the next higher class to obtain food, and so would raise their mortality. Consequently, Malthus concluded, supporting the poor would only spread poverty to higher classes of society. This somewhat abstract conclusion stood side by side with one of Malthus's more practical remedies: allowing abandoned illegitimate children to die so as not to swell the ranks of the poor, and forcing their parents to pay for their upbringing if they wanted them to live.[61] It was left to John Stuart Mill, Malthus's mid-nineteenth-century interpreter, to elevate these claims to the status of utilitarian principle: "Everyone has a right to live. We will suppose this granted. But no one has a right to bring creatures into life, to be supported by other people."[62] In other words, Malthus and Mill called for the regulation of poor people's reproduction as a service to the "population" as a whole.

At the center of Malthus's claim about the population and its reproduction, Catherine Gallagher argues, was a disjuncture between the health of the individual body and that of the body politic. Unlike the ideas of most of his contemporaries, who imagined a correlation between a healthy society and healthy individual members, Malthus's theories suggested that the health of the individual body would, through reproduction, "eventually generate a feeble social organism." As a result, "the healthy, and consequently *reproducing*, body . . . is a harbinger of the disordered society of starving bodies."[63] To check this disorder, Malthus offered the remedy of sexual continence. Foreshadowing late nineteenth-century imperial discourses that linked sexual control to white, bourgeois masculinity, Malthus regarded sexual continence "as a criterion of civilization and even a major element in the civilizing process."[64] Thus, although Malthus may not have called himself a philosopher of sexuality, his concerns about overpopulation were intimately connected to fears about the oversexuality of poor and "uncivilized" classes and nations. In Mervyn Nicholson's terms, "population in Malthus's text is also a codeword for sex: the result (population) stands metonymically for its cause (sex)."[65] The sexuality of the poor, by resulting in overreproduction, becomes a powerful threat to a status quo that divides the propertied and laboring classes, the civilized from the uncivilized. Moreover, as Alison Bashford demonstrates in her "spatial history of Malthusianism," population was rendered *over*population for Malthus when it surpassed the food-producing capacities of available land; that is, reproductive sex became a problem when it overturned the balance with space.[66] Consequently, in a Malthusian calibration of life, sexuality and reproduction were balanced against land and economy.

By the late nineteenth century, some British administrators, especially at the higher levels, looked to Malthusian theories to explain famine. They understood events in India as proof of Malthus's argument that population would overrun its means of subsistence. Administrators speculated that the colony had already reached a Malthusian limit and that population was out of balance with the land available. In the midst of famine in 1877, the viceroy, Lord Lytton, made these concerns public, suggesting that the Indian population "has a tendency to increase more rapidly than the food it raises from the soil."[67] In the aftermath of the famine, the government-appointed Famine Commission reinforced Lytton's assessment, concluding that "the numbers who have no other employment than agriculture, are in large parts of the country greatly in excess of what is needed for the thorough cultivation of the land."[68] The balance between sex and space had been overturned.

This assessment of Indian overpopulation did not depend upon any demonstrable increase in population numbers. Too little information existed, in any case, for contemporaries to make definitive claims about whether or not population was increasing, since census data was just beginning to be collected. We know in retrospect, however, that in most parts of the subcontinent, population was relatively stagnant between 1870 and 1920, though there was some slow growth after 1880. We know, as well, that there was substantial regional variation in population growth rates. According to Sumit Guha, peninsular and eastern India witnessed relatively rapid growth between 1800 and 1870, whereas the central Indo-Gangetic plain did not experience a similar population increase.[69] However, more than numbers, the fact of famine itself seemed to provide colonial administrators with proof of overpopulation. They suggested that the death of so many Indian peasants confirmed that the land they inhabited could not sustain all those who depended upon it. Such was the view of James Caird, an agricultural scientist and member of the Famine Commission. "The greatest difficulty with which the Indian statesman is confronted," Caird wrote in 1879, "is over-population, with constant increase." This was a problem, since India was a "country already full of people, whose habits and religion promote increase without restraint."[70] One of Caird's correspondents went even further. Famine in Madras and the Deccan, he argued, was due to the "radical dangers and ultimate result of Indian social life and habits." Specifically, he claimed that "Malthusian practice of marriage," by which he may have meant reproduction without regard to population growth, was pursued "without the slightest reference to the consequences." Only "nature" could restore the balance by carrying off "tens of millions" through repeated famines.[71]

This image of the overly prolific and hypersexual "native" is not new to scholars of imperial history, who have demonstrated that the production of a racialized, bourgeois, and masculine European sexuality was premised on an "other" that was not white, not bourgeois, and not masculine.[72] Colonial representations of famine contributed to this sexual discourse by bringing Indian conjugal and reproductive practices forcefully into the realm of economy; they held the "native" responsible not only for sexual perversion but also for his or her own poverty and starvation. As the undersecretary of state for India, Louis Mallet, thus concluded, "a people with such practices as prevail in India with regard to marriage and inheritance must be miserable."[73] This supposed connection between reproduction and famine appears starkly in a document that one historian terms the "most Malthusian" in colonial famine administration. In a memo to Viceroy Lord Ripon, Finance Secretary Sir George Couper insisted that the famine was affecting only the lowest stratum of the population: "If the famine mortality in 1879 be tested, it will be found that about 80 per cent of the deaths come from the laboring classes." These laborers died in large numbers, but "still they reproduce themselves with sufficient rapidity to overcrowd every employment that is opened to them." In classic Malthusian fashion, Couper argued that keeping this class alive would only push wages down further while threatening the classes above it. Indeed, Couper concluded, any change in famine policy that would maintain the laboring classes "to the full span of human existence, without at the same time providing safeguards against their reproduction" would only exacerbate problems of Indian poverty.[74]

In its final report, the Famine Commission brought together these various strands of debate to conclude that British rule in India had changed the balance between life and death in the country. With little empirical evidence, it claimed that British technology and civilization had "fundamentally changed the position of the people for the better" by giving "a check to some of the great causes of mortality among them." This reduced mortality rate, however, brought its own grave consequences, which the report defined as "an increase of the population" and a "pressure on the means of subsistence."[75] In this view, vulnerability to famine was due to population growth brought about by British civilization and was thus a mark of the *success* of the imperial administration, rather than its failure. In the Famine Commission's Financial Statement, Sir Evelyn Baring made this point even more directly, noting that "every benevolent attempt made to mitigate the effects of famine . . . serves but to enhance the evils resulting from overpopulation."[76] Too many lives saved through famine relief would only increase poor people's reproductive capacities. Thus, when life was calibrated against the price of its sustenance, reproduction threatened to tip the balance—to push the scales into a Malthusian "overpopulation." In the context of famine, reproduction thus became an economic cost that had to be accounted for.

Marriage and National Malthusianism

In the waning days of famine, the *Quarterly Journal of the Poona Sarvajanik Sabha* similarly counted reproduction as an economic cost in an article titled "Over-Population and Marriage Customs." Appearing alongside the Sabha's detailed "famine narratives" about the impact of the crisis on specific villages and districts, the article took a more expansive view on the causes and consequences of famine in India. The author, who remained anonymous, suggested that Hindu marriage practices had led to the rapid growth of population, which in turn exacerbated the country's poverty and ultimately led to famine. Consequently, he argued, "among the principal causes of the brutal ignorance and degraded poverty and pauperism of the people of India must be reckoned the Hindu law and custom of marriage." It was a "source of fearful diseases and plagues, and of more fearful famines." Having witnessed the terrible suffering of the famine's victims, the author concluded that it was time to make radical changes in Indian reproductive practices.[77]

The anonymous author of "Over-Population and Marriage Customs" was likely Mahadev Govind Ranade, a lawyer and judge active in Poona's public life who was among the chief architects of Indian economic nationalism in the late nineteenth century. Ranade was a founding member of the Poona Sarvajanik Sabha in 1876, and he played a leading role in the organization's efforts to collect information about the famine. The *Quarterly Journal* was created at his instigation.[78] The article reflects this kind of personal experience with the famine, which the author describes as having "seen with our own eyes."[79] It also resonates with Ranade's developing critique of colonial political economy and with his documented attempts to reform marriage practices. Thus, although I have not located definitive proof of authorship, I follow other historians in suggesting that Ranade is the most likely author of the text.[80]

Ranade's article welds his rejection of Hindu marriage practices to a critique of the political economy of colonial rule. Beginning from the Malthusian premise that there was an "over-growth" of population in India, as evidenced by the recent famine, Ranade argues that the country could no longer sustain its rate of reproduction. Whereas population growth may have been necessary in earlier eras of human history, the constraints of colonialism now mandated a new balance between the life of the population and its economic prospects. In other words, Indian reproduction had to account for the country's poverty. In terms that anticipated the economic nationalist critique that Ranade would develop—alongside Dadabhai Naoroji, Romesh Chunder Dutt, and others—"Over-Population and Marriage Customs" indicts colonial economic policy as the chief cause of this poverty. India's unfavorable balance of trade with Britain, alongside the "home charges" that funded the colonial administration, had drained the country's savings. Meanwhile, the imperial government supported the interests of the British textile industry at the expense of Indian manufacturing, thus "inflict[ing] upon the land all the evils, without most of the blessings of a so-called free trade policy." Ranade also lamented soil exhaustion due to "pauper cultivation" and lambasted the "stress of rack-rent and rigid [land revenue] settlements" that had forced peasants to cultivate uncultivable land. Finally, the government had not encouraged emigration as a means to relieve the pressures on the land. By listing these factors, the article challenges Malthusian arguments that stressed a natural propensity of all species to reproduce beyond their means of subsistence. Instead, Ranade develops a historical critique of colonial policies making the population unsustainable. He insists that the problem in colonial India has been, more than any "natural" increase in numbers, the "slow development of [the population's] means of subsistence" under British rule.[81] Indian reproduction only magnified a poverty whose fundamental origins were found in the colonial economy.

Given these impoverished conditions, Ranade argues, it became imperative that Indians reform their marriage practices. For "in these days, nobody will be prepared to dispute the position that the law and custom of marriage in any country are closely connected with the economical condition of the bulk of its population."[82] Such recognition was prompted, for Ranade, by the fact of famine itself: "If the multiplication of the population had not been encouraged and ensured by the supposed sanction of religion and caste opinion, and each man and woman had been left to exercise a prudential restraint on the instinct of propagation, there would not have been such helplessness and such fearful pauperism in this country, nor such devastating famines."[83] Ranade targeted two conjugal customs that prevented this "prudential restraint" on propagation: marriages that occurred before puberty and universal marriage. The custom of prepuberty marriage violated true Hindu tradition, which insisted on four "Ashrams or divisions of human life." Of these four, the married condition was only one, and for Ranade, it lasted "between the age of 20 and 45 years of a man's life." Before and after those years, he maintained that "the single or celibate life is enjoined as a virtue and a duty upon all." But in contemporary times, people had ignored this call to celibacy by marrying girls even before puberty and commencing sexual intimacy soon thereafter and thus had increased their numbers rapidly. This increase was exacerbated by an imperative for universal marriage. In contrast to Europe, where peasants would not marry unless they could provide for children, Ranade claims, Indian peasants believed that "their religion inculcates marriage as a sacred duty."[84]

From this perspective, Indian "overpopulation" was the product of a specific intersection of colonial policies with customary conjugal practices of universal and prepuberty marriage. The article called upon readers to question these practices as a way to bring reproduction in line with colonial economic constraints. For Ranade, such a shift in marriage could not occur via legislation by a foreign government; it required the "educated and reflective" among the native population to change public opinion among the masses.[85] He figures the middle-class intelligentsia—men very much like himself—as the central historical actors, capable of effecting change in the reproductive sexualities and economic fortunes of its "own" peasantry. Despite their political disenfranchisement, and without access to financial capital, these men could still intervene in the economic life of the nation through the reform of marriage.

I term Ranade's intervention a national rereading of Malthus because it adopts core Malthusian principles about population but refutes colonial discourses that claimed Indian overpopulation was the sole cause for poverty. This endeavor to theorize overpopulation and poverty in the context of specific colonial conditions parallels Ranade's more influential work on political economy, in which he proposed an Indian inquiry that challenged the supposedly universal principles of the discipline.[86] The result, in "Over-Population and Marriage Customs," is a reading of Indian reproduction that is at once pro-Malthusian and anticolonial. Moreover, in mobilizing a middle-class intelligentsia to transform the nation's reproductive practices, the text sidelines the colonial regime and centers a section of the Indian population as the agents of change for the nation. Ranade understands marriage reform as offering "economic" advantage, insofar as it can reduce famine and impoverishment. These reforms also offered "cultural" benefits, since they returned Hindus to their earlier traditions of celibacy and sexual restraint and, as he argued elsewhere, were necessary on moral and humanitarian grounds. Consequently, the text's national Malthusianism joins together arguments about economic policies and cultural practices in India—about colonial impoverishment and indigenous marriage—to stake its claims about reproduction and population.

Just a few years after the publication of "Over-Population and Marriage Customs," these connections among marriage, population, and economy reappeared in one of the most significant public interventions on Hindu-Indian conjugality in the late nineteenth century, Behramji Malabari's

"Notes on Infant Marriage and Enforced Widowhood" (1884). Malabari, a Parsi publicist and reformer residing in Bombay, made a forceful plea to end the practice of marrying Hindu girls before puberty and supported the remarriage of Hindu "child widows." He circulated his "Notes" among British administrators and Western-educated Indians and received numerous responses. This marked the beginning of a fraught debate about child marriage that would consume public attention during the 1880s and early 1890s, eventually leading to the Age of Consent Act of 1891, which legislated a minimum age of consent of twelve for all girls in British India.

Like Ranade, Malabari insisted that the marriage of girls before puberty held grave economic consequences for India. The practice resulted in "a too early consummation of the nuptial troth . . . the birth of sickly children, the necessity of feeding too many mouths, poverty and dependence."[87] Taken together, these individual catastrophes contributed to a national crisis of poverty caused by overpopulation: "Here we are confronted with that grave economic problem—over-population in poverty. If over-population is felt as an evil in advanced and wealthy countries, where natural and artificial means exist to hold it in check, what must be the effect of over-population in a poor and backward country, where the evil is actively stimulated by unnatural means?"[88] These "unnatural means"—prepuberty marriage— produced a rapidly growing population that a country like India was ill equipped to handle. Because of these "economic" consequences of Hindu conjugality, as I noted in the introduction, Malabari called for the colonial state to legislate a minimum age of marriage for girls. A foreign government might hesitate to intervene in the cultural or religious practices of its subjects, Malabari conceded, but surely it could not ignore the "economic phase of the evil." Indeed, the low age of marriage threatened both the wealth and the governability of the Indian colony: "Taking infant marriage as a purely economic question, as a source of over-population and consequent disturbances, can the State do nothing to check it?"[89] Thus, in Malabari's hands, marriage became a legitimate public question, subject to a foreign government's jurisdiction, precisely because of its connections to population and poverty. However, in contrast to Ranade's "Over-Population and Marriage Customs," the "Notes" did not offer a simultaneous critique of both colonial impoverishment and prolific reproduction; Malabari indicted "infant marriage" while exonerating the policies of free-trade imperialism. Following from this argument, the Indian middle class did not figure as the agents of reform. Instead, Malabari's critique of prepuberty marriage prompted new engagements with the state.

Malabari's Malthusian analysis of Indian conjugality remained largely unquestioned among his respondents. Neither supporters nor opponents disputed his assertion that "infant marriage" increased the population by leading to motherhood soon after puberty or that population growth impoverished families and the nation. According to Keshavlal Madhavdas, for example, early marriages became customary at a time of "great prosperity in India and abundance of food, so that no one cared for increase in the number of family members." The custom was ill suited to the less prosperous present, when "the wealth of India is being diverted into several channels by which it flows abroad."[90] Others identified additional economic impacts of "infant marriage." For Gopalrao Hari Deshmukh, early marriage led to universal marriage among Hindus. Echoing Ranade's suggestion that some people ought to remain unmarried, Deshmukh lamented that every country required "a number of bachelors who could venture upon enterprise, foreign travel, & c." However, in India, this was impossible since "every man has a family. Even little boys are burdened with wives and children."[91] The result of these conjugal practices was a country in which people were unfit for either agriculture or trade and lived in conditions of poverty and economic stagnation.

Among the best-known respondents to Malabari's "Notes" was Ranade himself. While assuring Malabari of his support, Ranade questioned whether economic considerations alone would provide sufficient motivation for changes in marriage customs. He suggested that "mere considerations of expediency or economical calculations of gains or losses can never nerve a community to undertake and carry through social reforms" in marriage. This is a curious argument, given the contents of "Over-Population and Marriage Customs." Perhaps disappointed by the failure of his own economic arguments to promote change in marriage practices, Ranade seems to be rethinking the wisdom of this strategy just a few years later. Without refuting his national Malthusianism, Ranade instead speculates that fears about poverty or the promise of prosperity would not convince people to change sexual customs that mandated prepuberty marriage. Anxiety about overpopulation, in short, would not convince anyone to postpone their marriage. Instead, for Ranade, "only a religious revival" could offer the "moral strength" to make lasting and fundamental reform in Hindu conjugality.[92] He calls for religion, rather than economic rationality, to be the basis of reproductive reform.

In immediate terms, Ranade's forecast was correct. The late nineteenth-century battle over child marriage was fought not over "economical calculations," but in the terms of an emergent Hindu cultural nationalism. Public

ECONOMIES OF REPRODUCTION 53

attention focused less on claims about poverty or overpopulation and more on the situation of the child bride, heralded as a symbol of Hindu tradition but also of a degradation of that tradition. Two specific cases brought these debates to a head. In 1889, the ten-year-old Phulmoni died after sexual intercourse with her adult husband, Hari Mohan Maiti. Maiti's trial received widespread media coverage, propelling the case into the heart of questions about the nature of child marriage and its wider implications for Hindu society. Equally controversial was the case of Rakhmabai, a former child bride who, at age twenty, refused to live with her husband on the grounds of personal incompatibility. Here, too, questions about the "consent" of child brides reverberated across wider debates about the nature of Hindu marriage. As Tanika Sarkar demonstrates, these debates engaged in complex negotiations of community and individual rights. Linking the fate of the "Hindu wife" to that of a "Hindu nation," they helped to produce a new cultural nationalist politics in the late nineteenth century.[93]

Meanwhile, even as the child marriage debates provoked a distinct cultural nationalism, nationalists also began to delineate "the economy" in new ways. A pivotal figure in this emerging economic nationalism was Dadabhai Naoroji, who expressly rejected Malthusian thinking about population and reproduction in his major work, *Poverty and Un-British Rule in India* (1901). A former mathematics professor, Naoroji drew upon regimes of quantification and measurement in his number-filled analysis of the causes of Indian poverty, concluding that a "drain of wealth" from India to Britain left the colony impoverished. To make this argument, Naoroji had to contend with colonial discourses that looked to overpopulation as the primary cause of Indian poverty. Claims that India was overpopulated, he insisted, were merely a "favorite excuse" of "Anglo-Indians."[94] Under current conditions, he wrote, "it is absurd to talk of over-population—i.e., the country's incapability by its food or other produce, to supply the means of support to its people—if the country is unceasingly and forcibly deprived of its means of capital. Let the country keep what it produces, for only then can any right judgment be formed whether it is over-populated or not."[95] Conditions in India were thus not the result of "economic laws" of free trade or population growth but of the "pitiless *perversion*" of these laws under British rule.[96]

Naoroji's rejection of Malthusian analysis helped to frame the Indian economy as a site of critique that stood apart from marriage and sexuality. Therefore, for Naoroji, unlike for Ranade or Malabari, the problem of poverty could not be addressed by a middle-class intelligentsia that reformed their own marriages, their own bodies, and their "own" peasantry. There was no biopolitical solution, in other words, to the economic problems posed by a colonial drain of wealth.[97] Instead, *Poverty and Un-British Rule* insists that "the economy" must be addressed and transformed *prior* to any consideration of questions about overpopulation and reproduction. Consequently, Naoroji offers no recuperation of Malthus, repurposed in the name of national economic development; the text's critique of colonial and national Malthusianisms, and their attendant reproductive politics, charts a different terrain of struggle.

Birth Control in an Imperial World

While concerns about Indian famine prompted men like Ranade and Malabari to call for reforms in Indian marriage, and for Naoroji to excoriate a colonial drain of wealth, the same conjuncture helped to fuel a campaign for birth control led by a woman, Annie Besant. Her campaign began from the familiar Malthusian premise that human reproduction would increase beyond its means of subsistence, but Besant also brought something radically new to the reproductive politics of the late nineteenth century. That is, she called for control over reproductive capacities not via raising the age of marriage or encouraging celibacy but through contraception. Moreover, although Besant was based in London, her case for birth control depended on India. Arguing that the recent Indian famine provided proof that the colony was overpopulated, she recommended contraception as the best remedy to prevent the starvation of many millions of Indians. Controlling births, in other words, was the best means to bring the Indian population into balance with food and finance. In this way, Besant's campaign for birth control rendered contraception into a reproductive technology that claimed to address the economies of impoverishment in an imperial world.

Besant insisted that birth control was the best means to regulate reproduction since it enabled the expression of "natural desire" while controlling its consequences.[98] In her trial defense when charged with obscenity for publishing Knowlton's birth control manual, Besant thus argued that any attempt to delay marriage or enforce celibacy was bound to fail because it ignored sexual desire. Meanwhile, poor people, both in Britain and across its empire, suffered the most from these failures, since they lived in conditions where there was "food enough for two but not enough for twelve."[99] Under these circumstances, Besant called birth control the only rational response to poverty. She and her supporters termed this argument a "neo-Malthusian" call for contraception, since it adopted Malthus's arguments about population but rejected his ideas about birth control. At her trial, Besant built this case meticulously, citing Malthus as well as his utilitarian followers, including John Stuart Mill, to make what she termed an economic case for reproductive regulation.

Following her acquittal, Besant continued her campaign for birth control. She and Charles Bradlaugh founded a Malthusian League in July 1877, with the goal of spreading "among the people by lectures, cheap books, leaflets, and all practicable means a knowledge of the law of population, and of its practical application."[100] The League's first members were drawn from the Defence Committee constituted in support of Bradlaugh and Besant during their trial, but Besant invited others to join, especially the "poor, above all for whom the struggle is being fought."[101] While building the Malthusian League, Besant also authored *The Law of Population*, a text she hoped might replace Knowlton's *Fruits of Philosophy*. The pamphlet explained the mechanism of fertilization and listed several birth control techniques, including condoms, withdrawal, and Besant's most favored method, the contraceptive sponge.[102] The text appeared with advertisements about contraceptive devices, and Besant herself recommended specific types of syringes, sponges, and pessaries and provided information about where to obtain them. *The Law of Population* was immensely successful, selling 40,000 copies in its first three years.[103] By 1891, it had sold 175,000 copies in England, had been reprinted in the United States and Australia, and had been translated into German, Dutch, Italian, and French—making it among the most widely circulated tracts on contraception in its time.[104] Although Besant's text was not an official publication of the Malthusian League, the organization advertised and distributed it, recommending it especially to those who sought "practical advice" on contraceptive methods.[105]

Indian famine gave energy and urgency to Besant's argument that birth control would bring reproduction into balance with the economy. In terms that would have been familiar to colonial administrators, she wrote that British rule had lowered mortality in India, even while Indian reproductive practices encouraged prolific growth. The result was famine: "It appears that our civilization in India, taking away the ordinary natural checks to population, *and introducing no others in their stead*, brings about a famine which has already destroyed more than 500,000 in one Presidency alone, and has thrown about one-and-a-half million more on charity." These circumstances put India in an untenable bind: "the law of population is 'an irrefragable truth' and these people are starved to death according to natural law; early marriages, large families, these are the premises; famine and disease, these are the conclusions."[106] Prefiguring the findings of the government's Famine Commission Report, Besant opined that Indian practices of marriage led inevitably to rapid reproduction and that, in the absence of Malthusian "positive" or "preventive" checks, famine was the necessary result. Yet whereas colonial administrators and famine commissioners had merely lamented this fact or suggested policies of emigration and agricultural modernization, Besant turned to birth control for a solution. Indeed, given Indian conditions, contraception was even more important for the Indian colony than for the British metropole. In Besant's terms, "Even our philanthropy [in famine relief] is misjudged and but aggravates the evil it seeks to allay. Our rebellion against the teaching of Malthus and [John Stuart] Mill is sad enough in its effects at home; in India it promises a harvest of two hundred millions in starvelings."[107] In other words, for Besant Indian conditions of famine fueled a Malthusian campaign for birth control both at "home" in England and more widely across the British Empire and the world.

In making this neo-Malthusian argument, Besant turned away from potential alternative frameworks of contraceptive advocacy, namely the sexual radicalism of early European socialist movements and the campaigns of Victorian feminists. Besant was familiar with Owenite socialism through her work with the National Secular Society and was undoubtedly aware of the movement's call for the collectivization of reproductive labor and commitments to "the liberation of sexual pleasure from the burdens of procreation."[108] Her defense of sexuality as a "natural" and necessary part of human existence for both men and women gestured to these Owenite ideals, and she retained this argument both in her trial and in *The Law of Population*. Besant was equally aware of the Victorian feminist movement, which, though it did not support birth control, developed a powerful critique of marital norms.[109] She was a vocal advocate for women's rights in her own personal life and wrote at length about women's inequality in marriage. Nevertheless, in her contraceptive advocacy, Besant avoided such critiques and argued instead that birth control would support earlier marriage and more genuinely monogamous conjugality. Her relentless attention to the doctrines of Malthus posited birth control as a scientific response to the economic problems of empire.

On one level, this neo-Malthusian framework of birth control advocacy offered Besant a way to challenge Victorian assumptions that deemed public discussion of sexuality, especially by a woman, to be obscene. The references to poverty and its alleviation in the Indian colony cloaked her support for contraception in more respectable vestments. Birth control was now harnessed to a mission of civilizational uplift and imperial responsibility. Moreover, her focus on poor and starving people situated Besant firmly within nineteenth-century humanitarian discourse on hunger, which marked starvation as the product of an unjust society.[110] As I have argued elsewhere, all this may have lent her birth control advocacy an aura of respectability and greater acceptance at a moment when, in both her personal and her political life, Besant faced accusations of sexual immorality and unfit motherhood.[111] Yet on another level, the choice to link birth control so firmly to famine and Malthusian overpopulation had far-reaching implications. Beyond simply energizing a Malthusian worldview, her argument made birth control a critical component of debate about the causes, consequences, and remedies for poverty. At a moment when new imperial axes of inequality were being crystallized, Besant called attention to Indian famine as a critical imperial problem and offered birth control as a solution. In other words, she suggested that contraception was a necessary feature of struggle against poverty in the British Empire. If this logic sounds startlingly contemporary, this is perhaps because it is. By the mid-twentieth century, as we shall see in later chapters, contraception had become a critical component of population control campaigns that claimed to target "Third World" poverty. Decades earlier, by referencing the famine in India, Besant was among the first to make birth control a tool for poverty alleviation, thus articulating a relationship between reproductive regulation and economic prosperity that would prove enduring.

Even as India came to figure so prominently in Besant's case for birth control, Indian writers and publicists also became important to the imperial circulation of neo-Malthusian ideas. Their participation helped to validate claims that overpopulation was an Indian problem and shaped the contours of an imperial contraceptive advocacy. The Besant-Bradlaugh trial, reported extensively in the English-language media in India, offered one site for this circulation of ideas.[112] Indian responses to the trial centered on Madras, a city profoundly affected by the famine. In the wake of the trial, the *Philosophic Inquirer*, a "weekly Anglo-Tamil Freethought journal" published in Madras and edited by Murugesa Mudaliar, contacted the Malthusian League in London to praise the "neo-Malthusian views so steadfastly and so bravely held by Mr. Bradlaugh and Mrs. Besant."[113] The League's official publication, the *Malthusian*, responded with its "hearty greeting to our fellow labourers and brethren of the new Malthusian faith in Hindostan."[114]

Mudaliar thereafter joined the League's international correspondents—drawn primarily from European countries and Australia—in circulating neo-Malthusian propaganda. He requested copies of the Malthusian League's pamphlets and in 1880 became a vice president of the League, thus occupying an important place in the organization's claim to connect neo-Malthusians globally.[115]

Mudaliar and the *Philosophic Inquirer* accepted Besant's insistence on the centrality of India in the supposedly global crisis of overpopulation, but the journal also charted out the specifics of India's population problem. In a striking parallel to Ranade's and Malabari's interventions, the journal identified child marriage as the central Malthusian issue among Hindus. According to an article by the pseudonymous "Veritas," "ever since the birth of the Code of Manu, the system and practice of early marriage is viewed by the faith-bound Hindus with a favorable eye." As a result, "the country is deplorably laboring under the burden of over-population, and the misery the laboring classes are suffering from is so enormously greater in magnitude that all our attempts to depict them in detail are an utter failure." Even the "great diminution [of population], owing to the late monstrous famine" in Madras and the Deccan had been insufficient to return a balance between population and resources. Consequently, "Veritas" looked to neo-Malthusianism as a solution to the problem of Hindu reproduction, since "conjugal prudence" would result in fewer children and a smaller population.[116] The Malthusian League, for its part, welcomed this message for its importance to the "teeming nations" of India.[117]

These nascent connections between neo-Malthusians in Madras and London took additional institutional form in 1882 with the founding of the Madras Malthusian League, an organization whose principles were the "same as those of the Parent League of London."[118] The Madras League was established just five years after its English counterpart and a mere four years after the official end of the famine, but there is little in the historical record attesting to the activities of the organization or its founders, Muthiah Naidu, Lakshmi Narasu, and Mooneswamy Naiker.[119] Yet the very existence of the Madras League, its goal of propagating contraception, and its stated affiliation with the Malthusian League in London are significant. Rooted both in the historical experience of famine in Madras and the Deccan and in an emergent neo-Malthusian discourse, in which India played a critical role, the Madras Malthusian League suggests the contours of a reproductive politics that connected an Indian economy to Indian sexual practices and that moved from the Indian colony to the British metropole and back again.

Besant herself would eventually move to India, but not as a birth control activist. After meeting the occultist and philosopher Helena Blavatsky in 1890, Besant shifted away from her radical secular politics and became a member of the Theosophical Society. In that capacity, she traveled to India, where she became president of the organization, and lived in Madras, where its international headquarters were located. Active in Indian nationalist politics, she became a leader of the Home Rule League during World War I and was elected president of the Indian National Congress in 1917. Besant's shifting political and geographic locations changed her reproductive politics as well, and in 1891, she withdrew *The Law of Population* from circulation. Writing of her decision in *Theosophy and the Law of Population* in 1896, Besant did not completely disavow her earlier Malthusian concerns with poverty, and she acknowledged that birth control might serve as a "palliative" for the poor. However, as a theosophist, she claimed to look away from the "material plane" that had been the basis of her support for birth control in the 1870s and proposed that control over "sexual instincts" was "the task to which humanity should set itself." Foreshadowing Gandhi's more famous call for *brahmacharya*, Besant called for "self-restraint within marriage" and rejected birth control. Removing reproduction from a question about economy, *Theosophy and the Law of Population* looked instead to "spiritual intelligence" to make change.[120] Yet, despite Besant's ultimate rejection of birth control, her neo-Malthusian claims about famine, poverty, and contraception continued to resonate throughout the nineteenth century and into the twentieth. As we shall see in the following chapters, some of India's earliest birth control advocates would draw inspiration from Besant, both in her contraceptive advocacy and in her Indian nationalism. While Besant herself never brought these parts of her life together, her successors would eventually call for contraception as a means for nationalist economic progress.

Conclusion

During the last decades of the nineteenth century, conditions in India prompted a rearticulation of reproduction as an economic question. This new economy of reproduction depended, in part, upon a new regime of numbers, which quantified the population and made it a target of administration. These processes of quantification occurred in the context of famine, and this, too, shaped how reproduction entered into public debate. As famine seemed to provide empirical proof of Malthusian theories, the colonial state weighed the life of the population against the costs of its sustenance. Within this calibration of life, colonial administrators like Richard Temple and Indian reformers like M. G. Ranade represented population as an economic cost and suggested that reforming reproductive practice to control population growth would bring economic benefit. This was the context that enabled Malabari to demand colonial legislation on child marriage as an economic question and supported Annie Besant's conviction that birth control could remedy poverty in the British Empire. In short, reforming reproductive practices seemed to promise a way to grapple with the period's major crises of subsistence.

Reproduction was economized even as the broad contours of a new economic nationalism took shape in late nineteenth-century India. Ranade and Naoroji, among others, made the emergent category of the economy foundational to a national imaginary. In other words, they could imagine India as a bounded territorial entity, as a nation-in-the-making, in part through demarcating its national economy. This vision of the national economy, as Manu Goswami argues, emerged from a critique of colonialism and classical political economy, alongside a "naturalization of the interlinked categories of nation, economy, and territory."[121] Consequently, the question of reproduction was not asked and answered in preexisting economic terms. Rather, what "the economy" was—what it included and excluded, how it mapped onto India as nation and territorial entity—was being worked out even as reproduction was economized. These categories of thought overlapped and were co-constituted.

Ultimately, however, the dominant strands of Indian economic nationalism moved away from reproduction, and from Malthusian population theories in their critique of colonialism. Ranade himself would keep his work in "social reform"—regarding practices of child marriage, widow remarriage, or religious custom—largely distinct from his theories of Indian political economy. His ideas in "Over-Population and Marriage Customs" thus did not reappear in his major interventions in the field.[122] Organizations like the Madras Malthusian League, which centered reproduction in their analysis of Indian poverty, were likely short-lived. Malabari's campaigns against infant marriage eventually turned toward "religion" and "culture" as key battlegrounds. Even Besant—perhaps the most committed Malthusian— would disavow her own advocacy of both Malthus and birth control as she joined the cause of Indian nationalism.

Yet the economizing of reproduction that first emerged in the context of famine in the late nineteenth century would have a long life in colonial and postcolonial India. In particular, the notion that Indian conjugality con-tributed to Indian impoverishment endured across the decades and was taken up both by reformers and by defenders of the status quo. As the next chapter demonstrates, this idea gained new life during the interwar decades, when feminist and eugenic movements recentered reproduction within a national body politic.

CHAPTER 2

FERTILITY, SOVEREIGNTY, AND THE GLOBAL COLOR LINE

TO COMMEMORATE ITS INITIATIVES IN MATERNAL AND INFANT welfare, the municipal government of Madras held a "City Health and Baby Week" in 1930. Exhibits showcased services such as a milk depot and health clinics. Public health posters offered parenting advice alongside more general suggestions about clean water, latrines, refuse disposal, and intestinal parasites.[1] Meanwhile, advertisers looked to the Health and Baby Week to promote their products. An advertisement for "Rajdosan elixir" proclaimed that "Beautiful Mothers" produced "Beautiful Offsprings," and the nerve tonic Jeevamrutam offered to "assist you to fulfill your desire."[2] The municipal government was keen to use the baby week to document its ongoing interventions in pre- and postnatal care for women and their babies. A commemorative volume released for the event noted that efforts had begun in 1917, when the city government had hired four midwives and one "lady doctor" to help reduce maternal and infant mortality. The program expanded through the 1920s, and by 1930 the city's "Maternity and Child Welfare Scheme" offered registration of expectant mothers, free midwifery for all women below a certain income, and free advice to expectant and nursing mothers. In addition, the program made available health visitors to conduct "inspections of babies" in their homes for the first year and provided free cow's milk to "poor infants." The result, the city claimed, was a substantial reduction in both infant and maternal mortality.[3] Perhaps in recognition of these municipal efforts, the city sponsored several "best baby" competitions during the week, in which infants were categorized by age, race, class, religion, and caste. Visitors to the exhibit could thus enter their infants in categories such as "Best Musalman Baby," "Best Non-Brahmin

(Hindu) Baby," "Best Indian Christian Baby," "Best European Baby," and others, who would share the title of "Best Baby of the Whole Show."[4]

The Health and Baby Week in Madras resonated with similar events across India and beyond.[5] As part of public health campaigns, they modeled a reproductive politics that made population "quality" an essential determinant of national economic progress and political status. Commentators viewed the Madras week with an eye toward other countries, noting with concern that India had fallen behind on the world stage. According to one observer, baby weeks were "an important item in the constructive nation-building programme designed to enable India to take her rightful place in the progressive nations of the world."[6] Indeed, such events were essential, since anyone who "aspire[s] to attain at least the same measure of national efficiency as is reached in England, and the other Dominions, and claim equality with them, cannot afford to neglect problems of health, such as affect the health and vitality of our people."[7] The chief minister of Madras, P. Subbaroyan, apparently agreed, drawing a direct connection between Madras's "best babies" and India's economic goals; in his words, "the prosperity of a nation depends on the welfare of its children," but in India high rates of infant mortality jeopardized this prosperity.[8] The promise of the Health and Baby Week thus extended beyond the health of the individual infant to chart possibilities and goals for the nation's progress.

The Madras Health and Baby Week offers one glimpse into an emergent reproductive politics in interwar India that invested biological reproduction with new meanings. The concerns about pregnancy, labor and delivery, infant health, and "best babies" that fueled the baby week were one part of a broader public debate about how best to reproduce the national body politic in order to foster its genetic "fitness" and racial "vitality" during the late colonial decades. The reproducing body thus became implicated in a range of claims about the future of the Indian nation, and its relationship to the British Empire and other nations of the world. As I argue in this chapter, these claims hinged on two sets of questions. The first concerned political sovereignty: Which bodies, and which populations, could rule themselves, and which must be subject to the rule of others? Which bodily practices, including reproduction, might make populations fit for self-rule? The second set of questions concerned rights to land, migration, and territorial possession. In other words, which populations had the right to increase and to colonize new territories? Which bodies, and which peoples, were fit to populate the earth, and which were supposedly dying out or fit only to remain in place, restricted by a global "color line"? Nationalists and imperialists, eugenicists and neo-Malthusians, public health officials and census administrators, Gandhians and women's rights activists all turned to reproduction to ask and answer these questions.

They targeted reproduction not only because of its impact on individuals and families but also because of its supposed implications for the Indian nation's health, prosperity, sovereignty, and geopolitical status. To trace this imbrication of reproduction with a set of national questions, this chapter begins with the publication of Katherine Mayo's *Mother India* (1927), a sensationalist text that attributed India's political subjugation to the population's sexual and reproductive practices. I read *Mother India*, alongside Indian responses to the text, to investigate an entanglement of reproduction with transnational debates about race, migration, and rights to land. While some Indian reformers refuted Mayo and challenged her imperialist and racialized analysis of bodies and land rights globally, by the 1930s debates about Indian reproduction began to shift away from these transnational frames and settle more firmly within the boundaries of the nation. The second part of the chapter thus explores varied attempts to solve the supposed problems of "Indian" reproduction within the territorial framework of "India" itself. I consider how reproductive reform became a means to control the quantity of the national population and the bodily "quality" of its citizens. As was the case in the late nineteenth century, the abolition of child marriage and the neo-Malthusian advocacy of birth control became key flash points in this process. These reforms rearticulated reproduction along nationalist lines, promising not only the country's best babies but also its best political futures.

Reproduction, Migration, and Rights to Land

In 1927, the American journalist Katherine Mayo published the enormously controversial book *Mother India*. Not one to understate her case, Mayo declared that "the whole pyramid of the Indian's woes, material and spiritual" rested upon a "rock-bottom physical base. This base is, simply his manner of getting into the world and his sex-life thenceforward." Mayo supported this assertion with lurid descriptions of the suffering of child wives and mothers, highlighting especially the *dai*, or birth attendant, whom she described as a "Witch-of-Endor."[9] A critique of Indian reproduction was at the heart of *Mother India*, and the book condemned how Indians married, engaged in heterosexual intimacy, bore their children, and raised them. Mayo's book quickly became a media sensation and sparked a massive public outcry in India. Thousands of people attended public meetings to voice their opposition to *Mother India*, and more than fifty books and pamphlets were published to challenge Mayo's conclusions. Gandhi famously dismissed the book as a "drain inspector's report," but concerned about the damage it might do to American perceptions of India, he sent Sarojini Naidu on a US tour to provide audiences with a different view of Indian society and political aspirations. The publication of *Mother India* thus became a notable event in the history of Indian nationalism and, as Mrinalini Sinha demonstrates, served to realign social and political spheres during the interwar decades.[10]

The controversy over *Mother India* was also a remarkable event in the Indian and transnational history of reproduction. In particular, I read the debates surrounding the book to map emergent connections between a biopolitics of reproduction, on the one hand, and a geopolitics of land and migration on the other. That is, reproduction became one way to distinguish between those "races" that had the rights to sovereignty and global mobility and those whose reproduction rendered them both politically subordinate and geographically immobile. Thus, although historians of global population suggest that a focus on the global geopolitics of land gave way to a biopolitical concern with bodies and reproduction in the early twentieth century,[11] I read Mayo's work and its attendant controversies to examine how a concern with bodies related directly to anxieties about land and migration during the 1920s and 1930s. At least in late colonial India, biopolitics did not overcome, or remain separate from, an imperial geopolitics; each shaped the other.

At its core, *Mother India* argued that Indians' sexual and reproductive practices rendered their bodies unfit for political sovereignty. In Mayo's terms:

> Given men who enter the world physical bankrupts out of bankrupt stock, rear them through childhood in influences and practices that devour their vitality; launch them at the dawn of maturity on an unrestrained outpouring of their whole provision of creative energy in one single direction; find them, at the age when the Anglo-Saxon is just coming into full glory of manhood, broken-nerved, low-spirited, petulant ancients; and need you, while this remains unchanged, seek for other reasons why they are poor and sick and dying and why their hands are too weak, too fluttering, to seize or to hold the reins of Government?[12]

The passage draws upon eugenic language, which I discuss in more detail below, to make political sovereignty a question of bodily and racial fitness to rule, and India emerges as entirely wanting in this regard. Comparing Indians to a manly Anglo-Saxon race, Mayo suggests that the former are entirely responsible for their own corporeal degeneration, manifest in their "weak" and "fluttering" hands that cannot govern. Significantly, *Mother India* frames this as a problem of public health. From her first chapter, Mayo alerts her audience that the book will leave "untouched the realms of religion, of politics, and of the arts" and instead limit "inquiry to such workaday ground as public health and its contributing factors."[13]

This framework had several implications for Mayo's broader claims about sovereignty and governance. Within India, the Montagu-Chelmsford Reforms of 1919 had devolved greater, though still limited, power to Indian governing bodies. Public health was among the areas transferred to increased Indian control, and it became a key arena for Indian politicians to introduce policy and legislation. The Madras Health and Baby Week was one example of these new initiatives. Moreover, as Rahul Nair has argued, public health officials played a key role in articulating an interwar "population question" that raised alarms about both the "quality" and growing quantity of the Indian population and, in some cases, called for birth control as a necessary reproductive reform.[14] Linking population, reproduction, and governance, Mayo's focus on public health thus placed *Mother India* at the heart of ongoing debates in Indian public life.

Public health was equally central to an emerging transnational sphere of governance during the interwar decades. The League of Nations spearheaded the collection of vast bodies of health-related data and produced reports on birth and death rates, population density, age profiles, maternal and infant mortality, epidemic disease, and caloric intake. The organization of this data facilitated easy comparison across geographic spaces and put Indian numbers in conversation with global norms and averages. At the same time, a focus on public health was important to discourses of US imperialism, with organizations like the Rockefeller Foundation launching campaigns in India to improve public health.[15] All of this helped Mayo to emphasize the global relevance of Indian conditions. Disease in India, she claimed, put the health of the world at risk. In a chapter entitled "The World-Menace," Mayo considers these risks in some detail to "estimate[e] the safety of the United States from infection." Each epidemic, she claims, would produce some "healthy carriers" whose ability to "spread disease lasts from one hundred and one days to permanency." Since "India is scarcely a month removed from New York or San Francisco," the United States was at risk from Indian bodies that might appear healthy but were in fact carriers of contagion.[16]

Mayo's argument, as Sinha demonstrates, rested on an anti-immigrant sentiment shared by American organizations like the Asiatic Exclusion League.[17] In the years preceding *Mother India*'s publication, this sentiment had been institutionalized in US law. The Supreme Court ruled in 1923 in *United States v. Bhagat Singh Thind* that Indians were not entitled to US citizenship on the grounds that they did not belong to the white race. A year later, the Immigration Act of 1924 (Johnson-Reed Act) introduced national quotas for some countries while ending Asian immigration. Moreover, American anti-immigration policies resonated within a wider Anglo-American world, in which the British Dominions of Australia, Canada, New Zealand, and South Africa imagined themselves as "white men's countries" inhabiting lands reserved for a white, Anglo-Saxon race.[18] During the first decades of the twentieth century, this politics was expressed through increased restrictions on Asian and African immigration, leading to the African American leader W. E. B. DuBois's prescient declaration in 1900 that the problem of the twentieth century was "the problem of the color line."[19]

Mother India's critique of Indian reproduction aimed to strengthen this color line, which divided white from nonwhite populations globally. The division was necessary, Mayo argued, because Indian disease and weakness threatened Anglo-Saxon whiteness. Toward the end of the book, she noted that "infant marriage, sexual recklessness and venereal infections" were so prevalent in India that "one is driven to speculate as to how peoples so living and so bred can have continued to exist." This fantasy about the disappearance of an Indian "race" echoes rhetoric more often used about indigenous peoples by white settlers, who suggested that the former might simply die out and clear space for the settler colony to become a white possession. Mayo attributed Indians' continued existence, despite the circumstances of their birth and breeding, to the "virile races of the north"—British Anglo-Saxons—who had reduced mortality through controlling war and famine. These imperial efforts, however, had led to unchecked population growth, and herein, for Mayo, lay the true danger of Indian reproduction: "The prospects it unfolds, of sheer volume of humanity piling up as the decades pass, is staggering. For, deprived of infanticide, of suttee, and of her native escape-valves, yet still clinging to early marriage and unlimited propagation," India's population was controlled only by disease.[20] This made population containment—through continued British colonialism and ongoing immigration restrictions—a central task for global public health. If Indian "early marriage and unlimited propagation" threatened to overwhelm the planet, then the only solution was to restrict Indians to the subcontinent while maintaining Anglo-Saxon political control.

Indian commentators rejected these connections between Mayo's anti-immigration stance and her critique of Indian reproductive practices. Their analysis was likely informed by debates about Indian migration, most notably about the movement of indentured laborers to British colonies. Although thinkers like M. G. Ranade had promoted labor migration as a remedy for India's economic problems in the 1870s and 1880s, the living and working conditions of Indians indentured abroad had drawn increasing nationalist concern in the early decades of the twentieth century. Nationalists noted the discriminatory legislation against indentured workers, alongside exploitative wage rates, in many receiving countries. They expressed anxiety about the gender imbalance among labor migrants and the consequent implications for sexual and family relations among workers. Prompted in part by Gandhi's campaigns among such workers in South Africa, nationalists lambasted the colonial government for failing to protect Indians abroad and for acquiescing to their second-class status in other British colonies. Their outcry eventually led to the abolition of indenture in 1920 and a stated commitment by the Indian government that subsequent labor migrants be protected from exploitation and receive full equality in the receiving country. Despite these professions, the reception that Indian migrants received abroad was still deeply racialized after 1920. In South Africa, where former indentured laborers were part of a substantial Indian population, they faced an erosion of rights.[21] In the Dominion colonies of Australia, Canada, and New Zealand, which had not taken indentured laborers before, Indians confronted increased restrictions to entry. In sum, despite nationalist calls for ensuring the free migration of Indians outside India, the 1920s witnessed the establishment of restrictions that prevented movement and limited rights.

Uma Nehru, who published *Mother India aur uska jawab* (Mother India and its reply) in Hindi in 1928, was a perceptive critic of these race-based restrictions. Nehru was active in the Indian women's movement and a participant in nationalist struggle. *Mother India aur uska jawab* drew from both strands of her political thinking to argue that the foreignness of British rule was responsible for India's social, economic, and political problems. Moreover, Nehru challenged the immigration restrictions that prevented the free global movement of Indians. In a startling move, she compared caste—one topic of Mayo's critique—to Anglo-American discrimination against migrants. According to Nehru, Indian caste prejudice was confined to "the field of social relations as in dining and marriage regulations."

> In the West, however, these prejudices have been allowed to infect the political realm. In the name of "national pride" and "security," therefore, Western rulers have enacted discriminatory regulations in their nations against Asians and other races, limited their access to work, and are further regulating their free movement. In ancient times, even before the advent of history, the Brahmans on the strength of their religious superstitions had made a section of their own society into untouchables. Today, in these modern times, Europe is the New Brahman that is reducing the rest of the world to untouchables.[22]

In short, Western anti-immigrant sentiment was a form of caste prejudice. Nehru turned the problem of Indian reproduction, as posed by Mayo, on its head. Rather than asking how to contain a supposedly weak and diseased population within India, she suggested that these practices of containment were themselves the problem. "Discriminatory regulations" against Asian workers, far from being a necessary response to Asian migration, were evidence of a political failing in the British Empire. Thus, Nehru responded to Mayo's critique of Indian reproduction by challenging the divide between white and nonwhite that constituted the global color line.

In the years following the publication of *Mother India*, even after the controversy surrounding the book had waned, the politics of reproduction remained enmeshed in race and immigration. Understanding these intersections of biopolitics and geopolitics—of the regulation of reproducing bodies and of migrating ones—helps to explain why reproduction remained such a fraught public question throughout the 1930s. These connections appear repeatedly in the work of Radhakamal Mukherjee, who was among India's foremost theorists of population during the interwar decades. Mukherjee, a professor of economics and vice chancellor at the University of Lucknow, chaired the National Planning Committee's subcommittee on population, which was created in 1937 by the Congress Party and tasked with formulating a population policy for independent India. During this period, he also authored two books. His *Migrant Asia* (1936) made a case for Asian migration across the globe. Two years later, Mukherjee's *Food Planning for Four Hundred Millions* (1938), as its title suggests, asked how

India might feed its growing population. While the two books tackled different topics, we may productively read them together—and in conversation with Mayo and her critics—to trace the imbrications of reproduction with migration.

Mukherjee's *Migrant Asia* argued that Indian, Chinese, and Japanese populations were the ideal colonizers of "tropical lands," including in Australia, East and South Africa, and the Americas. This was due to their bodily capacities. With a lower basal metabolism, smaller body surface, and lower weight, Mukherjee alleged, the "Asiatic peoples" required less protein and thus needed less land to produce the food for their survival. "With much less food and clothing and various physiological adjustments to a warm climate which are part of his racial make-up, the Asiatic colonist is at a far greater economic advantage in the tropical and sub-tropical lands than the European."[23] Although Mukherjee was not writing in explicit response to *Mother India*, his claims rejected the anti-immigrant sentiment that shaped Mayo's work and suggested that, in the aftermath of indenture, Indians were not just laborers but could also be colonizers. Mobilizing a language of environmental and racial determinism, *Migrant Asia* argued that Indians and other Asians were best suited for the economies of colonization and that their bodily adaptability to tropical climates gave them superior rights to the land, a right that superseded the claims of a "white race." Thus, while anti-immigrant discourses faulted Asian immigrants for undercutting white workers by accepting lower wages, Mukherjee argued that this was in fact a sign of Asian advantage and a foundation for Asian land rights. From this position, Mukherjee launched a critique of racial exclusion policies in these settler colonies. The claims of white settlers in these places had no basis, he insisted, since those settlers could not make the most efficient and profitable use of the land.[24]

Mukherjee's attack on Asian exclusion, which may be read as anti-imperialist in its challenge to white supremacy, depended upon a profound racialization of climate, economy, and people, whereby the Asian colonists' rights were rooted in corporal adaptations unique to the race.[25] His argument was also deeply implicated in a settler-colonial logic about indigeneity and supposedly "empty" lands. While rejecting the claims of white settlers, he retained the argument that "the vast empty spaces of North America, Australia, and Central and South Africa" could not "long remain thinly inhabited or inadequately utilized."[26] Although Mukherjee called for a "judicious recognition of the need of native tribes for natural expansion, and the maintenance of tribal integrity and individual self-respect," this assumption of emptiness was precisely the rationale that had driven the European colonization of Australia and the Americas and underpinned a possessive logic that fueled such initiatives as the White Australia campaign.[27] Mukherjee's conception of empty lands, in short, participated in a set of discourses that disavowed indigenous rights.

With its turn toward migration, *Migrant Asia* refused to pose reproduction as a problem for the Indian body politic. That is, the management of Indian population growth did not call for reproductive regulation within the subcontinent but required a global framework of migration that would see Indians welcomed everywhere. Consequently, Mukherjee called for a "scientific" reordering of population in global terms, proposing that an international body such as the League of Nations determine migration policies for global economic benefit.[28] However, soon after the publication of *Migrant Asia*, Mukherjee posed the question of population and reproduction quite differently in *Food Planning for Four Hundred Millions*.[29] Here, he asked how "India," as a bounded territorial entity, could produce food for a growing national population. Mukherjee offered several solutions for the problem of national food scarcity, including agricultural reform, industrialization, and—notably—reproductive reform via birth control.

Mukherjee's case for contraception in *Food Planning* moved away from *Migrant Asia*'s emphasis on the superior adaptability of Asians to the tropics and focused instead on the improvement of an Indian "race" within national boundaries. In particular, he outlined the threat that the supposedly prolific reproduction of "inferior social strata" posed to Hindu upper castes and classes. Adopting the communal and eugenic ideas circulating at the time, and mobilizing the language of differential fertility, which I discuss in more detail below, Mukherjee argued that Hindu lower castes and Muslims reproduced at vastly higher rates than their Hindu upper-caste counterparts. Indian reproduction was thus "dysgenic," since "the most fertile social strata in India are inferior," displaying a tremendous gap between "fecundity and culture."[30] As long as the "lower social strata" continued to reproduce rapidly, they would overtake the more "prudent" members of the Hindu upper castes, a category which included, not coincidentally, Mukherjee himself. By controlling the reproduction of Muslims and lower castes, Mukherjee argued, contraception could improve the "race" while making it fit to advance the Indian nation.

Throughout the 1930s, Mukherjee retained this dual focus on migration and reproduction, suggesting Indian emigration in some contexts and birth control in others. He understood Indian population growth as at once a global and a national problem that required the movement of Asian bodies across borders and the regulation of fertility among the "lower strata" within India. While historians have tended to highlight either one or the other aspect of his thought, my reading of *Migrant Asia* alongside *Food Planning* suggests a crucial point of connection between Mukherjee's anti-imperialism in a transnational context and his reassertion of class and caste hierarchies within a national space.[31] His anti-imperialist challenge to white settlement depended upon his assertion of a class- and caste-based Indian national "fitness" to rule India and to settle lands abroad. That is, Mukherjee's critique of a global color line depended upon a reassertion of lines of hierarchy among castes and classes in India.

However, for many other contributors to the population debates, Mukherjee's dual focus was not sustainable. They increasingly viewed reproductive regulation—especially birth control—as the only viable solution to Indian population problems. The Tamil writer T. S. Chokkalingam, for example, rejected the argument that Indians could migrate to "less populated countries," improve their economic position, and provide resources for the national freedom struggle. Such a goal was impossible when Indians "in these countries are treated like animals. . . . Places like South Africa and America are white people's countries, and they have created laws against Indians."[32] Hemmed in by racist immigration laws, Chokkalingam argued, Indians had no alternative but to restrict their own numbers via birth control. Perhaps the strongest rejection of migration as a solution came from the statistician P. K. Wattal. Given the global economic depression, he suggested in *Population Problem in India*, Indian migration to Ceylon, Malaya, and South Africa had been reduced. Indians were "not welcome anywhere," and in any case, "dumping, whether of goods or populations, is equally objectionable, and nations have every right to protect themselves against either."[33]

Not all writers were as explicit about migration as Chokkalingam or Wattal. Nevertheless, across a wide spectrum, a turn toward reproductive self-regulation was premised on the assumption that migration was not a viable option. Controlling birth, in other words, became an appealing solution when it became impossible to control land. If Indians were unwelcome outside India and treated "like animals" when they ventured abroad, then a national solution appeared to be the only option. Reproductive regulation seemed to offer the preeminent means to turn inward toward the nation, the family, and the body itself. Controlling individual reproduction in order to regulate national population at a moment when imperial power, anti-immigrant sentiment, and a global color line seemed to deny this national control: this was the heady promise of reproductive reform in interwar India.

Child Marriage and the National Body Politic

Just two years after the publication of *Mother India*, the Child Marriage Restraint Act (CMRA) promised a measure of reproductive reform in service of national goals. Instituting fourteen as the minimum age of marriage for all girls in British India, the new law provoked immense controversy about Indian sexuality and reproduction. Proponents and opponents debated the moral, religious, corporeal, economic, and public health effects of prepuberty marriage and negotiated questions about the age at which girls and women might commence sexual intercourse, become pregnant, and deliver babies. Although these debates were shaped by *Mother India*'s denunciation of Indian reproductive sexuality, efforts to raise the marriage age predated the publication of Mayo's book. During the mid-1920s, several Indian legislators introduced bills to raise the existing age of consent from twelve, as instituted by the Age of Consent Act of 1891, to thirteen or fourteen. Fearful of controversy, the government was generally reluctant to support these bills, but in 1925, public pressure forced the passage of a law raising the age of consent to thirteen. This rather negligible change did not satisfy reformers, who pressed for an even higher age of consent and a minimum age of marriage. In 1927, Harbilas Sarda introduced a bill in the Indian Legislative Assembly to establish a minimum marriage age for Hindus at twelve for girls and fourteen for boys. Meanwhile, the government appointed the Age of Consent Committee, which, after investigating conditions across British India, recommended not only a higher age of consent but also a legal minimum age of marriage. Sarda amended his act, now called the Child Marriage Restraint Act, to make fourteen the minimum marriage age for all girls regardless of their religious affiliation.

In making their case against child marriage, reformers drew upon an emerging interwar discourse that linked the bodily and sexual fitness of citizens to the progress of the nation as a whole. Gandhi was a major proponent of such claims; his famous advocacy of celibacy linked sexuality to a biomoral and somatic fitness to rule both oneself and the nation. More specifically, he was a critic of child marriage: "We sing hymns of praise and thanks to God when a child is born of a boy father and a girl mother! Could anything be more dreadful? Do we think that the world is going to be saved by the countless swarms of such impotent children endlessly multiplying in India and elsewhere?"[34] Practices of child marriage, in other words, resulted in an excessive number of "impotent children" who were ill suited to the tasks of national regeneration.

Connecting reproductive practices, bodily vitality, and national vigor, Gandhi spoke regularly of his fears that Indian reproduction would produce a "race of cowardly, emasculated, and spiritless creatures" rather than the strong servants the Indian nation needed.[35] Harbilas Sarda, as the legislative sponsor of the CMRA, agreed. In his terms, with the elimination of child marriage, "every man, woman, and child in this country [could] grow to his or her full growth and be able to work without shackles for the good of the country till we reach the goal we have set for ourselves."[36] Child marriage legislation thus became a means to improve Indian bodies—to enable their full growth, to make them virile and efficient—in service to the Indian nation. Moreover, it was an action that Indians could take for themselves, and a reform that they could institute within their own families and communities. Turning inward toward their individual bodies, Indians might together revitalize the national body politic.

The bodies in question were, of course, gendered, and the body of the girl/woman became a flash point for these claims about the vitality of the nation. The Indian women's movement played a critical role in centering women by highlighting the corporeal suffering of young wives and mothers. For instance, the feminist and nationalist Muthulakshmi Reddi, who was a leader of the Women's Indian Association as well as a physician and legislator, recounted to her colleagues in the Madras Legislative Council the suffering of girls who were married before puberty. These included one "child wife" who was burned to death because she would not satisfy her "husband's animal passions" and another girl of ten who was forced to live with her forty-year-old husband prior to her menarche. In her medical capacity, Reddi had spent many "nights and days with a heavy heart vainly moaning over their miserable condition," and she demanded that her fellow legislators acknowledge and remedy this pain. If they would not take action to save girls like these, Reddi told council members, they must at least acknowledge the national implications of child marriage practices. "If we want to grow into a strong, robust and self-respecting nation, if we want to reach our full physical and mental height, the system of child marriage must go." Reddi's words echoed aspects of *Mother India* and, like Mayo, she described the bodily consequences of "blind meaningless custom" in Indian society, while hinting at evidence of even worse horrors.[37] Yet, unlike Mayo, Reddi offered a different set of solutions. Indian reproduction, she argued, could be reformed through the efforts of Indians themselves; child marriage legislation was the first step on a path toward national development and progress.

The Indian women's movement advanced this argument, which centered women in projects of national reproductive reform, at multiple levels. Members of the Women's Indian Association (WIA) and the All India Women's Conference (AIWC) lobbied legislators and engaged in public debates in support of child marriage legislation. The AIWC managed to get one of its leaders, Rameshwari Nehru, appointed to the Age of Consent Committee, and members including Kamaladevi Chattopadhyay and Muthulakshmi Reddi offered evidence before that committee. Throughout their campaign, they connected reproductive reform to nationalist goals and inserted their voices—as women speaking for other women—in support of raising the age of marriage. In a joint memorandum to Sarda, the AIWC and WIA made their position clear: "At this psychological moment when Miss Mayo has focused the attention of the world on the sex life of India . . . you men think yourselves reformers when you fix the age of 12 as the proper age for girls. To make this age legal against the wishes of the organized, vocal, and progressive women will do more to retard Home Rule than you have at all realized. You will give the impression that Indian manhood approves of what other races in the world consider the sex standard of the degenerate."[38] India's claim to political sovereignty, they argued, required rejecting the "sex standard of the degenerate." Especially in the wake of the *Mother India* controversy, India's hopes for Home Rule hinged on reproductive reforms. Moreover, the memo asserts that the "organized, vocal, and progressive women" represented by the AIWC and WIA were the best positioned to determine these reforms and to instruct "Indian manhood" on the directions of change, since "we women ache even more than men do to save the widows and the child-mothers, and we say it can be done."[39]

These claims about reproduction developed with an eye toward India's status—both as a colony within the British Empire and on the larger world stage. Activists crafted a rationale for legislation that made the task of national revitalization through reproductive reform central to asserting India's geopolitical position. Ultimately, the Age of Consent Committee recommended a minimum age of marriage on these grounds, arguing that in anticipation of Indian independence, the country's status among the nations of the world would depend upon reproductive reform: "There can be no doubt that, now that India is soon to take her place in the comity of nations, it is all the more necessary that we should put her domestic affairs in order; the offspring of weaklings are generally physically degenerates and incapable of sustained physical or mental exertion."[40] Reforming the nation's own "domestic affairs" by regulating the intimate biopolitics of reproduction and sexuality became the precondition for Indian entry into a global geopolitics.

Contraception and the National Population

In the immediate aftermath of legislation on child marriage, birth control became a new focus of reproductive reform. However, while the campaign against child marriage centered on changes to the law, legislative efforts to involve the government in birth control met with failure. Attempts at municipal, provincial, and central levels to require the state to provide contraceptive advice and information were all voted down.[41] The single exception to this trend was the princely state of Mysore, where the government opened three birth control clinics in 1930. Across the rest of India, the campaign for contraception occurred in other venues: in the resolutions passed by feminist, eugenic, and medical organizations; in the creation of private birth control clinics; and in the publication of new magazines and journals promoting contraceptive methods. In these varied spaces, contraceptive advocates argued that birth control—like marriage reform—offered a means to promote national sovereignty by regulating reproduction and improving health. In this sense, birth control was a reform internal to the nation that would align the bodies of individual citizens to the needs of a national body politic. Moreover, as the Indian women's movement became a leading force in support of birth control, activists centered women and their bodies in this national project, promoting contraception as a means for women to contribute to the development of the nation.

These arguments for birth control developed in the context of economic crisis, specifically the global economic depression that began in 1929 and intensified during the early 1930s. In India, the depression vastly exacerbated economic dislocations that had followed World War I, and among its most drastic effects was a collapse of agricultural prices. Although the massive famines that closed the nineteenth century did not recur, the specter of hunger nevertheless stalked many millions of peasants, and economic stagnation continued to characterize these decades.[42] Some reformers connected their support for birth control directly to this economic crisis. For instance, the mover of the AIWC's first successful resolution on birth control, Vimala Deshpande, argued that the country "cannot afford to feed these unwanted children, and the world-wide unemployment and economic condition cannot be changed without practicing the birth control."[43] A supporter of Deshpande's resolution, Phulawati Shukla, added that, given global economic depression, it would be irresponsible to bring more children into the world "whom we do not have the means to look after."[44] Drawing upon long-standing neo-Malthusian discourse, these commentators argued that economic conditions made birth control an urgent necessity.

Their economic concerns intensified with the publication of the Indian census of 1931. The decennial count revealed an increase of more than 10 percent in the country's population, to 352 million. Although this rate of growth was not unprecedented, either in India or globally, the increase in absolute numbers seemed very substantial to contemporary observers, especially in comparison to previous decades.[45] The census did not by itself spark fears of Indian overpopulation, which, as we have seen, was a long-standing Malthusian feature of Indian political discourse. However, as Rahul Nair suggests, it did become a focus for a "population anxiety," in which Indians debated how to feed, house, and employ the country's 352 million while limiting future growth.[46] Birth control became one aspect of this debate, as the limitation of numbers seemed to require some mechanism of reproductive regulation. Even the census commissioner, J. H. Hutton, made this connection between census data, population increase, and reproduction. Voicing concerns about the "present rate of increase" of the Indian population, he warned that "efforts to reduce the rate of infantile mortality should be preceded by precautions to reduce the birth-rate." That is, "if the luxury of 'baby weeks' be permitted they should at least be accompanied by instruction in birth control."[47] Hutton's argument drew upon a building concern among public health officials, who had been raising alarms about high rates of maternal and infant mortality in India. Interpreting these rates as evidence of Indian overpopulation, these officials offered birth control as a means to control the population while also reducing mortality.[48]

The "science" of eugenics offered a powerful ideological framework for these developing connections among birth control, population, and economy. In India, as elsewhere in the world, there was an explosion of scientific and public interest in eugenics during the interwar decades, and it became part of the mainstream of research and discourse on race, heredity, population, and reproduction. The term *eugenics* was first coined by the British scientist Sir Francis Galton in the late nineteenth century. Influenced by Malthusian ideas about population numbers and by his cousin Charles Darwin's arguments about natural selection, Galton saw eugenics as a means to manipulate natural selection within the human species. Eugenicists examined the heritability of various traits and aimed for the conscious improvement of bodies, populations, and "races." Eugenic thinking, as Alison Bashford and Philippa Levine argue, always had an "evaluative logic at its core," whereby some people's lives—and their reproduction— were seen as intrinsically more valuable than others.[49] We can see this logic play out in the history of racist eugenic sterilization laws in the United States, first instituted in Indiana in 1907, whose models were later adopted by the Nazi regime in Germany.

However, as many historians note, during the interwar decades eugenics was an ideology of both the political right and the left. Eugenic rationales were adopted by "liberals and leftists," as Laura Briggs argues for Puerto Rico, seeking to improve health, lower infant and maternal mortality, and counter the racialism of tropical medicine.[50] Similarly, as Sarah Hodges demonstrates for India, eugenics "in a poverty-stricken colonial context provide[d] a powerful and enduring template for connecting reproductive behavior to the task of revitalizing the nation as a whole."[51] In addition to birth control, it could support initiatives in nutrition, sanitation, and health care. Adopted by feminists, anticolonial nationalists, and other reformers, eugenic discourse could signal a vision of modernization that sidestepped imperial constraints to call for action among the colonized themselves. Recognizing these multiple aspects of eugenics—while attending to its evaluative logics—helps to explain how and why birth control supporters drew so heavily upon eugenics in making their case for contraception.

Within these political and ideological contexts, the Indian women's movement was at the forefront of promoting birth control throughout the 1930s. The issue was first debated formally at the AIWC's annual meeting in Madras in 1931, when Lakshmibai Rajwade introduced a resolution calling for a committee of "medical women" to educate "the public to regulate the size of their families." Rajwade had trained as a physician and, like Reddi in the case of child marriage, drew upon her medical authority to argue that birth control was a measure to promote women's health. Speaking of the country's high rates of maternal and infant mortality, Rajwade noted that the condition of "mothers is physically and mentally extremely pitiable." They were forced into frequent pregnancies and suffered from the loss of their infants. She connected these problems of individual health

to the nation's health and economy, arguing that birth control was necessary due to the "immense increase in the population of the country and
having regard to the poverty and low physical standard of the people."
Finally, she concluded, birth control was a matter of national sovereignty:
"If India is to take her place in the comity of nations she must produce men
and women who will be worthy of that name. We must bring the science of
eugenics into our practical lives."[52] Birth control would enable this more
"eugenic" reproduction by reducing maternal and infant mortality, thus
improving the health of individuals, families, and the nation itself.

Rajwade's resolution met with strenuous opposition. Her opponents did
not question the connections she made between women's reproduction and
national health and economy, but they debated the merits of birth control
in relation to other methods of reproductive regulation. Muthulakshmi
Reddi led this opposition; she rejected "unnatural methods" to reduce family
size and called for spiritual education on the "virtue of self-restraint and
self-control."[53] Acknowledging the suffering attendant upon "premature"
pregnancy and motherhood and its national and eugenic implications,
Reddi offered Gandhian self-regulation as the solution, calling for married
couples to control their sexuality in order to limit their reproduction. Eventually, her views carried the day, and Rajwade's resolution failed.[54] Just one
year later, however, thanks in part to Rajwade's intensive lobbying efforts
with local AIWC branches, the organization formally endorsed birth control; it promoted contraception at each subsequent annual conference
throughout the decade.[55]

Echoing Rajwade's initial resolution, AIWC activists called for birth control on multiple grounds. They claimed it would improve women's health,
curb population growth, address economic constraints, and promote
eugenic improvement. They argued, moreover, that birth control would
especially benefit poor women, since "educated and rich" women were
already aware of birth control methods. According to Rameshwari Nehru,
for instance, the AIWC's endorsement of birth control would have little
impact on its own membership. Rather, "it is the ignorant and poor who
have no such means at their disposal who are crushed under the weight of
frequent births and who need our guidance and advice."[56] The organization's
first successful resolution on the subject, passed in 1932, brought together
these varying reasons: "The Conference feels that on account of the low phy-
sique of women, high infant mortality and increasing poverty of the country, married men and women should be instructed in methods of Birth
Control in recognized clinics."[57] The resolution thus linked birth control

firmly to marriage and implicitly separated contraception from nonmarital sexualities. At the same time, in what Sanjam Ahluwalia terms a "polyvocal" advocacy of contraception, the AIWC did not identify a single primary reason for birth control but insisted that it could address numerous problems simultaneously.[58]

For AIWC activists, therefore, birth control was not solely a women's issue, linked only to women's well-being or autonomy. Rather, through contraception, they made women's reproduction central to addressing the problems of the body politic. By linking women's health directly to population and economy, the AIWC's polyvocal advocacy of contraception inserted birth control into a set of debates about national development. Indeed, as Lakshmi Menon—one of the AIWC's earliest contraceptive advocates—claimed, birth control was a necessary remedy in light of the failure or impossibility of national development by other means. As she noted in support of Rajwade's initial birth control resolution, the population of the country was increasing, but the amount of cultivated agricultural land had remained stagnant. Under the constraints of British rule, Indian industries had not been developed. There could be no relief for "excess" population through colonization, since all land was already occupied. If the world was thus closing in on India, and the country's population was limited to its own borders, Menon suggested, birth control was a "last resort" for the nation.[59] It could jump-start development when all other avenues were unavailable to Indians, and it made women critical to the development process. S. N. Ray made this argument even more directly, suggesting that other remedies for population and poverty, such as increased production or better redistribution of resources, could not address the scale of India's problems: "A Population, born in misery and bred in squalor, is not what India needs. Unless there is a considerable restriction in numbers with her present productive capacity it is physically impossible for her to raise a generation healthy and strong—in mind and body—to be able to work for her proper place in the comity of nations."[60] For Ray, birth control would ease the suffering of Indian women subjected to repeated childbirth; perhaps even more importantly, it would enable Indians to carve out their "proper place" among the nations of the world.

While making birth control a national concern, the AIWC was also eager to forge transnational alliances around the issue. In 1935, the organization invited the American birth control activist Margaret Sanger to India.[61] For the AIWC, hosting Sanger would raise the public profile of their contraceptive advocacy. For Sanger, India offered a new stage for activism at a moment when she was concerned that US interest in birth control was flag-ging.[62] She thus accepted the AIWC's invitation and would later publicize the organization's resolutions on birth control as a model for other women's organizations globally.[63] Sanger began her visit to India with an address to the AIWC's annual meeting in Trivandrum, where she described her trip as undertaken in a "spirit of atonement" to "undo the false and mischie-vous impressions created regarding India" by another American woman, Katherine Mayo.[64] Thus distancing herself from Mayo, Sanger advanced an argument that birth control would benefit women globally and Indian national aspirations specifically.

Like the AIWC, Sanger's support for birth control was polyvocal. Per-haps this commonality helped to solidify her alliance with AIWC activists and shaped their common language of contraceptive advocacy. In her decades of activism, Sanger had espoused numerous reasons for contracep-tion and had been willing to ally with individuals and organizations from a range of political perspectives. Thus, in line with the growing enthusiasm for eugenics during the 1930s, she had established ties with American eugen-icists and eugenic organizations to advance her case for contraception.[65] When in India, Sanger embraced eugenic alongside Malthusian concerns to advocate birth control. After her time with the AIWC in Trivandrum, Sanger and the British suffragist Edith How-Martyn launched a propaganda tour across the country. Perhaps Sanger's most famous encounter on this tour was with Gandhi at his ashram in Wardha. Although she was unsuc-cessful in persuading Gandhi—who was devoted to marital celibacy—to embrace birth control, this meeting raised the profile of contraception, and of Sanger herself, in India.[66] Her visit, alongside numerous public speeches, radio addresses, and private meetings, helped to solidify the connections the Indian women's movement had been making between birth control and India's population, economy, and global standing. Like the AIWC's resolutions on contraception, Sanger's Indian tour centered women's bod-ies as key sites of national development.

Although Sanger and the AIWC thus linked birth control to national goals, their polyvocal framework of contraceptive advocacy did not entirely subsume other feminist voices. Activists sometimes offered dif-ferent reasons for supporting birth control and centered priorities other than the health or economic growth of the nation. From within the women's movement, the most prominent of these alternative voices came from Kamaladevi Chattopadhyay, whose 1952 address to the Inter-national Committee for Planned Parenthood I discussed in the introduction. A few biographical details of Chattopadhyay's somewhat unorthodox personal life may help to contextualize her contraceptive advocacy. Married and then widowed while still a girl, she entered Madras University in 1918. Soon thereafter, she took an unusual step for a Brahmin widow by marrying Harindranath Chattopadhyay. The Chattopadhyay family, which included the Marxist revolutionary Virendranath Chattopadhyay—whose partner Agnes Smedley had connections to Sanger—and the nationalist-feminist Sarojini Naidu, was deeply influential in the young Kamaladevi's politics. While in Madras, Chattopadhyay also came into contact with Annie Besant, who along with Margaret Cousins were important to Chattopadhyay's involvement in the women's movement. She became a founding member and the first organizing secretary of the AIWC in 1927, and in this capacity she testified before the Age of Consent Committee. Two years later, she resigned from her AIWC position to devote herself more fully to the nationalist movement and eventually helped to establish the Congress Socialists, a group that remained within the Indian National Congress, in 1934. Chattopadhyay was not active in the AIWC during the mid-1930s, when the organization passed its resolutions on birth control, but she was a staunch supporter of contraception.[67]

Chattopadhyay argued that birth control could emancipate women from patriarchal control. As she wrote in "Women's Movement in India" (1939), a "masculine-dominated society always stresses the importance of women as a breeder." But with contraception, a woman "freed from the penalty of undesired motherhood will deal a death blow to man's vested interest in her. He can no more chain and enslave her through children."[68] Consequently, for Chattopadhyay, women's lack of control over their own reproductive capacity became a central component of patriarchy, and contraception offered them a tool of resistance: "This war which woman is waging today against man, against society, against nature itself, is against her sexual dependence. For as long as woman cannot control her own body and escape the sentence that nature seems to have decreed upon her, social and economic freedom would be innocuous."[69] Chattopadhyay's championing of birth control differs substantially from the AIWC's resolutions, which, as we have seen, highlighted women's health, more than women's liberation. For Chattopadhyay in this passage, the promise of birth control did not lie primarily in its ability to foster national development, or promote economic or political progress. Rather, contraception promised to attack the very foundations of women's oppression not only in India but more universally as well.

However, even this forthright antipatriarchal critique did not prevent Chattopadhyay from also drawing upon the eugenic and neo-Malthusian currents of support for contraception that swirled across Indian public discourse. In the same essay, she highlighted the "economic and eugenic" reasons for birth control and argued it would lead to a "clean and healthy nation." While critical of the Malthusian claim that a large population was the cause of poverty, Chattopadhyay agreed with neo-Malthusians that population increase could add to the "burden of the poor" and that birth control offered a remedy.[70] Her support for reproductive reform thus combined a radical case for women's self-emancipation with a range of other rationales for birth control, and neither argument precluded the other.

Differential Fertility and National Reproduction

The connections that women like Rajwade and Sanger, and even Chattopadhyay, made between birth control and the Indian nation depended upon eugenic logics. Proponents of eugenics suggested that Indians—not their British colonizers—could best manage their own reproduction and, through this, "breed a better India."[71] In other words, their reproductive self-governance modeled Indians' fitness for political sovereignty, while also creating the strong bodies necessary to take control of the nation's future. However, when connected to a national project, the evaluative logics of eugenics also raised fundamental questions about which bodies would best reproduce the nation. Whose reproduction might improve the racial or genetic fitness of the national body politic, and whose reproductive sexuality threatened to produce an "overpopulation"? Whose reproduction might be encouraged and whose discouraged in the pursuit of national modernity or development? These concerns underpinned the eugenic advocacy of birth control in interwar India, both within the women's movement and among various eugenic organizations.

In line with the growing global popularity of eugenics, several eugenic societies were established in India during the 1920s and 1930s. The earliest of these was the Indian Eugenics Society, founded in Lahore in 1921. It was followed by the Sholapur Eugenics Education Society (1929), the Madras Neo-Malthusian League (1929), the Eugenic Society of Bombay (1930), and the Society for the Study and Promotion of Family Hygiene (1935). Each of these groups connected eugenic and neo-Malthusian rationales for birth control and aimed to spread its ideas through publications, public meetings, and clinics. The leaders of these organizations were men, some of whom became prominent in eugenicist circles both in India and abroad. Perhaps most notable among them was A. P. Pillay. A regular correspondent of Western eugenicists, Pillay hosted Sanger when she visited Bombay. He served as honorary director of the Sholapur Eugenics Education Society and helped to establish the Society for the Study and Promotion of Family Hygiene.[72] He was also the founder and editor of the international scientific journal *Marriage Hygiene*, which aimed to "publish scientific contributions treating marriage as a social and biological institution."[73] The journal ran articles by Indian, other Asian, European, and American authors on aspects of sexuality, birth control, population, and eugenics. Among *Marriage Hygiene*'s contributors was the statistician P. K. Wattal, who, as I discussed above, rejected migration as a solution to population problems. Employed as an assistant accountant-general in the Bombay government's Finance Department, Wattal advanced an argument about differential fertility among religious groups, which, as I argue in more detail below, became central to his call for the eugenic reform of reproduction. Other key participants in this eugenics discourse included Sir Vepa Ramesam and Sivasami Iyer, who were founders of the Madras Neo-Malthusian League and supporters of the League's magazine, the *Madras Birth Control Bulletin*.

Eugenicist supporters of birth control investigated differences in fertility rates along class, caste, and religious lines and expressed anxieties about what these differentials might mean for the nation's future. This was a chief concern for Wattal, for instance. Mining census data to compare fertility across social groups and noting correlations between fertility and occupation, he concluded that "fertility is in inverse ratio to standard of living and intellectual development. . . . The well-to-do have many interests in life and more than one outlet for their nervous energy, but the poor have very few. Sex life for the poor means much more than it does for the well-to-do."[74] This excessive sexuality of the poor, he continued, led to their greater reproduction and stood in contrast to the supposedly more controlled sexuality, and varied intellectual pursuits, of their wealthier counterparts. Wattal also cited the "dignity and worth of life" among various social groups, concluding that "among aboriginal tribes" such dignity was lowest, even while fertility was high. For Wattal, the implication was clear: the overreproduction of the poor threatened to overwhelm the more constrained reproductive sexuality of the rich.

Others shared Wattal's concerns about fertility differentials between rich and poor. This was a driving impetus, as I discussed above, of Mukherjee's *Migrant Asia*. It was also important to the Madras Neo-Malthusian League's establishment of a birth control clinic in the working-class neighborhood of Chintadripet in Madras in 1938. The organization had been holding regular public meetings, running a small library, and sponsoring publications such as the *Madras Birth Control Bulletin* for some time. However, in expanding its efforts to create the clinic, the League aimed to reach the "semi-starved and half naked teeming millions of Mother India."[75] The organizing committee for the clinic, which included Wattal alongside Pillay, enlisted a "male doctor and a lady doctor," assisted by nurses, to offer free consultation to "the poor" for three afternoons each week.[76] This outreach was necessary to spread knowledge of birth control beyond the city's elite classes: "It is the illiterate and poor who are not aware of such methods [for contraception] but it is they who need it most desperately."[77] One writer in the *Madras Birth Control Bulletin* was clear that if only wealthy citizens used contraceptives, it would intensify existing fertility differentials between classes. He thus called upon "statesmen" to ensure that birth control was "made available to the class of people (poor and illiterate) who are in more need of it than others, as otherwise it will prove to be an evil rather than a blessing."[78]

Alongside class difference, caste became another key axis of eugenic concerns about differential fertility. In Madras, with its growing anti-caste Dravidian politics, the question hinged on Brahmin reproduction and sexuality. For instance, according to Murari S. Krishnamurthi Ayyar, who was a medical practitioner and the joint secretary of the Madras Neo-Malthusian League, Brahmins naturally had a lower birthrate than other castes. His book *Population and Birth Control in India* attributes this difference to the impact of their vegetarianism on their sexuality. Amplifying this "natural" difference was the fact that some upper castes and classes already had knowledge of birth control, in contrast to lower castes, whose supposedly higher fertility was unconstrained by contraception.[79] This emphasis on the restrained sexuality of Brahmins—especially of Brahmin men like Krishnamurthi Ayyar himself—asserted Brahmin superiority. Within the evaluative logics of eugenics, this made Brahmins the most appropriate reproducers of the nation.

The eugenic framework of differential fertility also applied to Hindus and Muslims, as a "communalization of demographic issues" made Muslim reproduction seem a threat to a supposedly diminishing Hindu community.[80] Many of these claims centered on male bodies, making their reproductive sexualities central to assertions of nationhood. Krishnamurthi Ayyar, for instance, suggested that Muslims had higher birthrates than Brahmin Hindus. One reason, he speculated, may have been that Muslim men were circumcised, making their penises less sensitive and prolonging their ejaculation: "This delay in turn greatly increases the chance of the female orgasm. . . . This favours conception as during female orgasm the mouth of the cervix opens and sucks in the spermatozoa."[81] For Krishnamurthi Ayyar, this image of orgasmic women and their circumcised male partners paints a threatening picture, since it underpins the growth of Muslim populations vis-à-vis Hindu Brahmins.

Although Wattal did not enter into such physiological or sexual detail, he too proffered a picture of Muslim reproduction gone awry. In a 1937 lecture to the Madras Rotary Club, reprinted in *Marriage Hygiene*, Wattal claimed to trace the demographic decline of Hindus compared to Muslims in Bengal. He argued that, based on census figures, "the rate of increase of the Muslim population in Bengal for the last 50 years has been one per cent per annum and that of the Hindus less than half of that." Wattal declined to speculate on "whether an upward trend is a sign of virility and a downward trend one of decadence. . . . The framing of a sound population policy is, however, an urgent necessity for every country."[82] Wattal does not specify what this policy might be, but he invokes a specter of Muslim demographic domination that was a consistent strand in interwar public discourse and was sharpened with the creation of separate electorates and the broader communalization of Indian politics during these decades. As Charu Gupta documents, these Hindu concerns about Muslim population growth claimed that Muslim conjugal practices—notably polygamy and the remarriage of widows—placed Muslims at a demographic advantage over Hindus, and even put Hindu women at risk of the sexual predations of Muslim men.[83] In this gendered and communalized sexual discourse, upper-caste Hindu men, who were imagined as vegetarian and sexually restrained, were beleaguered by the supposedly uncontrolled reproduction of the nation's "others." Eugenic ideas could thus serve to elevate the reproduction of upper-caste Hindus as essential to national reproduction, while simultaneously disavowing the nation's "others" as dangerous reproducers. The result was a contraceptive politics that linked birth control to the national population while incorporating only some bodies as appropriate to reproduce the nation.

Birth Control and Self-Emancipation

Across these currents of debate about eugenics, neo-Malthusianism, and the nation's differential fertility, one 1930 editorial in the Tamil newspaper *Kuti Aracu* offered a starkly different vision for birth control. Its author was E. V. Ramasami, a sociopolitical radical and leader of the anticaste Self Respect movement. Known as Periyar among his followers, Ramasami was a major figure in Tamil public life and a long-standing supporter of birth control. However, when a birth control resolution was brought before the Madras Legislative Assembly in 1930 and the issue became a subject of public debate across the presidency, Ramasami was keen to distinguish himself from other supporters of contraception, especially the Brahmin leadership of the Madras Neo-Malthusian League: "The reasons given by us for birth control, and the reasons given by others, are different. We say birth control is necessary for women's freedom and independence. Others give reasons like the good of women's health, the energy of the children, the country's poverty, or to prevent the fragmentation of family property. Many Westerners give the same reasons. But our view is different. If having children comes in the way of women's personal freedom, then we say that women should stop having children altogether. Having many children also prevents men from living free and independent lives."[84] Ramasami rejects neo-Malthusian and eugenic arguments in favor of birth control and casts aside maternal and child health as primary reasons for his support of contraception. Refusing to valorize reproduction or motherhood, he encourages women to cease reproducing altogether if it interferes with "personal freedom," and suggests that birth control may liberate men as well.[85] Economic concerns—the "country's poverty"—are similarly cast aside in a bid for contraception as a technology of emancipation.

Ramasami's broad rejection of the dominant frameworks of birth control advocacy was in line with his position on reproductive reform, especially regarding marriage. Beginning in the 1920s, the Self Respect movement had pioneered a new form of wedding ceremony that rejected the trappings of caste Hindu marriage, and Ramasami himself had been central in promoting these weddings, and their associated anticaste politics. At the Self Respect annual conference in May 1931, several months before Rajwade's unsuccessful attempt to gain AIWC support for birth control, the movement passed a resolution declaring that childbearing was an obstacle to women's freedom and that contraception was important for their liberation.[86] Women leaders in the movement, such as S. Nilavati, agreed, noting that since "it is women who experience the benefits and difficulties that come with having children," they should be the ones to control reproduction.[87] Similarly, Indrani Balasubramaniam called for decisions about birth control to be made by women and not by the male-dominated Madras Legislative Council: "Who bears the children? Is it men? Or women? If the men who are opposed to birth control ever experienced the suffering of giving birth, they would never speak as they do."[88] For these activists, contraception offered a tool for women's self-emancipation, rather than for individual or national self-governance.

Consequently, they centered oppression and social change to make their case, arguing that contraception was a vehicle of resistance against class and gender inequalities. For instance, Self Respect writer T. D. Gopal noted that Tamil-Indian society had failed working-class mothers and their children. "What is the reply of these women," he asked, "to a society which treats them merely as 'child-manufacturing machines' and treats their children in an unjust manner?" These children were not given a proper education, shelter, or food, and their mothers were "deprived of a natural environment to care for their children." Perhaps, then, Gopal speculates, women will "say that they won't reproduce unless society stops maltreating their children. . . . Why can't women make a vast, collective wish and tell the society that they won't bear children until the wishes of a girl child in the poorest of families are fulfilled at once?"[89] Thus, in contrast to upper-caste eugenic and neo-Malthusian discourse, Gopal does not imagine poor and lower-caste women to be less desirable reproducers. Nor does he suggest that poverty was caused by bearing "too many" children, or that the children of the poor were less eugenically fit. Rather, he calls for poor women to control their reproductive capacity as a mode of revaluing their own labor—and their own children—under conditions of caste and class oppression. By allowing women to refuse childbirth in a society that so fundamentally undermined their gendered reproductive labor, birth control became a tool for poor women to craft their own liberation.

However, despite these sweeping claims about the emancipatory prospects of birth control, the Self Respect movement did not entirely jettison eugenic or neo-Malthusian frameworks in its contraceptive advocacy. The Self Respect newspaper, *Kuti Aracu*, regularly featured articles addressing the growth of the Indian population and the problems of poverty, especially in the context of economic depression. Birth control advocates, including Ramasami himself on occasion, emphasized that contraception could improve the "quality" and health of the population while controlling its increase: "In our country, the population is growing daily. Many people have no employment, and no means to live, and yet they go on having more and more children. They suffer without the strength to care for, or educate, these children."[90] These claims were in line with mainstream eugenic and neo-Malthusian population anxieties, even while they disavowed concerns of differential fertility. In this sense, the movement's insistence that birth control was a technology of self-emancipation did not entirely displace other rationales for contraception. We find instead that eugenic visions for improving the race existed alongside calls for poor and lower-caste women to use birth control to challenge patriarchal control over their bodies and labor.[91] Therefore, what distinguished Self Respect contraceptive advocacy was not its adherence to, or rejection of, eugenics and neo-Malthusianism but its refusal to link reproductive "fitness" to caste or class. In this regard, Self Respect discourse resonated with the anticaste politics of B. R. Ambedkar, who, as Shailaja Paik argues, centered reproductive labor in a materialist assessment of birth control.[92]

The Self Respect movement's reproductive politics, however, did not circulate beyond its Tamil audience. Although Ramasami and other Self Respect leaders were critical of child marriage, their campaigns for marriage reform did not engage with the women's movement on the issue. Self Respect writers debated Mayo's *Mother India* and reported on Sanger's visit to India, but this interest was not reciprocated.[93] The limited reach of Self Respect discourse thus forces us to consider which ideas about reproduction traveled—that is, became nationally or even transnationally relevant—and which stayed in place. The divide was, in part, linguistic: Self Respect publications were almost entirely in Tamil and did not move across national and transnational networks that were dominated by English. Moreover, through the interwar decades, claims about the eugenic reproduction of the nation gained political purchase and became a shared language of scientific research, public health efforts, international conferences, and transnational women's activism. This was emphatically not the case for the self-emancipatory politics of Self Respect, whose birth control advocacy did not claim to reproduce the nation, and whose caste critiques undermined upper-caste eugenic and neo-Malthusian claims about the fit and unfit reproducers of modern India.

Conclusion

As we have seen, reproduction became a national project in interwar India. Reformers imagined powerful connections between individual bodies and the body politic, arguing that changes to reproductive practice would promote national progress. Public health events like baby weeks, legislative efforts to end child marriage, and campaigns to support birth control all made reproductive politics central to efforts to reform bodies while asserting India's political status on a global stage. Connecting reproductive self-regulation to national sovereignty, reformers insisted that changes in how Indians married and engaged in sexual relations would promote nationalist claims for political independence, while challenging the racial politics of imperialism, migration restrictions, and a global color line. This was a politics, in short, that was both about bodies and about land. Biopolitical regulation of the reproducing body was meant to produce geopolitical shifts in India's relation with the world, supporting claims to sovereignty within the nation and the rights to mobility across the globe.

At the same time, concerns about differential fertility—and its supposed connections to caste, class, and religious affiliation—also shaped the contours of debate and demarcated between "fit" and "unfit" reproducers. Reproductive regulation thus did not apply to all Indians equally, but targeted some people's reproduction as "dysgenic" or as an excess that produced overpopulation. As economic crisis in the 1930s propelled these concerns about reproductive practice, the impetus to regulate population became increasingly urgent. These concerns would eventually become the foundation for the postcolonial state's investment in population control programs, as we shall see in the next chapter.

CHAPTER 3

FEMINISM, NATIONAL DEVELOPMENT, AND TRANSNATIONAL FAMILY PLANNING

AFTER 1947, DHANVANTHI RAMA RAU WAS ONE OF MANY LEADERS of the Indian women's movement who were reevaluating their work in light of the political changes heralded by independence. Rama Rau had served as president of the All India Women's Conference (AIWC) from 1946 to 1947, shepherding the organization through the transitions and traumas of the partition. She then accompanied her husband, a diplomat, to Japan and the United States, where the couple joined the ranks of representatives of the newly independent Indian state. Returning to her home in Bombay, Rama Rau reconnected with her AIWC colleagues, but as she writes in her memoir, she was unsure of how best to direct her energies. She then met a "welfare worker" who introduced her to two "tenement families." Rama Rau professed herself shocked by the poverty and poor health of both parents and children. "[W]hen I thought over these glimpses of slum life," she recounts, "it became perfectly clear to me that, however much our social workers tried to improve conditions, nothing could be accomplished while unlimited numbers of children continued to be born in crowded houses where expansion was impossible."[1]

In Rama Rau's retelling, this realization provoked her lifelong commitment to controlling India's population: "I knew then that I had found a new purpose in life. There was no question in my mind that I should work for family planning single-mindedly and intensively. The limiting of our population was a fundamental and pivotal necessity if we were to make the gigantic task of social and economic improvement successful."[2] She founded the Family Planning Association of India (FPAI) in 1949, and it soon became the country's largest nongovernmental organization in the field of population control. Three years later, she helped to create the International Planned Parenthood Federation (IPPF) and served as its president from 1963 to 1971.[3] In both the national and transnational arenas, Rama Rau established herself as a central figure in the drive to control population through reproductive regulation.

Rama Rau's trajectory, from her involvement in the Indian women's movement to her founding of India's premier family planning organization to her leadership of a transnational population control network, suggests important connections between feminism and family planning during India's transition to independence. Rama Rau herself represented this trajectory as seamless. She invoked sympathy and support for women as her motivation behind family planning; her encounter with the suffering mothers of Bombay tenements thus sparked her drive to create the FPAI. At the same time, Rama Rau linked family planning to population control in the service of national development, arguing that easing women's suffering via birth control was a foundational step in India's social and economic progress after independence. These national commitments, moreover, always developed with an eye toward transnational networks, and Rama Rau was an eager collaborator with an emerging global population establishment. In creating these connections, Rama Rau was not alone. During the transition to independence, activists in the women's movement were central to making family planning a key component of national, as well as women's, development.

This chapter explores the transitional decade, from the early 1940s, when the women's movement positioned birth control as a vehicle for economic and social development in independent India, to the early 1950s, when the ideological and institutional foundations of India's population control policies were put into place. Traversing independence in 1947, this was a period when hopes about independent India's future grappled with the tragedies of the partition and the lofty promises of anticolonial struggle confronted the realities of profound inequality. During this decade, new state institutions and ideologies developed in tandem with a rising concern that population growth was outpacing India's food supply. Increasingly, women's reproduction was targeted as a core reason for this imbalance between population and food, and family planners began to argue that reproductive regulation could be a tool of national development. Globally, these years also saw the end of World War II and the beginnings of decolonization. Among Western powers, concern about the growing demographic footprint of Asian, African, and Latin American countries sparked organizations like the IPPF to call for global population control to avert a supposedly world-wide crisis. As it had in the past, India seemed to be at the epicenter of global population concerns, and Indian family planners like Rama Rau contributed to a transnational movement to control population. Their efforts also pushed the independent Indian government to include population control within its overall drive for state-led development planning. In 1952, India became the world's first state to establish a program of population control, thus vindicating the aspirations of the FPAI, which had been founded just three short years before.

Feminists had an important, but often overlooked, role to play in this transformation of family planning into a pillar of India's development regime. I use the term *feminist* broadly here, to include activists, organizations, and ideas aligned with the Indian women's movement. In terms of personnel, the networks created by the leading women's organization of the colonial era—the All India Women's Conference—provided some of India's first postcolonial family planners. In addition to Rama Rau herself, a number of AIWC members helped to create and staff the FPAI, and a few came to occupy important roles in the state's health and social welfare programs, where they shaped the country's emergent family planning efforts in the early 1950s. The AIWC's institutional networks extended beyond national borders as well. The organization's connections with Margaret Sanger had influenced the AIWC's campaign for birth control in the 1930s, as we have seen. These connections were reinvigorated in 1952, when, as I described in the introduction, Sanger and Rama Rau collaborated to host the International Committee for Planned Parenthood conference in Bombay, a transnational effort that also boosted the FPAI's commitment to making birth control a vital component of national development.

Beyond specific individuals and their networks of allegiance, my attention to feminists and family planning also analyzes the framework of ideas that linked claims about women's rights to emergent regimes of population control. As we have seen, the AIWC's first resolutions in favor of birth control in the 1930s offered multiple reasons why contraception benefited women—including eugenic and neo-Malthusian concerns about population, interventions in maternal and infant health, and women's sexual and reproductive labor within families. This chapter suggests that during the transition to independence, these multiple rationales for birth control began to coalesce around the women's movement's commitment to national development. Family planning supported national development planning, AIWC members claimed, because access to birth control would improve women's health by reducing their childbearing and foster economic growth by controlling the population. Family planning via birth control could thus bring development to women and the nation. In effect, this approach to family planning centered the postcolonial nation-state as an agent of women's emancipation, while simultaneously linking feminist politics to the agenda of state-led development. This chapter maps these transitions through a close look at how family planning became such an important component of feminist activity.

Attention to these intersections between feminism and family planning during the 1940s and 1950s challenges three historiographic assumptions. First, that activists in the women's movement were simply co-opted by the state in the aftermath of independence.[4] Second, that the impetus to control population via family planning was driven exclusively by men as technocratic experts.[5] And third, that the first postindependence decade was, at most, just a prehistory to the rise of state-led population control in the 1960s and 1970s.[6] While it is true that many feminist activists turned to the postindependence state as a site for their politics—and thus turned away from movement-building outside the state—they did not set aside their own agendas to accept already existing state policies. Rather, as the campaign for family planning suggests, feminists actively helped to make reproduction the terrain for state interventions into women's bodies and lives.[7] Overlooking this role leads to the assumption that population control was entirely a male-led enterprise, with its agenda and implementation set exclusively by male demographers, development experts, and bureaucrats. As we shall see, women both inside and outside state institutions worked alongside—and sometimes at odds with—male policy-makers to determine what "family planning" was and how it was linked to state-led development. Moreover, they often did so *as women*, claiming family planning as a gendered space that connected women to development projects. Finally, although the 1960s and 1970s witnessed the vast expansion of population control, as discussed in the next chapter, we cannot understand this expansion without attention to the ideological and institutional assumptions that made "family planning" so central to imagining and implementing "development" in the context of independence.

To map this history, the chapter turns first to the years immediately before 1947, when the women's movement established its commitments to planning for national development. These commitments took further institutional shape in 1949, with the creation of the FPAI. Building upon its links to the women's movement, the FPAI also mobilized transnational networks and helped to make India central to forging a global campaign around the question of population. The last section of the chapter investigates the terms by which family planning was folded into a process of state-led national planning with the First Five Year Plan in 1952. As I argue, family planning offered a means to bridge a series of tensions within the planning process by claiming to alleviate poverty without tackling structures of inequality and by promoting women's development while leaving the question of patriarchy unanswered.

Ultimately, the women's movement's commitment to family planning advanced a population control agenda that would have little interest in challenging the structures and ideologies of women's oppression. Instead, middle-class women family planners targeted the bodies and sexualities of poor and working-class women in the service of postcolonial development. Consequently, in suggesting that feminist thinking influenced an Indian development regime during the first postcolonial decade, I do not imply that "development" was therefore emancipatory or gender egalitarian. Rather, this chapter asks how a range of family planning policies that had so little interest in challenging gender, caste, and class inequalities became justified in the name of poor and lower-caste women's advancement. To answer this question, I do not claim to uncover family planners' individual intent or motivations, although I highlight their claims about intent whenever it becomes visible in the historical archive.[8] More than intent, this chapter considers the far-reaching impact of discourses and actions that connected claims about women's needs and rights so firmly to a top-down model of family planning. Historians must grapple with this impact if we are to understand either feminism or the politics of family planning during the transitional decade of independence.

Planning Families for Women and the Nation

A decade or so before independence, and anticipating the end of colonial rule, several prominent leaders of the women's movement plunged into planning for national development. Under the leadership of Lakshmibai Rajwade, who had introduced the AIWC's first resolution on birth control in 1931, they joined the Congress Party's National Planning Committee to produce a report titled *Woman's Role in the Planned Economy* (WRPE). The WRPE report gave prominent mention to birth control, arguing that contraception would not only improve Indian women's lives but also contribute to the nation's development by controlling population, reducing food scarcity, and alleviating poverty. Consequently, the authors argued, family planning was a critical vehicle to bring women into the state's development mandate. They called for the state to ensure women's access to family planning services; at the same time, they called upon women to take responsibility for limiting their families in service to the nation. Their arguments became the foundation for the women's movement's commitment to reproductive regulation as a component of national planning for women.

The WRPE was one of a series of reports produced by various subcommittees of the National Planning Committee, which the Congress Party established in 1938 under the chairmanship of Jawaharlal Nehru to create a program of India's planned development with a view toward independence. The subcommittee on women, which produced the WRPE report, included in addition to Rajwade many leading figures of the women's movement, such as Aruna Asaf Ali, Vijayalakshmi Pandit, Rameshwari Nehru, Hansa Mehta, Sarojini Naidu, Durgabai Joshi, Begum Shareefah Hamid Ali, and Muthulakshmi Reddi.[9] Their report broke radical ground, stepping away from the largely middle-class-centered agenda of the colonial-era women's movement, as Maitrayee Chaudhuri demonstrates, by focusing on women as workers and by bringing women's labor firmly into consideration as part of the national economy. At the same time, however, the WRPE foreclosed the more revolutionary implications of its own analysis, reverting instead to an emphasis on bourgeois rights of property ownership and citizenship. Chaudhuri traces this contradiction to a realignment between the Congress Party and Indian business interests, which led the NPC overall to offer a radical class analysis while dismissing the possibility of its realization.[10]

We see similar contradictions between a deep-rooted analysis and limited conclusions in the WRPE's discussion of families, sexualities, and contraception. The report develops a thorough critique of familial patriarchies but appears to ignore the implications of this critique in its recommendations for birth control. For instance, the authors condemn joint families for their oppression of women: "The present position of woman in the Joint Hindu Family system is incompatible with her emancipation or her free development as an individual . . . her position is considered only in virtue of her relationship to man, as wife, mother or daughter."[11] Alongside this rejection of the joint family, the report challenges norms about women's responsibilities as mothers: "We would like to displace the picture so deeply impressed upon the racial imagination of man striding forward to conquer new worlds, woman following wearily behind with a baby in her arms. The picture which we now envisage is that of man and woman, comrades of the road, going forward together, the child joyously shared by both."[12] This passage positions reproduction—and in particular the work of social reproduction—as a burdensome form of labor that has hindered women's ability to "conquer new worlds." The WRPE imagines a new division of labor whereby parenting is a shared task, which would enable women's fuller participation in the life and work of the nation. This potentially radical challenge to the gendering of domestic and reproductive labor could offer the ideological grounds for linking birth control to the WRPE's calls for gender equality. Freed from the reproductive labors of constant childbearing and child-rearing, women as workers could take a new place alongside men as "comrades of the road" in building the nation.

However, the WRPE disregards this antipatriarchal critique in its chapter titled "Birth Control or Limitation of the Family." Without reference to their earlier analysis of women's reproductive labor or subordination within families, the authors use neo-Malthusian ideas to argue that limiting the number of children would "help to relieve the people of poverty, unemployment, malnutrition, and other miseries due to over population." Therefore, family limitation is in the interests of "the children, the parents as well as the nation." The report also adopts a "eugenic point of view" to add that "the Indian stock is definitely deteriorating." To remedy this racial degeneration, the WRPE calls for "the right kinds of persons [to] marry," to properly space their children, and to limit their children to suit their family income. The report concludes these goals "can be achieved if men and women have sufficient knowledge of the methods of birth control."[13]

The WRPE's argument that reproduction is responsible for poverty and racial decline turns away from the report's own concern with patriarchy and gender inequality. Contraception is not offered as a means to tackle women's subordination within patriarchal families, nor their limited access to the labor force—both problems the WRPE had already identified. Indeed, the chapter on birth control does not even pose inequality and oppression— whether of gender, caste, or class—as problems for national development to address. Instead, population growth becomes the core development obstacle to national development, and the WRPE makes birth control a technological means to overcome it. In other words, although the authors of the WRPE mobilized feminist rhetoric to argue that women had a role in national development, they sidelined this argument when bringing birth control into the purview of the national state. The political impetus for challenging women's oppression, so prominent in the report's analysis of women's role in the planned economy, thus faded away in the WRPE's recommendation for family planning.

As a result, despite all its feminist leanings, the women's subcommittee did not differ very much in its birth control recommendations from other subcommittees of the National Planning Committee that addressed the question. The subcommittee on population, chaired by Radhakamal Mukherjee, similarly lamented the "dysgenic" practices of the Indian population and its excessive increase.[14] The subcommittee on health called attention to "too many and too frequent births" which added to the "prevailing poverty."[15] All three reports—on women, population, and health—focused on birth control as a tool for improving population "quality" and reducing its quantity. Not even the WRPE's call to reorganize gendered reproductive labor could bring contraception out of this framework, whereby "family planning" would serve to align women's reproduction with the needs of national economic development.

Throughout the decade, AIWC leaders strengthened this alignment through their contraceptive advocacy. This move helped to legitimize population control as a vital component of development for both women and the nation. Consider, for example, the AIWC presidential address by Hansa Mehta in 1946:

> Woman shall have a right to limit her family. It is the woman who has to suffer bearing children, looking after them and bringing them up in a civilized way. The right to decide the family should therefore belong to her. Woman should be conscious of this right which she must learn to exercise for her own good, for the good of the family and for the good of the country. India is over-populated and its population is going up while her resources are limited. Unless something is done to check this upward curve of the population, poverty, starvation and all the evils that follow in their train will be our lot.[16]

In Mehta's terms, birth control is a woman's right because of her responsibilities toward her children; women's reproductive labor is thus at the center of her analysis of contraception. However, Mehta also harnesses this labor to the service of the nation, and specifically to national problems of overpopulation. Women's rights to birth control are thus of national benefit, since they can bring into balance the relationship between resources and population within India. The cause of expanding women's rights, and of easing their reproductive burdens, is thus perfectly aligned with national population policies. Mehta leaves little room for these dual interests to diverge, since she insists that women must exercise their reproductive rights for the "good of the family and for the good of the country."

A few months after Mehta's address, the AIWC pursued these connections between women's rights to contraception and the nation's need for population control still further. The organization's "Indian Woman's Charter of Rights and Duties" was drafted in anticipation of independence and aimed to secure for women their rights within the national state. The charter contained a specific provision for birth control: "Woman shall have a right to limit her family. It will be the duty of the state to provide the necessary knowledge to married women who desire to have it for health and economic reasons only through recognized hospitals or maternity homes."[17] As in Mehta's address, the AIWC document frames "family limitation" as a component of women's rights. But in contrast to Mehta's emphasis on women's exercising these rights for familial and national benefit, the charter introduces the state as the guarantor of women's contraceptive rights via a system of "hospitals" and "maternity homes." Moreover, when turning the focus from women onto the state, the charter narrows the reasons for state intervention in birth control. The government's responsibilities are limited to "married women," who are assumed to need contraception for "health and economic reasons."

At the first AIWC national conference after independence and partition, the organization's president, Anasuyabai Kale, cemented this move by calling for the state to make birth control a centerpiece of development projects geared toward women. Speaking to conference members in December 1947, Kale noted the range of issues facing the country. The economy had been in turmoil due to partition and the influx of refugees, and industrialization was a key priority to raise living standards. Within this context, Kale invited "the attention of the Government to one more important problem which cuts at the very root of all and that is the alarming increase of population . . . until we regulate this abnormal increase by artificial means the economy of the whole country will collapse."[18] In particular, she added, the population was out of balance with the food available. Domestic production of food grains was insufficient to meet the demands of India's growing population, and longer-term plans to increase agricultural production would take time. Meanwhile, the government's struggle to meet food needs reduced the capital available for industrialization, and thus "the question of population" threatened to upend even the best-laid national development goals. Finally, India's high maternal and infant mortality rates decreased the "vitality" of the population, and thus became another block to development. In Kale's terms, birth control would at once improve women and children's health, increase the country's food security, and promote industrial development. This combined benefit to both women and the nation was the basis of Kale's appeal to the state.

Similarly, Begum Shareefah Hamid Ali, an AIWC leader and member of the National Planning Committee's subcommittee on women, invited attention to this imbalance among food, population, and resources. She exhorted the readers of the AIWC magazine *Roshni* to support national development goals by becoming ambassadors for reproductive regulation. "For Heaven's sake teach your daughters, your neighbours, and every woman in her home the urgent necessity of controlling our population. We simply cannot survive if we go on increasing at the rate we have been increasing in the last twenty years. No enemy need come and attack our country—we shall be dead through sheer starvation!"[19] Neither Hamid Ali nor Kale mentions women's "rights" to contraception; they do not even address the arguments the AIWC had previously invoked, of women protecting their own health or controlling their own reproductive labor. Instead, birth control becomes an aspect of women's responsibility to the nation. The Indian state serves as a necessary partner in this process, as women leaders like Hamid Ali and Kale made controlling reproduction a matter for state-led development.

This turn toward the state suggests the faith that Indian feminists had in the postindependence regime's interest and ability to foster social change—including changes for women. In this transitional moment of decolonization, when the nation-state was still in formation, many AIWC women argued that obtaining state power and turning it in the direction of women's development would represent the culmination of the colonial-era feminist struggle. This faith in the state was not unique to feminists but widely shared across the political spectrum. Arguably, however, this reliance on the state disregarded its caste and class composition, and the resultant limitations on fundamental social or economic transformation, as Maitrayee Chaudhuri suggests.[20] Indeed, the AIWC women who would occupy positions of state power and influence after independence shared in this caste and class privilege—which enabled their entrance into the institutions that created the family planning bureaucracy. I consider the results of these alliances and aspirations in the next section, on the institutionalization of family planning.

Family Planning as National Social Service

After independence and partition, women's activists mobilized to bring family planning to the state's attention. The most important initiative in this direction came from the Family Planning Association of India (FPAI). The FPAI drew from the ideological and institutional legacies of colonial-era feminism, most notably through its connection to the AIWC. But the organization also marked its differences from the women's movement's campaigns for contraception by actively involving men and by claiming the authority of scientific and technical expertise. As a result, I argue, the FPAI linked the language of Indian feminism with emerging demographic science to mark family planning as a form of social service aligned with national development goals.

According to its founding members, the FPAI was created because of growing interest in family planning within both the women's movement and the scientific community. As Avabai Wadia, who would become the FPAI's second president, recounts, the question of family planning was first raised to her by Elfriede Vembu, a social worker in Bombay. Vembu approached Wadia, who was serving as the editor of the AIWC magazine *Roshni*, for assistance in publicizing birth control among women. Wadia was interested in helping, especially since the time seemed right. The Bombay Municipal Corporation had recently decided to introduce family planning services at two of its maternity centers, while the Bhagini Samaj, a Bombay women's organization, had begun a birth control clinic. *Roshni* could support these efforts, but Wadia was concerned that the English-language magazine was not the best way to reach out to the "underprivileged and largely illiterate mothers" who were, in her view, the target for birth control. In line with AIWC frameworks of contraceptive advocacy, Wadia assumed that members of the organization themselves did not need contraceptive advice, perhaps because they already had access to the information they required or because they were not responsible for the problem of "overpopulation." Instead, she imagined another target in the "illiterate mothers" who could not read *Roshni*.[21]

In Wadia's telling, her concern for such women had been sparked by Lakshmibai Rajwade. She was deeply affected when reading a speech by Rajwade, "who said that Indian women were fated to a life that 'oscillated between gestation and lactation until death wound up the sorry tale.'" Wadia's turn to family planning was prompted by a desire to free women from "the trap of biological compulsion and of the societal pressures for frequent childbearing." To this end, and in hopes of reaching women in need, Wadia recalls in her memoir, "We got together a group of experienced social workers and medical practitioners, both men and women, and formed the Family Planning Committee, which soon became the Family Planning Association of India."[22] Wadia's is one of several origin stories told about the FPAI. Rama Rau puts forward a slightly different version, marking her visit to the Bombay tenements as a key moment, as we saw above. Across these varied accounts, however, there is a common theme: both Wadia and Rama Rau represent birth control as a service offered to poor women by their more privileged or elite "sisters." This was a model of service with long genealogies in the colonial-era women's movement, as well as in Gandhian ideals of citizenship.[23] Wadia, Rama Rau, and their FPAI allies repurposed this ideal into the FPAI's support for postcolonial family planning.

Rama Rau and Wadia drew upon their AIWC networks to staff the new FPAI. These AIWC members included Mithan J. Lam, who served as president of the AIWC and vice president of the FPAI and even used her desk in the AIWC offices to conduct her family planning work.[24] Wadia recalls that all three women worked well together as a team for the FPAI. They "were on the same wavelength. All three of us had Theosophical Society influences behind us and believed in giving social service. We worked together in the AIWC and continued to have many discussions and shared jokes together. . . . We knew each other's families."[25] Other AIWC members who were involved included M. S. H. Jhabvala and Vaidehi Char as joint honorary treasurers of the FPAI. Additional women members included Elfriede Vembu, the social worker who had approached Wadia at *Roshni*, and Sushila Gore, a medical doctor.[26]

While drawing from these AIWC networks, Rama Rau also aimed to expand the FPAI's leadership. She argued that "it was important to have men on the new committee" whose scientific and medical expertise would lend authority to the FPAI's activities. The scientific "experts" who helped to found the FPAI included several prominent men—physicians, demographers, and birth control advocates. Among the organization's joint directors were the Bombay gynecologist V. N. Shirodkar and the renowned eugenicist and sexologist, A. P. Pillay, whom I discussed in chapter 2.[27] The executive committee included R. D. Karve, a longtime birth control advocate, social reformer, eugenicist, and former professor of mathematics.[28] In this way, the FPAI claimed a scientific agenda at a moment when, globally and in India, medical science and technocratic expertise reigned supreme.

Bringing together experiences and networks from the women's movement with this scientific expertise, the FPAI aimed to provide information about family planning as a form of social service for poor women.

Consequently, one of the new organization's first initiatives was to establish a birth control clinic in Bombay. This clinic, the Family Welfare Center (Kutumb Sudhar Kendra), purposefully targeted the inhabitants of the city's "slums." According to Rama Rau, "many of the slum dwellers in our neighborhood came to visit our doctor for medical help of all sorts. Here we began to educate them in the simplest, least-threatening terms about the need for controlling the size of their families."[29] Given the technologies of the time, the clinic likely focused on distributing pessaries or contraceptive sponges to women. Eventually, some FPAI branches also experimented with using pads soaked in oil.[30] By introducing its patients to birth control methods, the clinic aimed at once to improve women's health, alleviate their poverty, and reduce the "drudgery" of their reproductive labor. In Wadia's terms, the Family Welfare Center thus continued a project of service to impoverished women that the AIWC had initiated over a decade earlier, both in the organization's support for birth control and in its outreach efforts on women's health.[31] But significantly, it did so within the scientific space of the clinic—thus linking the women's movement's legacies of "service" to an agenda of scientifically managed modernization. This allowed the FPAI to position its birth control advocacy as a scientific approach to women's welfare.

While cultivating the targets for its birth control advice among the "slum dwellers" of Bombay, the FPAI also aimed to mobilize another constituency to support family planning. These were the social workers, medical professionals, and scientists, alongside a variety of volunteers, who the organization hoped would build a public interest in birth control as a vehicle for national development. To that end, the FPAI organized independent India's first national conference on the subject in December 1951.[32] The two-day session was attended by 110 individuals, "experts" in the field alongside ordinary citizens. The goal, in Rama Rau's terms, was both to promote interest in family planning and to "establish a scientific and practical course of action" to enable the education of "illiterate men and women on the desirability of smaller families."[33] As in the case of the clinic, through the conference, the FPAI positioned family planning as a form of social service that experts and middle-class volunteers could provide on a scientific basis to lower-caste and lower-class recipients. This bifurcation between the middle-class agents of service and their subaltern targets was apparent in the structure of the conference itself. It invited medical and social scientific studies of contraceptive use while advancing demographic and other rationales for family planning. The conference's imagined audiences were thus not those who might need or want access to birth control but rather those whose scientific and voluntary commitments would bring family planning to the "illiterate men and women" who might visit a clinic or be targeted for outreach. The conference in 1951 thus provided a platform for the FPAI to cultivate middle-class interest in its programs and highlight its scientific credentials—all while making the case that family planning was a form of social service that required state support.

While organizing and promoting the national conference, the FPAI was simultaneously lobbying the state. After independence, the government had embarked upon a planning process that built upon the Congress Party's earlier initiative with the National Planning Committee. Under Jawaharlal Nehru, a new entity, the National Planning Commission (NPC), was established and tasked with producing a Five Year Plan for economic development. Keen to engage the NPC and bring family planning into the First Five Year Plan, the FPAI called upon Wadia to draft a memo presenting the organization's views. Wadia aimed to "express our ideas about the need for family planning—to promote the health of mothers and children, and also as a means by which population growth could be slowed—and to outline some of the ways in which this could be done."[34] This resulting FPAI document, "The Growth of Population in Relation to the Growth of Economic Development," outlined a program of propaganda, clinics, training, field studies, and research. It insisted that voluntary organizations operate alongside the state in order to "prepar[e] the minds of the people for the practice of family spacing and limitation."[35]

The planning commissioners were apparently willing to consider these ideas, which resonated both with the Congress Party's earlier planning exercises and with a growing national and transnational interest in population control as a component of planned development. The NPC invited Rama Rau and Wadia to sit on its Advisory Health Panel and Advisory Social Welfare Panel, respectively.[36] The FPAI would subsequently develop a close alliance with the Indian state, and perhaps we might mark this moment—when Rama Rau and Wadia formally joined the planning process—as one step toward developing these ties between the FPAI's "voluntary" work in family planning and the government's emerging commitment to state-led population control. In particular, Rama Rau seemed ideally positioned to forge these connections. In addition to her credentials with the women's movement, she had access to government circles through her husband, a diplomat and chair of the Reserve Bank of India from 1949 to 1957. Mobilizing these networks, she set her sights on making "family planning" not only an element of social service within the women's movement, as it had been, but also an official arm of the postcolonial state. As we will see below, she met with considerable success when the First Five Year Plan allocated state funds to a family planning program in 1951. But first, let us turn to another set of ideas and networks that shaped family planning's emergence as a component of planned development. That was the growing transnational movement for population control.

Family Planning and Transnational Development Regimes

Building upon their early initiatives within an Indian national context, FPAI leaders also began to mobilize transnational networks in support of their family planning agenda. To do so, Rama Rau, Wadia, and their allies drew from the women's movement's existing connections, which had been forged during the AIWC's campaign for birth control in the 1930s. The FPAI took a major step in furthering these connections when it hosted the conference of the International Committee for Planned Parenthood (ICPP) in Bombay in 1952. As noted in the introduction, Rama Rau agreed to host the conference at the invitation of Margaret Sanger, and it became the first international gathering of its kind to be held in independent India. Its outcome was equally momentous; on the last day of the conference, delegates voted to create the International Planned Parenthood Federation (IPPF). Within this chapter's history of feminism and family planning in India, the Bombay conference marks a watershed moment for at least three reasons. First, it linked Dhanvanthi Rama Rau closely to Margaret Sanger and helped both women argue that population control was a continuation of a long-standing history of feminist support for contraception. Second, the conference helped to sideline alternative visions of family planning to put forward a neo-Malthusian agenda that insisted contraception was necessary for population control, and ultimately for modernization and economic development in the "Third World." This agenda would come to govern family planning programs both in India and abroad in the decades to come. Third, the Bombay conference connected Indians more closely to an emerging network of population controllers who had hitherto been mostly American and Western European but who had wider aspirations. In so doing, it also made India a critical site for shaping policies on population and reproduction that extended beyond national borders. That is, India was not simply the ground upon which a global population control agenda was enacted. Rather, India's specific historical conditions and the efforts of Indian family planners helped to shape what "global" population control would look like. India would help define the course of the movement worldwide.

Margaret Sanger may not have had all these outcomes in mind when she wrote to Rama Rau in 1951 asking the FPAI to host the conference. But in retrospect, it is clear that Sanger captured a moment when, both globally and in India, growing concern about world population was reshaping the politics of reproduction. Fears about global population increase—and especially the growing portion of that increase taking place in Asia, Africa, and Latin America—were prompted in part by the specter of food scarcity, made real during World War II and its aftermath. These fears spurred not only agricultural research but also a renewed search for means to control population growth on a worldwide scale. Americans and Western Europeans were especially disturbed by signs of differential fertility between their countries and the rest of the world. In the wake of decolonization, some were alarmed by a future that would be dominated demographically by Asians and Africans, and we can see in their writings during the 1940s and 1950s the precursors to what later became a full-blown panic about a global "population explosion."[37] These fears were fueled by the geopolitics of the Cold War. A large and growing population in places like India raised questions about whether poverty could be alleviated and living standards raised quickly enough to avert sociopolitical unrest. For some worried Americans, the Communist revolution in China had already shown this possibility, and India seemed to be the next battlefield in a global war against population. In response to these varied fears and aspirations, Americans took a leading role in creating new organizations to support population control transnationally, many of which took a keen interest in India as a site for research, funding, and policy-making. The most prominent of these organizations, the Population Council, was founded in 1951, just one year before Sanger and Rama Rau's Bombay conference.

An additional, potentially less US-centered avenue for transnational networking on population was the growing field of international health, in the form of the World Health Organization (WHO), a UN agency founded in 1948. For a brief period at its inception, various member states and observers aimed to involve the WHO in birth control as a global health issue.[38] In 1951, the Indian government sought WHO support for a study of the rhythm method as a technology of family planning. This study proved to be short-lived, and the WHO soon turned away from birth control research. Nevertheless, when Rama Rau and Sanger began their collaboration for the Bombay conference, the WHO remained another potential site for advancing their goals and was part of the broader transnational network that both women tapped into and helped to build.

Sanger came to this collaboration with some experience in India, since she had worked closely with the AIWC, traveled extensively across the country in support of birth control in 1935 and 1936, and met with Gandhi on the subject, as we saw in chapter 2. Turning to India again more than a decade later, Sanger professed herself to be impressed by Indian family planning efforts. She wrote to Rama Rau of her interest in the FPAI's proposed national conference and was hopeful that the organization might expand its work by bringing the International Committee for Planned Parenthood to India in the following year. The ICPP had held a previous international conference, at Cheltenham in England in 1948, where, coincidentally, Wadia had been in attendance.[39] Sanger was eager to continue these efforts in Bombay. Rama Rau agreed to Sanger's proposal but also sought to dampen the latter's expectations: "You realize that this is the first time that an All India Conference on this topic has been arranged, and we are still not sure what the attendance will be, or how much interest will be aroused in the country." Nevertheless, Rama Rau proposed that the Planned Parenthood conference be held soon after two other international conferences in India, on social work and on child welfare. She was hopeful the conferences might share common delegates and thus help to bolster numbers.[40] And although the FPAI was a new organization, Rama Rau assured Sanger that they could expect the support and cooperation of the more established AIWC.[41] Consequently, from the very outset of conference planning, Rama Rau linked the FPAI ideologically and institutionally both to the women's movement and to emerging ideas about social service and social welfare.

For Rama Rau and the FPAI, the collaboration with Sanger brought several benefits, namely opportunities for technical training and funding from European and American sources. Key financial support for the conference came from Ellen Watamull, an American associate of Margaret Sanger's whose husband was Indian. Along with providing five thousand dollars toward conference expenses,[42] Watamull sent six models of the female pelvis, a donation that Elfriede Vembu noted was in immediate demand for birth control education.[43] Meanwhile, A. P. Pillay requested that Sanger bring contraceptive supplies with her during her voyage to Bombay, specifically dyes for pessaries, which he hoped could subsequently be produced more cheaply in India.[44] During the conference itself, the FPAI arranged for visiting medical professionals to train Indian doctors in contraceptive methods; the organization paid women daily to come to the Bombay clinic, where they served as patients for the doctors demonstrating and learning new techniques.[45] More generally, the conference allowed Indian family planners—most of whom had few opportunities to travel abroad— to join transnational conversations about contraceptive technologies and global population control.

These benefits did not flow only in one direction. Sanger's global aspirations received a political and ideological boost from her alliance with the FPAI. As she wrote to Rama Rau, Sanger hoped to create a permanent world organization devoted to family planning. She was concerned, however, that "global" population control was perceived as an exclusively Western concern and tainted by association with racism, imperialism, and Cold War politics. Indeed, as Wadia later recalled, these associations had disturbed her when she first encountered the birth control movement in the 1930s, and they had resurfaced at the 1948 Cheltenham conference.[46] Sanger hoped that taking the conference outside of the US and Europe and holding it in India might push back against such criticisms and could bolster the new organization's global legitimacy and credentials. Perhaps it was this logic that led Sanger to make a unilateral decision, bypassing the ICPP, to hold the conference in Bombay.[47] Rama Rau agreed that meeting in Bombay would bring in Asian countries "much more wholeheartedly than you will be able to draw them in" if in Europe.[48] India, in this sense, served as a gateway to Asia and a link to the "global."

Beyond recognizing the political expediency of holding the conference outside the West, Sanger must have seen an ideological resonance between her vision for the global birth control movement and events that were unfolding in India. The ICPP was operating amid a jostling mix of ideas about the meaning and purposes of family planning. Some members of the organization espoused eugenic ideals as a primary motivation for their family planning work; the ICPP was in fact housed within the premises of the Eugenics Society in London. Others highlighted sex education, in particular the importance of addressing sexuality apart from reproduction, as a key mission for family planners. Some were primarily interested in the mechanisms of contraception and its dissemination via clinics.[49] However, Sanger argued that a truly global movement for "planned parenthood" needed to demonstrate the relationship between population control and economic development, especially in the newly decolonizing world. The

FPAI was already making such connections in India, and Sanger was eager to take the global movement in these Indian directions. Holding the conference in Bombay could make a powerful statement about what kinds of activities and agendas the new world organization on planned parenthood might pursue.

Sanger and Rama Rau advanced this agenda while sidelining alternative visions of the Planned Parenthood movement. In particular, Sanger was determined to deemphasize sex education, and in this maneuver, she went directly against the Dutch delegation's position. The two Dutch representatives to the ICPP, Dr. Conrad Van Emde Boas and Dr. A. Storm, were insistent that the conference be held in Sweden, as the ICPP had previously agreed, rather than in India. They called for a program with "more stress on the cultural aspects of the sexual problem than on the neo-Malthusian ones."[50] They were skeptical of the motives of population controllers and wary of associating birth control exclusively with neo-Malthusian fears about the dangers of population growth. Sanger was dismissive of these claims, writing to Rama Rau that "the Dutch representatives have been trouble makers on the Committee always. They both have a Marxian attitude about Population. They want the Committee to interest itself only in Sex Education."[51] Hosting the conference in India, Sanger implied, would move Planned Parenthood away from these "Marxian attitudes" that challenged the growing dominance of neo-Malthusianism in the global population movement. Instead, Indian interest in (over)population, and the FPAI's own neo-Malthusian perspectives, would anchor the new world organization.

The conference opened in Bombay in November 1952 and was attended by 487 delegates and observers from fourteen countries. This did not include the Dutch delegation, which boycotted the conference. Rama Rau chaired the local organizing committee, and she was joined by Mithan Lam and Wadia. Other FPAI members, notably A. P. Pillay and V. N. Shirodkar, were involved in the local arrangements as well. Indian attendees included several individuals who would later become leaders in India's family planning bureaucracy and in the Health Ministry.[52] The conference itself was inaugurated by the vice president, Sarvepalli Radhakrishnan. For any observer at the opening ceremonies witnessing the series of prominent politicians, scientists, and policy-makers, perhaps "family planning" seemed like a global movement whose time had come. In her statement opening the volume of conference proceedings, Rama Rau capitalized on this moment. She expressed hope that the conference would focus attention in India "on this very vital question of population control at a time when important plans for the development of the country were being initiated for the raising of the standards of living of the people." Having thus bound population firmly to the cause of national development, Rama Rau reminded her readers that the government of India had just recently made family planning one of its health priorities in the First Five Year Plan. The moment was thus right, she insisted, to bring the "whole of this important question to public discussion."[53] And indeed, the conference did so. An entire section of the proceedings was devoted to "population problems." Even more importantly, neo-Malthusian concern about the impact of population growth on economic development provided the context—and the political urgency— behind many of the papers presented. Sanger and Rama Rau's careful engineering of the agenda seemed to have succeeded in shaping a global movement for family planning around the questions of population and development.[54]

Nevertheless, there remained voices of dissent in Bombay. Conference delegates encountered one such voice at the very outset, when Kamaladevi Chattopadhyay greeted the attendees in her welcoming address. Chattopadhyay brought a powerful set of credentials to her position as chair of the Bombay conference's reception committee. As discussed in the last chapter, during the 1930s Chattopadhyay had been a forceful advocate of birth control, which she linked to a broader critique of patriarchal structures of family and sexuality. Her address to the delegates in Bombay did not return to this earlier antipatriarchal critique but offered an anti-imperialist and antiracist vision for a global family planning movement, as I noted in the introduction. Chattopadhyay challenged two foundational assumptions of the conference organizers: the notion that family planning was primarily a component of national planning and the neo-Malthusian premise behind the idea of Indian "overpopulation."

In the face of the demographers, doctors, and other "experts" in population control who were among the conference delegates, Chattopadhyay insisted that decisions about sexuality and childbearing could never be subject to top-down planning. Moreover, she reminded her audience that "planning is a means to an end, not an end in itself"; the end was "the fulfillment of human beings." Aiming to disentangle birth control from development planning goals, Chattopadhyay suggested that "planned parenthood" was relevant to all states and societies—not just those of the colonized or postcolonial world. Consequently, she refused to "accept any theories as to why there should be a planned family, whether economic or health, or any other reason because life is really much larger than any single purpose." At the core of her position, she added, was the "inherent right of parents to determine for themselves the size of their families."[55] Chattopadhyay's address walked back from her previous insistence that the primary purpose of birth control was to overthrow patriarchal controls over women's sexuality, and she instead privileged the "family" as locus of agency and decision-making. Yet, from her prominent position in the conference, Chattopadhyay's focus on the welfare of the "individual family" challenged the growing assumption that "family planning" was entirely subservient to an economic development regime.

Moreover, Chattopadhyay's vision for family planning rejected a neo-Malthusian framework and turned instead toward a geopolitics of land, food, and migration. The problem was not that some countries were overpopulated, she suggested, but that land was not equally available to all people. Chattopadhyay thus indicted countries "in Africa"—an implicit reference to the white settler colonies in South Africa and Rhodesia—that allowed a small minority to hold all resources and forced the majority of the population into small territories. Chattopadhyay also reminded her audience that some countries had plenty of land available—an implicit reference to the United States, Canada, and Australia—but had closed their doors to immigrants.[56] Such racist policies concerning land and migration, she argued, were a key part of the global "population problem," and she called upon conference delegates to include it in their discussions. Chattopadhyay's critique of a global color line and her insistence on understanding land in relation to population should remind us of an earlier strand of population discourse, advanced by Radhakamal Mukherjee, among others, that did not privilege reproduction as the primary solution to the problem of population. It hearkened back to a geopolitics that understood population as a transnational question that was not limited to the national boundaries of any single state. Her avowedly anti-imperialist and antiracist analysis thus refused to territorialize "overpopulation" as a problem for the independent Indian nation to confront via reproductive regulation. Instead, she challenged the assumption that "population" would have to be contained within the existing borders of nation-states—an assumption that underpinned the ICPP's international agenda.

There is no record of how Chattopadhyay's speech was received, but she may have found a sympathetic ear among at least some of the delegates. Among them was likely Sripati Chandrasekhar, a conference attendee who would go on to become the minister of health and family planning in 1967. Two years after the Bombay conference, Chandrasekhar published an analysis of the geopolitics of population, titled *Hungry People and Empty Lands: An Essay on Population Problems and International Tensions*.[57] Echoing Chattopadhyay, Chandrasekhar critiqued race-based immigration laws and challenged a global color line that prevented "hungry people" from accessing the resources of so-called "empty" lands. He thus linked the freedom from hunger to a freedom of global mobility and argued that the contemporary distribution of world population was neither necessary nor inevitable but the product of imperial rule. At the same time, like Mukherjee before him, Chandrasekhar relied upon imperial discourses about the supposed emptiness of land populated by indigenous people. This claim to "emptiness," in turn, became the basis of his calls to overturn imperialist immigration law to solve problems of population in Asia. At least in 1954, when *Hungry People and Empty Lands* was published, Chandrasekhar's geopolitics of land and migration turned away from reproductive regulation. In this sense, he shared with Chattopadhyay a suspicion of population control. Yet by 1967, as health minister, Chandrasekhar would join—even lead—the population control bandwagon, turning away from his earlier critique of migration policies while becoming a forceful advocate of increasingly intensive means of reproductive control.

Chandrasekhar's personal turn away from the geopolitics of migration toward an intensified regulation of reproduction mapped the trajectories of family planning both in India and globally. Challenges to racial immigration policies, alongside calls for individual choices in family planning, gave way during the late 1950s and 1960s to a quest to reduce Indian fertility rates to meet centrally planned development targets. In this sense, Sanger and Rama Rau's vision for the Bombay conference, whereby birth control would become a global concern precisely through its connection to population control, became the dominant discursive and policy framework. Rama Rau and Sanger solidified this vision on the last day of the conference, when delegates passed a resolution to create the International Planned Parenthood Federation.[58] The delegates determined, further, that the new Federation would comprise various national organizations—of which the FPAI was one—as members. The IPPF was thus a transnational network, operating across national borders. At the same time, it reterritorialized global population as a series of national problems and routed its personnel and finances through organizations that operated within the boundaries of the nation-state. Meanwhile, the Indian government took up the challenge issued at Bombay and began to develop a state-directed program of population control, to which we turn next.

Family Planning as Population Control

The government of India's First Five Year Plan, which was announced in 1951 and commenced in 1952, allocated funds for a family planning program. In many ways, the Plan's vision of family planning aligned with the FPAI's agenda as it had developed since 1949 and with the goals of an international movement as laid out during the Bombay conference. The Plan document asserted that population growth was a critical factor in India's economic development and recommended that the state conduct research on contraceptive methods, provide its citizens with access to birth control, and encourage them to plan their families. To this end, it situated family planning services within the government's Ministry of Health and allocated an initial budget of 6.5 million rupees. While this was a small proportion of the 178 million rupees provided in the health budget overall, the incorporation of family planning into India's national planning process was a momentous step within India, and also transnationally.[59] After decades of debate within Indian nationalism about the causes of Indian poverty and the role of Gandhian sexual continence in shaping a national citizenry, the Plan document came down firmly on the side of those who linked regulating reproductive sexuality to alleviating poverty.

However, when family planning became a component of national planning, it also became enmeshed in the latter's tensions and contradictions. Specifically, the call for birth control grappled between a stated commitment to universal health, welfare, and democratization on the one hand and the exigencies of a top-down and antidemocratic drive to control population growth on the other. As we have seen already, both these trajectories—birth control as a vehicle for liberation and for an intensified and intimate biopolitical regulation—had been present within the women's movement, and within broader reproductive politics, for decades. When family planning became a vehicle for national planning, these contradictions mapped onto a broader tension within Indian nationalism itself.

The National Planning Commission decided to support family planning in a context of some public pressure and lobbying. As we have seen, the FPAI took a leading role in mobilizing public opinion in favor of birth control and calling for its inclusion in the First Five Year Plan. These arguments likely found some support on the NPC, including from Durgabai Deshmukh, who was the only woman member of the commission and an AIWC member. At the same time, the planning commissioners were also concerned with food and famine. Increasing agricultural production was a central goal in the First Plan, and the NPC apportioned state resources accordingly. This focus on food was prompted by concerns that India's population would outpace the country's food supply and stymie the nation's development. While these fears had a long history, as we have seen throughout this book, they also had a more recent context in the horrors of the Bengal famine in 1943. The famine—widely understood to have been a human-made calamity due to British wartime policies—was the first on its scale since the turn of the twentieth century. For observers of the widespread starvation in 1943, including the AIWC delegation sent to Bengal to report back to the wider membership, experiences with famine relief shaped understandings of food crises and population in India.[60] As Rama Rau, a member of that delegation, later recounted, witnessing the famine further fueled her commitments to make reproductive control an aspect of planned development.[61] Meanwhile, continuing food shortages and widespread food rationing kept the question of hunger at the forefront of public debate.[62]

In the midst of these concerns and pressures, the census of 1951, the first conducted since partition, documented that the country's population had increased by nearly 45 million people, to 360 million, in the course of a decade.[63] This increase, according to census commissioner R. A. Gopalaswami, was due to the conjuncture of a falling death rate with ongoing high birthrates. Although rates of maternal and infant mortality remained high—India's were among the highest in the world—the number of births still outpaced the number of deaths, leading to significant population growth. As Gopalaswami suggested in more polemical terms, "improvident maternity," which he defined as births occurring to women with three or more children, was among the causes of India's population increase.[64] This widely circulated phrase, which was repeated across media and policy circles, helped to shape a growing consensus among Indian elites that women's childbearing was to blame for population increase and, in turn, for hunger and food scarcity. Targeting the birthrate, and the women whose supposed "improvidence" was its cause, seemed to offer a solution to India's (over) population. The NPC apparently agreed.

When the NPC brought population control into its purview, reproductive regulation became part of, and furthered, a set of tensions and contradictions within the planning process itself. Broadly speaking, state-directed planning negotiated the gap between goals that were transformational in their stated aims but limited in their policy implementation, which focused only on the formal sectors of the economy.[65] The rhetoric of socioeconomic transformation grew out of the history of Indian nationalism itself, more specifically from debates about the causes of Indian poverty and "underde-velopment." Economic nationalists like Dadabhai Naoroji had long argued that the British "drain of wealth" was the chief cause of Indian poverty, and this critique of colonial economic policy helped to produce India as a space of nationalist governance. Confronting rising popular pressures for trans-formational change, leaders like Nehru drew from this legacy when they insisted that a national government—not an imperial one—was best posi-tioned to bring economic development to its people. They offered develop-ment as an anticolonial answer to the problems of empire, and during the 1930s, the Congress Party staked its legitimacy, in part, upon this promise to foster development.[66] After independence, planned development came to offer a rationale for the new, independent, democratic state. Planning both represented a reason for the state's existence and marked its responsi-bilities toward its citizens. This insistence that state-led development could fulfill the promises of anticolonial struggle thus underpinned the transfor-mational rhetoric of postcolonial planning.

Even as the postindependence state remained wedded to these rhetorics of transformation, which Maitrayee Chaudhuri identifies as both socialist and feminist, it was "constitutive of social classes whose interests ran counter to these stated aims."[67] In other words, the state's upper-caste and upper-class composition starkly limited the kind of transformation that the NPC would pursue. Confronting popular pressures for change without disavow-ing elite interests, the Congress regime was forced to negotiate both "elite desires for power as well as popular desires for emancipation." This was a reflection, as Pranav Jani reminds us, of the "heterogeneous" character of Indian anticolonial nationalism during the transitional period around inde-pendence.[68] Consequently, during the 1940s and 1950s, the state's planning process gestured toward a vision of democratizing development while also solidifying its alliance with capital and business interests. These tensions played out within and outside the Congress Party in debates about the pur-poses and goals of state planning, which were also debates about the prior-ity of capitalist economic growth versus any form of democratic social transformation.[69] Ultimately, the planning process negotiated a "twin prob-lem," which Partha Chatterjee identifies as the need to secure both the accumulation of capital and the political legitimation of its social costs.[70]

A program of state-directed family planning that was aligned with the national planning process was perfectly positioned to negotiate this tension. Family planning aimed to address poverty, a central goal of postindepen-dence planned development. However, such a program avoided discussion of inequality, thus sidestepping any need to confront elite interests within the planning process. Rather than tackling systematic inequalities of land ownership, the disenfranchisement of Dalit and Adivasi populations, or the gendered hierarchies within households, it understood reproduction as the cause of the problem and the site of its solution. Consequently, family planning became a program of poverty alleviation that left hierarchies of class, caste, and gender almost entirely unchallenged. This, indeed, was the promise of population control in postcolonial India. It was also the promise of Indian population planning within a Cold War context. Divorced from geopolitical critiques of racist immigration policies and calls for the freer migration of people across the globe, an "Indian" program of family planning implicitly promised to contain "India's" growing population within its territorial boundaries. Kamaladevi Chattopadhyay's anti-imperialist reading of world population, which she voiced at the Bombay conference, thus disappeared from its nationalist framing within the First Five Year Plan.

These negotiations between elite and popular interests, and between globally anti-imperialist and more narrowly nation-bound readings of population, played out in the emerging institutions of family planning and their relationship to the organized women's movement. For instance, the caste-class composition of the state shaped women's access to the levers of state power and to the planning process itself. The largely middle- and upper-class members of the organized women's movement, as we have seen, were able to transition into positions within the state bureaucracy and to bring their case for family planning directly to the NPC's attention. This included not only Rama Rau and Wadia, but also NPC member Durgabai Deshmukh and independent India's first minister of health, Rajkumari Amrit Kaur. The planning process potentially amplified their voices, since the composition and structure of the NPC and its various advisory boards elevated the recommendations of bureaucratic and technocratic "experts" at the expense of ordinary citizens in charting the directions of social and economic change. Meanwhile, Wadia and Rama Rau's repeated insistence that "voluntary organizations" must play an essential role in bringing family planning to ordinary people further solidified the mediating role of the FPAI, the AIWC, and their cadre of middle-class women volunteers. Within this institutional framework, the stage was set for the NPC to pioneer a top-down approach to family planning that would mobilize the nation's elites—including its elite women—to provide a "service" to its subalterns by bringing them technologies of birth control. As we know, this claim to serve impoverished women had been a pillar of the AIWC's contraceptive advocacy during the 1930s. By the 1950s, this motivation became folded into the state's development agenda and made family planning a component of social service and social welfare. I discuss the political implications of this model of middle-class service further in the next chapter.

For now, I focus on family planning's promise to alleviate poverty without addressing inequality. This claim rested upon long-standing neo-Malthusian foundations, which tended to blame poverty on the over-reproduction of the poor. However, by the mid-twentieth century, family planners also began to situate their arguments within a new intellectual paradigm: the theory of the demographic transition. Beginning in the late 1940s, the first generation of American academic demographers, most notably Kingsley Davis and Frank Notestein, outlined a sequence of steps that all societies would ostensibly take on a common road to modernization. At first, industrializing societies would reduce their death rates while birthrates remained high; this would lead to population growth. However, as a society reached "socioeconomic maturity," people's values would shift toward limiting their families, and birthrates would eventually fall, leading to a stabilization of the population. All modernizing societies would pass through this moment of demographic transition. From a population control perspective, the question was how quickly such a transition would occur within any given society. However, academic demographers noted a problem when applying theories of demographic transition to the former colonies. They argued that unlike in Europe, where falling death rates had led to concurrent declines in birthrates, in Asia and Africa death rates had fallen well in advance of the socioeconomic changes that would lead to lower fertility. Therefore, countries like India were stuck in a position of lower death rates but ongoing high birthrates, leading to rapid population growth. Further, they theorized that in the "Third World," unlike in the European and American past, population growth and its associated problems would prevent the "modernization" necessary for shifting social attitudes toward childbearing.[71]

Therefore, in the eyes of demographic transition theorists, India was mired in a demographic trap. Its death rates had fallen far in advance of social attitudes that would limit birthrates; at the same time, its burgeoning population would prevent the economic development that might prompt people to limit the size of their families. In response to this perceived problem, scholars who applied demographic transition theory to explain a transition *after the fact* in Europe made the theoretical apparatus *prescriptive* in India, as in other parts of Asia and Africa. As Karl Ittmann argues, the result was "an emphasis on increasing access to contraception rather than waiting for social change to generate fertility decline."[72] Birth control, in short, was the spark necessary to produce a demographic transition outside of Europe and the United States. Demographic transition theory thus offered a new promise. The countries of Asia and Africa could modernize their economies by regulating how their populations reproduced. They could circumvent the problems of poverty and inequality—produced in part by their "stalled transition" to low birthrates—by convincing people to limit their childbearing by using contraception.

The NPC latched onto this promise of a "demographic progression to modernity."[73] The First Plan document noted an imbalance between falling death rates and ongoing high birthrates, thus situating India within an early, pretransition phase of demographic development. However, the planners noted, any attempt to rebalance birth and death rates would confront a further problem. Birthrates might come down "as a result of improvements in the standards of living," such that a wealthier population might produce fewer children. Yet "such improvements are not likely to materialize if there is a concurrent increase of population." For the planning commissioners, this was India's demographic trap in a nutshell: a vicious cycle encouraged poor people to have many children, which in turn led to their further impoverishment, which again increased their fertility. State-led population planning could extricate India from this demographic quagmire. This was a necessary component of the development process—or, in the Plan's terms, "Population control can be achieved only by the reduction of the birth rate to the extent necessary to stabilize population at a level consistent with the requirements of national economy."[74] In this way, the First Plan made population a manipulable component of its economic plans; stabilizing population growth through state-led planning would enable the government to reach its development goals.

The NPC situated its quest to stabilize population within the state's programs for health. Planning for health, like the process of planned development overall, negotiated multiple and competing claims during this transitional period. Within the transformational rhetorics of state-led planning, health was represented as a basic human right. Long denied by the colonial state, it became the responsibility of the postindependence regime. With the creation of the WHO, health could also serve as a site of internationalist aspiration, a universal human right that set the peoples of the formerly colonized world on equal footing with their former colonizers.

Yet, as Sunil Amrith reminds us, these universalist and rights-based rhe-torics of health existed simultaneously with state planners' drive for health interventions that would improve the Indian "race" and make it more effi-cient and governable. This approach to health meshed with long-standing elite concerns about racial and caste purity and degeneration and prom-ised to contain the supposed threat of lower-caste reproduction. Conse-quently, state intervention in health stemmed at once "from an egalitarian commitment to welfare, and a far-from-egalitarian fear of the rising num-bers of the lower castes."[75]

Family planning again served to bridge the gap. It promised to improve the health of impoverished mothers and their children and also to contain and regulate their reproduction. This was the ground upon which health expenditures for family planning became a critical component of economic development: "[Stabilization of population] can be secured only by the real-ization of the need for family limitation on a wide scale by the people. The main appeal for family planning is based on considerations of the health and welfare of the family. Family limitation or spacing of the children is necessary and desirable in order to secure better health for the mother and better care and upbringing of the children. Measures directed to this end should, therefore, form part of the public health programme."[76] The goal here is economic development via stabilizing population growth. However, its appeal is health. That is, the people of India would not simply come to a "realization of the need for family limitation" based on the state's develop-ment goals. Instead, they would become more governable—more willing to submit themselves to the state's development regime—when they saw its health benefits. Family planning was thus a component of the universaliz-ing drive for health as a basic human right; it could serve the goals of improving the welfare of children, mothers, and their families. At the same time, it was also a means to promote the hegemonic claims of state-led planning; it could persuade the "people" of the legitimacy of development and, by extension, of the state itself.

The NPC's rhetorics of family planning as a component of women's and children's health precisely echoed a long-standing argument of the women's movement. From Rajwade's first birth control resolution in the AIWC to the WRPE report to Rama Rau's claims that the suffering women of the Bombay tenements had inspired the creation of the FPAI, feminist women had promoted health as a critical rationale for birth control. In this, they joined women like Margaret Sanger—and even Annie Besant before her—who emphasized mothers' corporeal suffering and declining health to argue that birth control was a woman's right. In fact, as we have seen, women's movements were important in making health a priority within dominant neo-Malthusian and eugenicist frameworks of contraceptive advocacy. They had also negotiated this health right as a component of development, thus merging its egalitarian and inegalitarian aspects, well before Indian independence. The First Five Year Plan adopted and intensified this language.

Even while situating its family planning budget within these transformational rhetorics of health, the NPC was far from certain about how such funding should be used. The allocation called for collecting information about public attitudes toward fertility regulation, as well as conducting field experiments on the effectiveness of family planning programs. But it did not specify which methods of fertility regulation would be studied. The government turned, first, to the rhythm method, preferred by minister of health Rajkumari Amrit Kaur. Amrit Kaur was a member of the princely family of Kapurthala in Punjab whose father had converted from Sikhism to Catholicism. A close associate of Gandhi's as a well as a former president of the AIWC, she brought to the Health Ministry a Gandhian commitment to public health alongside an interest in promoting "measures for family limitation so as to make some adjustment between the number of people and the resources that are available to them."[77] Perhaps she believed that the rhythm method could meet all these needs, especially since it was the only method that Gandhi had eventually endorsed—albeit with reluctance— during his discussions with Margaret Sanger.

Alongside others in the government, Amrit Kaur likely shared the view that rhythm was a culturally appropriate form in India because it could draw upon existing sexual norms about periodic abstinence within heterosexual marriage.[78] Moreover, it would cost nothing, another important factor in the drive to find an appropriate contraceptive method that was accessible to all people. Taken together, these apparent benefits propelled the rhythm method to the forefront of the government's initial foray into family planning. In 1951, the same year the draft Five Year Plan was first announced, the government invited the WHO to conduct a pilot project on the rhythm method in India.[79] This initiative situated family planning and population control firmly within the field of international public health and thus aligned with the Plan's broader organization and vision.

The WHO sent Dr. Abraham Stone, a physician and medical researcher who headed the Margaret Sanger Research Bureau in New York. Stone was directed to center his investigations on rhythm, and alongside a small team of investigators, he piloted studies in one urban area (in Lodi in Delhi), and in one rural one (in Ramnagaram in the state of Mysore). Stone had already been studying the rhythm method in New York, and in India he and his team devised a way that women could keep track of "safe" and "unsafe" days for sexual intercourse by using a string of beads of different colors and shapes.[80] They would move one bead each day to keep track of their menstrual cycles. Stone's team tried several designs in order to make the bead necklace workable, eventually incorporating a safety catch to avoid any confusion about which direction to move the beads. Other barriers, however, proved more difficult to overcome. Reports soon surfaced that some women and men believed that simply owning or wearing the necklace had contraceptive effects; others believed that the beads violated their privacy, since it marked their menstrual cycle in public.[81] Couples soon began to drop out of the study, and it eventually ended with little success.[82] This marked the end of the WHO's investigations in India since, in 1952, opposition from several member states led the organization to withdraw from the field of family planning.[83]

The Indian government's short-lived experiment with the rhythm method should remind us that during the early 1950s, despite the state's rapid movement toward population control, the course of its planning program had still not taken shape. Multiple ideas about the directions of family planning, and its relationship to contraceptive technology and reproductive sexuality, were still in contestation. In the case of the WHO study, this contest pitted Amrit Kaur against her former colleagues and associates in the AIWC and in the FPAI. Although she seemed committed to the rhythm method, the AIWC denounced Stone's study as a waste of state funds, and its members offered to use the money themselves in order to conduct more useful studies of contraceptive methods.[84] Dhanvanthi Rama Rau was suspicious about the effectiveness of rhythm, especially among India's largely illiterate population. When Stone stayed with her in Bombay in 1951, she took the opportunity to express her frustrations directly: "I also told him that a number of us felt that he would be undermining the work we had been doing" by seeming to advocate a "Safe Period theory in preference to contraceptives."[85] Other FPAI members, notably A. P. Pillay and R. D. Karve, challenged rhythm's effectiveness and the ability of ordinary women to calculate their safe days properly.[86] Meanwhile, the FPAI and its various branches continued to seek other methods, including the contraceptive sponges designed by Marie Stopes.[87] Challenging Amrit Kaur and the Indian government's endorsement, therefore, a growing network of AIWC and FPAI members did not believe that the rhythm method aligned with the goal of bringing scientific expertise to the dissemination of family planning.[88] This divide was visible at the international conference in Bombay, which Amrit Kaur—despite her position as health minister and stated commitment to controlling population—refused to support.[89]

However, the Indian government would soon move toward other technologies of birth control. Longer lasting was the First Five Year Plan's transformational rhetoric, which linked family planning to maternal and infant welfare and to a vision of universal public health and democratizing development more broadly. Alongside this set of rhetorical claims, as we have seen, reproductive regulation claimed to address poverty without challenging existing inequalities. This too, was a legacy of the First Plan's vision of family planning within its national development regime.

Conclusion

Looking back from the mid-1950s, just a few years after the creation of the FPAI, Dhanvanthi Rama Rau and her colleagues in the organization may well have found reason for satisfaction. The FPAI was a growing organization that had begun to expand from its Bombay headquarters to other parts of the country, all the while working closely with the Indian government. Meanwhile, via the First Five Year Plan, the government had adopted the principle that population control was a vehicle for national development and had targeted contraception as a means to control population growth. Moreover, family planners in India were increasingly connected to a transnational population establishment, and the FPAI had become a constituent member of the IPPF. Within this transnational arena, the broad frameworks of neo-Malthusianism and the more specific analysis of demographic transition theorists helped to link birth control to economic development and modernization in the "Third World." India was not merely a site to enact these ideologies but was crucial to shaping the directions of the global movement. Rama Rau's vision from the tenements of Bombay—in which she insisted that contraception was necessary to save both women and the nation—seemed on the verge of fulfillment.

As we have seen, the organized women's movement helped to shape the direction of these momentous events. During the transitional years surrounding independence, the AIWC's institutional networks served to recruit and organize the first generation of women family planners and connected Indian efforts to an emergent transnational population control movement. Feminist legacies were important to the discourses and rationales of family planning as well. Rama Rau and the FPAI drew upon the AIWC's long-standing argument that family planning was a women's issue. In the aftermath of independence, both the FPAI and the AIWC suggested that family planning could serve as a national response to the "women's question" by linking women's development to the nation. Recognizing a growing concern about population among Indian development planners, FPAI and AIWC leaders successfully linked family planning to population control, and argued that family planning centered primarily on women. Rama Rau and the FPAI's connection to Sanger helped to advance these claims in transnational contexts as well.

The success of feminist women's efforts depended upon alliances with many others—from demographers to eugenicists, physicians to planners—who pushed for population control as a vehicle for national (and "Third World") development. The result, as some historians suggest, brought together "strange bedfellows" in both national and transnational campaigns for family planning.[90] Yet perhaps these links were not entirely strange, given the women's movement's powerful commitment to India's emerging development regime. While drawing upon their feminist credentials and highlighting the centrality of women, Rama Rau, Wadia, Deshmukh, Rajwade, and other family planners nevertheless advanced an agenda that was less interested in addressing gender inequality than in bringing women's reproduction into the purview of state-led development. By positioning women in this way, family planners helped to advance the promise of state-led family planning to alleviate poverty without grappling with inequalities of gender, class, or caste. Indeed, feminism's connection to family planning rested less upon its claim to challenge patriarchy or women's subordination than its claim to bring poor women's reproductive lives more firmly into the embrace of the development state.

CHAPTER 4

REGULATING REPRODUCTION IN THE ERA OF
THE PLANETARY "POPULATION BOMB"

FOR TWO DAYS IN JUNE 1960, S. K. KHAN VISITED VILLAGES IN
Naini Tal to spread the message of family planning. As an honorary family
planning education leader, Khan had been appointed by the Indian government to "mobilize public opinion and form a network of voluntary
groups" to support state population control efforts.[1] With these goals in
mind and accompanied by a "Lady Social Worker," she visited ten houses
in the village of Mahomedpur, where she "spoke to the women and told
them what Family Planning was." Khan had hoped to reach a wider audience of women, but "it was not possible to hold a meeting there as the rumour
had been spread that the Family Planning people would give injections and
stop children being born completely. There was a certain amount of antag-
onism in this village, and I had to explain to the women what we stood
for."[2] Stymied by these obstacles, the honorary family planning education
leader left Mahomedpur, presumably disappointed by the prospects for
family planning in the village.

Khan's experience with the women of Mahomedpur represents one of
many such encounters between the messengers of family planning and their
intended targets. Their message—what Khan and her colleagues "stood
for"—linked reproductive regulation to national development. The targets
of this message were often women, and like in Khan's Mahomedpur ven-
tures, they were imagined to be ignorant of contraceptive technologies and
unwilling to regulate their fertility. The discourses of family planning represented their reproduction as a threat to the nation and aimed to contain
their fertility to defuse an explosion of population growth. Thus, the women
of Mahomedpur, like their counterparts across India, were tasked with

regulating their bodies and reproductive capacities to align with the demographic goals of the postcolonial state. Family planners expected women to accept a range of interventions to meet these goals: attending public meetings and being lectured by strangers on the virtues of birth control, visiting clinics and subjecting their bodies to new contraceptive technologies, and ultimately limiting their childbearing to two or three children.

Family planners understood their targets as reproductive subjects whose primary contribution to state-led development was limiting their fertility. They separated biological reproduction from other aspects of women's lives and made it the point of women's entry into development programs. Within the field of health specifically, family planning programs delinked contraception from maternal and child health and funded the former at the expense of the latter. These priorities shaped day-to-day interactions, such as Khan's meetings in Mahomedpur. Like her colleagues, Khan encountered women solely in order to discourage their reproduction, with little regard for the circumstances or needs that might prompt them to bear children. With no mandate to support their struggles to raise the children they already had, or to address any other aspect of women's lives, family planners like Khan simply explained that they "stood for" contraception as a means to serve national development goals.

While the women of Mahomedpur thus encountered the state's development agenda through their reproductive bodies, women like Khan demonstrated their commitment to development differently. By claiming to bring the message of family planning to impoverished rural and urban women, middle-class family planners like Khan became mediators between the state's development goals and its intended targets. Yet, as the Mahomedpur women's unwillingness to attend a public meeting suggests, this mediation was far from smooth. Women sometimes ignored, refused, or reinterpreted the family planner's message. They ascribed different meanings to their reproductive lives—meanings that did not hinge on the supposed threat posed by their bodies or by the explosive growth of population. In particular, women who did not fit within the boundaries of normative citizenship, which was marked as upper caste, Hindu, and middle class, found their reproduction to be doubly or triply stigmatized. Their encounters with family planners negotiated this stigma while offering alternative understandings of their bodies, families, and lives.

This chapter investigates a history of reproductive politics during an era of increasing anxiety about population from the 1950s to the 1970s. I begin in 1952, with the Indian government's official embrace of family planning in the First Five Year Plan. Successive Five Year Plans increased the funding for family planning while vastly expanding its ambitions. A growing number of workers, both volunteer and paid, took on the task of spreading contraceptives to the masses. Numerical targets for contraceptive use, alongside financial incentives for family planning "acceptors" and "motivators," became the hallmarks of India's emergent family planning bureaucracy. By the 1960s, crises of development, failures in food production, and concerns about national security had all combined to make "overpopulation" a site of heightened anxiety. Growing fears of a "population bomb," with its epicenter in South Asia, haunted the public imagination in both India and the West. Within India, this fueled the targeting of lower-caste, lower-class, and Adivasi women in desperate attempts to curtail their reproduction. In the West, racialized discourses marked black and brown women's bodies as responsible for global overpopulation. This urgency continued into the 1970s, when it was punctuated by the Emergency, a period from 1975 to 1977 when the mechanisms of parliamentary democracy were suspended by Prime Minister Indira Gandhi. The Emergency remains the most widely known and infamous chapter in India's family planning history, in part because it marked a temporary shift toward men's bodies as the grounds for fighting a war on population. However, although it is often assumed to be a historical aberration[3]—both in Indian democracy and in family planning—the Emergency also represented a culmination of the logic of reproductive regulation that had taken shape across the postindependence decades. This chapter thus situates the turn to men during the Emergency in relation to the logics and institutions that had long connected women's reproduction to population and economy.

India's scaled-up ambitions for family planning during this era depended, in part, upon new contraceptive technologies that enabled more absolute control over reproduction. The methods available in the 1950s were largely the same as those of earlier decades. Even in 1960, when Khan visited Mahomedpur, she would have spoken of contraceptive foams, jellies, and sponges, and possibly pessaries or diaphragms for women who could visit a physician. Just a few years later, the birth control pill, the intrauterine contraceptive device (IUD or IUCD), and the widespread use of surgical sterilization had changed the contraceptive landscape, both in India and globally. While these new technologies could enable people to control their own fertility more effectively than ever before, they also opened the door to more intensive modes of reproductive regulation by population controllers.

As we shall see, they also helped to position women's bodies as the figurative fuse of the "population bomb."

Consequently, while visits like Khan's to Mahomedpur aimed to teach women about contraception, their goals were also broader. As women's reproductive bodies became a site to enact development plans, the history of reproduction became thoroughly implicated in the history of postcolonial development. Contraceptive technologies were the means to make this link, quite literally connecting individual bodies to development goals. This chapter traces these close intersections between birth control and the intimate regulation of bodies, and between the fears of a "population explosion" and the emphasis on reproduction in India's development regime. I begin with the institutionalization of family planning during the 1950s and early 1960s. Although this period is sometimes overlooked in histories that focus on the more aggressive population control campaigns of later decades, the earlier years were central in bringing middle-class women—as family planners—into the state's development agenda, and in situating poor and working-class women as their targets. This targeting would intensify in the later 1960s, as Western funders and Indian government priorities aligned to make population control a focal point of Indian development, and women's bodies became the grounds to enact this development agenda. The chapter concludes with the intersection of surgical sterilization with states of emergency in the 1970s, examining the changing assumptions—about both gender and development—that underpinned reproductive politics in this era.

Targeting Women for Family Planning

The First Five Year Plan centered its implementation of family planning on women. It called for middle-class women volunteers to meet family planning goals and situated subaltern women as their targets.[4] Following middle-class assumptions about women's dependent roles in both family and economy, the planning commissioners largely ignored peasant and working-class women as producers and mentioned them primarily as recipients of social welfare. Simultaneously, the document distanced the state from such welfare activities, noting that "the main burden of organized activities for the welfare of women is to a large extent borne by voluntary agencies" rather than by central or state governments directly.[5] Family planning, alongside maternal and child health more broadly, thus came to occupy a space between state control and the work of voluntary actors and organizations. As I argue, this approach opened up a new field of national activity for middle-class women, who claimed it was their right and responsibility to bring contraceptive information and technology to their needier "sisters." Through their work in family planning, they argued, women volunteers could bring the promise of development to poor and working-class women and simultaneously solidify their own position as dutiful citizens of the new nation. To make this claim to citizenship and development, middle-class family planners depended upon subaltern women to receive their welfare services. However, as their accounts reveal, family planners who visited villages, organized public meetings, or ran birth control clinics often encountered women who questioned, ignored, or refused their services; sometimes, women asked for entirely different means of welfare support for themselves and their families. The result was a sometimes tense negotiation between the middle-class family planners who claimed to serve both women and the nation and the subaltern women who rejected that service.

The institutional structure of family planning, which combined state direction with women's voluntary work, was prompted in part by the efforts of Durgabai Deshmukh. A former AIWC president and activist in the freedom struggle, Deshmukh was the only woman member of the NPC that drafted the First Five Year Plan. Appointed to the commission after much of its work had already been completed, Deshmukh soon recognized that the commissioners had allocated no budget for "social welfare," which she defined as "services intended for individuals and groups in need of special attention," including women.[6] To remedy this, Deshmukh lobbied the other commissioners—including her future husband, C. D. Deshmukh—to create the Central Social Welfare Board (CSWB), a largely autonomous body tasked with coordinating collaboration between the state and nongovernmental or voluntary organizations. The government approved the creation of the CSWB in 1953, with Deshmukh at its head and a budget of 40 million rupees, including 6 million devoted to family planning.[7] By the Second Five Year Plan (1956 to 1961), a focus on women as targets of social welfare was further entrenched, as activities supporting women were located entirely under the CSWB. Health was among these "welfare" activities, and here the focus was on "family planning and other supporting programmes for raising the standard of health of the people."[8]

Deshmukh encouraged women's organizations to take up family planning and channeled most of the CSWB's initial family planning budget to these groups.[9] In an address to the AIWC, she noted that "women workers have been invited" by the government to propose measures for family planning and called upon the organization to prioritize its efforts in this direction. AIWC leadership evidently agreed, determining that they should "focus on collaborating with the Planning Commission," including on family planning.[10] These commitments prompted a spurt of activity centered on birth control clinics and propaganda, which figured the middle-class woman volunteer as a mediator between the state's population control goals and its women targets. For example, in Bombay, AIWC members supported the FPAI's newly established birth control clinic. One of the AIWC's volunteer workers, Shanta Navkal, spoke to meetings in the "poor areas" of greater Bombay to encourage people to adopt contraceptive methods.[11] Many other branches similarly did "outreach" work on birth control. According to the AIWC's Annual Report for 1953, for instance, the Mysore branch sent one woman volunteer to address women's gatherings in Bangalore, Bhadravathi, and the Kolar Gold Fields on family planning. The Madras branch conducted outreach work in the city while collaborating with the city corporation to start family planning clinics in hospitals. In Delhi, the AIWC worked to include three family planning clinics in municipal health centers and offered advice on birth spacing and on preventing children on medical and "economical grounds." According to the South Madhya Pradesh branch, eight "lady doctors" had opened family planning clinics "at the instance of the branch," while in the Madhya Bharat branch another doctor had attended trainings at the Planned Parenthood conference in Bombay.[12] The FPAI was even more active in these clinical and propaganda efforts. As Avabai Wadia reported in 1959, the FPAI had opened twenty-two branches across India, many of which supported clinics and held "educational meetings" to promote contraceptive use. The organization also expanded its Bombay clinic to include several branches and opened a supplies department to send contraceptives to "welfare clinics" around the country.[13] While these efforts were on a small scale, they testify to the importance of middle-class women workers in staffing the new family planning regime, and in marking it as a domain for women volunteers.

Among these volunteers were the honorary family planning education leaders, who were appointed by the state to support outreach and voluntary efforts in family planning. The government drew upon organizations like the FPAI and AIWC to select these voluntary workers, who were tasked with spreading information about birth control. Among them was Padmini Sengupta, a writer and CSWB member, who lamented that "constant breeding and care of children make women unfit to become intelligent members of an active society."[14] She reported to the AIWC about her activities in West Bengal in 1959. Sengupta met with jute-mill workers and sweepers in the "slum of Barrackpore"; she also appointed a number of women family planning educators to continue outreach projects.[15] Her colleague K. Meenakshi Amma, honorary family planning education leader for Kerala, reported that in April 1960 she held group meetings at Kozhencherry, Kummannoor, and Kottayam. She also visited fifty houses, formed a voluntary corps for family planning at a social welfare center in Kummannoor, addressed a meeting of women's organizations, and inaugurated a family planning camp of three hundred women and one hundred men.[16] Similarly, Prem Lata Gupta of Andhra Pradesh addressed numerous meetings in Hyderabad and in rural areas.[17] Other volunteer workers, including women who were not officially appointed family planning education leaders, engaged in similar tasks. For instance, Krishna Agarwal of the AIWC worked in the Indore region. Since her husband was a doctor, Agarwal claimed she had a greater "connection with the people." In a pilot project with the FPAI, she worked with four clinics in a "slum area" inhabited by five hundred mill families; she also addressed a meeting of Ayurvedic medical practitioners about the "Need of Family Planning and Psychological Effects of It on a Family."[18]

These accounts do not represent volunteer family planning workers as requiring specific training or expertise. Instead, literacy and an understanding of the purposes and mechanisms of birth control were the implicit qualifications. Perhaps most important, as Agarwal suggests, was the ability to forge a "connection" to the targets of family planning—figured here either as rural populations or as the working-class inhabitants of urban "slum" neighborhoods. As such, volunteer family planning work opened up a potentially vast terrain of activity for literate middle-class women, who were assumed to be familiar with birth control in their own lives and to have the requisite understanding of national development goals and population policy. Moreover, these middle-class women—with their ostensible connection to their poorer sisters—could bridge the gap between the state's development agenda and the ordinary women whose childbearing decisions would shape the timing and extent of a modernizing demographic transition. Thus, while elite women with connections to government like Dhanvanthi Rama Rau and Deshmukh engaged with family planning at the level of policy, there were many more educated, literate women—often the wives and daughters of doctors, lawyers, professors, and others—who made the case for birth control in homes and neighborhoods.

Eventually, as the scope and goals of the family planning bureaucracy became more ambitious, paid workers began to join the volunteers. For instance, the FPAI reported that while "voluntary members" continued family planning outreach, in 1961 the organization hired a full-time "trained social worker, Mrs. Pramila Thakore, BA." Thakore was tasked to conduct an "educational programme of meetings, lectures, film shows, etc. for audiences drawn mainly from the lower income groups." In her first year in her position, Thakore ran 349 meetings with a total attendance of more than 73,000 people, both in the city of Bombay and in the outskirts and rural areas, using the FPAI's mobile unit.[19] Alongside social workers like Thakore, the "lady doctor" was another critical paid worker in the family planning bureaucracy. Both the government and private organizations lamented the scarcity of women medical practitioners and sought them to staff clinics.[20]

Whether volunteer or paid, family planning workers claimed a gendered sphere of activity. So long as subaltern women were the targets of reproductive regulation, literate, middle-class woman volunteers and paid social workers and doctors were essential mediators between these women and the state. Thus, according to Prem Lata Gupta, who was then president of the Andhra Pradesh branch of the FPAI, women's voluntary service would bridge the gap between the goals of national development—which required the "control of population"—and the "welfare of the individual and the family [in which] women can and have to play the most vital and intimate role."[21] Women volunteers could explain to other women the benefits and methods of family limitation, thus "educating them properly" into appropriate reproductive roles. AIWC members insisted that these efforts to spread the message of family planning ultimately benefited poor women and, indeed, "would usher in a new age for the women of India. . . . Instead of merely slaving in the name of family, love, wifehood and motherhood, women gain better health, self respect and leisure."[22]

Yet, as women volunteers reminded themselves, poor women could never gain these benefits through their own efforts but required the gendered service of middle-class family planners. As Dr. Aleyamma George of the AIWC argued:

> Honestly speaking the educated and well-to-do class need not require any
> advice at all. . . . But it is in the slum areas among the poorer classes that
> this message has to be spread. We have seen women with bitter tears
> coming to us and talking to us about their miserable lives. They are not
> able to give proper clothing for their children. . . . It [family planning] is

really an uplift of the population. We are trying to bring them to a certain standard which is not the animal standard, if I may be excused such a word.[23]

George's comments demarcate two groups of women: those whose duty is to serve by offering family planning advice and those in need of social welfare measures to control their reproduction. This focus on service had a long history in the Indian women's movement, which was deeply influenced by Gandhian thought. It enabled Indian feminists to argue that their movement was not solely a middle-class project, even though most activists came from middle-class backgrounds. Rather, through a commitment to serving poor women, the women's movement advanced its claim to represent all Indian women—an argument first made during the during the interwar years.[24] Moreover, as Emily Rook-Koepsel has shown, this appeal to service had broad resonance in Indian society, where differences of caste, religion, class, and gender posed apparent barriers to claims of national unity and connection.[25] Family planning, by linking the volunteer worker to her target of service, claimed to surmount these barriers.

However, Gandhian ideals of service required not only a volunteer to provide service but also a needy target who would receive and accept that service.[26] A few family planners emphasized this grateful receipt of services, as in the case of an AIWC worker in Belgaum, who claimed that "village women were very keen to know the methods and also they demanded the means for Family Planning."[27] Yet many other AIWC and FPAI workers reported a tremendous gap between the family planner and the intended recipients of her message. Consider for example the efforts of Visakha Dixit, the AIWC's member in charge of family planning in Madhya Pradesh, who convened a meeting of village women in Sanver, in Indore District, to explain the "importance of family planning." About eighty women attended, and Dixit "had personal talks with them about their health problems." However, she concluded glumly, "there was very little response to family planning. Mostly the women seemed to be against it."[28]

Dixit's AIWC colleague in West Bengal, Aroti Dutt, confronted additional difficulties when working in the Darjeeling District. She was unable to arrange any large meetings due to bad weather and was reduced to speaking only to smaller groups of women. Moreover, as a native Bengali speaker, Dutt found it difficult to communicate with her targeted audience. She wrote that it was "important to know the local language Nepali to be able to speak to the women directly," and she decided to learn the language before visiting

Darjeeling again in six months.[29] Both Dutt and Dixit voice an anxiety that the targets of their service are uninterested in what they have to offer and may even be actively opposed. Representing family planning as a form of "service" to such unwilling and uninterested women became a deeply problematic exercise, and family planners' reports reveal a tense negotiation, justifying their efforts while grappling with limited and inadequate results.

On occasion, some family planning workers expressed frustration with the intended recipients of their services. This was especially the case when the targets were marked as religiously different and "other" from the family planner herself. Thus, for instance, Meenakshi Amma reported on her visit to fifty houses in two "backward wards" of Mulanthara and Kummannoor: "The Muslim section of the population, I found, could not be convinced about the necessity of birth control, though they are in most urgent need of it. In one of the houses, the owner Alipillai, aged fifty and father of fourteen healthy children ranging from 23 years to ten months, wanted to know whether the Central Government would give him any aid or grant for bringing up and educating them."[30] Meenakshi Amma does not recount her response to Alipillai's query, and its inclusion in her report was perhaps meant to suggest its impossibility—or even absurdity—rather than to discuss his request for state support. Moreover, her emphasis that Alipillai was part of the "Muslim section of the population" draws upon communal discourse about the differential fertility of Muslims and Hindus and the supposed national dangers posed by Muslim reproduction. Her mentioning Alipillai's fourteen children further fuels Hindu anxieties about Muslim population growth. At the same time, her comments mark the vast difference between the family planner as a rational, implicitly Hindu, normative citizen in service to the state, and the nation's problematic "others," who perversely refuse such service despite its ostensible personal and national benefits.

However, most family planners' reports did not emphasize religious or caste differences in such explicit ways. They were more guarded in their language, leaving the differences and hierarchies between the provider and recipient of service implicit when referencing the "slum women" or "backward" areas in which they served. On rare occasions, they spoke about the class differences that made it difficult for middle-class women to gain the trust of poor women, especially on matters of sexuality and reproduction. The family planner from Belgaum, for instance, acknowledged that the "villagers . . . at first felt shy" but eventually discussed the subject with her. Because they were "not ready" to attend government dispensaries and hospitals, she herself began to carry and distribute contraceptives.[31] The most direct recognition of the limitations in the family planner's mediation came from Hem Sanwal, a physician and family planning education leader in Uttar Pradesh. Based on work in the village of Gomet in Aligarh District, Sanwal argued, "If we depend on . . . the trained highly educated social workers mostly coming from urban areas and *not feeling one with the village and village women,* who are not even available in sufficient number to cover all the village population, we still remain very far from solving any population problem and would be depriving those who earnestly desire to adopt family planning methods."[32] Sanwal places some blame on the "highly educated social workers" who do not feel unity with the village women they supposedly serve. Taken further, her statement implicitly questions the very model of service that figures the middle-class family planner as the provider of social welfare measures to lower-class women.

This divide between the middle-class family planner and her subaltern targets of service highlights a "bifurcation of the female subject" that Asha Nadkarni locates in the aftermath of Indian independence. In Nadkarni's terms, even as "bourgeois rights for women [were] written into the Indian Constitution," working-class women were "forgotten as productive subjects, [and] targeted instead under the purview of education, maternal and child health, and family planning."[33] Family planners represented themselves as legal and juridical citizen-subjects within this bifurcated regime, becoming the beneficiaries of new legal rights for women alongside new opportunities for higher education and professionalization. Family planning offered middle-class women a terrain to assert their authority and professionalism as volunteers, social workers, and doctors who could spread the message of family planning. To enact this new citizenship and service, however, they needed poor, less educated urban and rural women. These women would encounter the state not through their legal and juridical rights as citizens but through their reproductive capacity. Within a bifurcated regime, their ability to reproduce—to make live, to limit fertility, to preserve life— rendered them the quintessential biopolitical subjects, whose citizenship became attached exclusively to their bodily capacities and sexual behaviors. Consequently, the middle-class family planner's ability to represent herself as a dutiful citizen-supporter of national progress depended upon her representation of subaltern women as reproductive subjects, whose entrance into economic and political life depended upon the regulation of fertility.

However, some women who were targeted by these development programs rejected this focus on their reproduction and challenged family planners' assumption that limiting childbearing was a necessary step on the path to modernizing progress. These critiques remain a rare presence in the archives, which were devoted to documenting the efforts of the family planner and took little interest in noting how ordinary women received these efforts. Indeed, the voices of targeted women appear only in fragmented form in archival texts, typically when a report's author recounts the difficulties she faced in convincing women to adopt birth control. Moreover, women's voices almost always enter in the aggregate; reports note only that women of a particular village, or of a specific caste or religious group, questioned or rejected the family planner's message. Thus, without assuming that these texts reveal women's full experiences with family planning, I ask how the fragments of women's responses that appear in the archives disrupt family planners' attempts to connect reproduction with development. That is, while family planning workers aimed to highlight subaltern women's biological reproductivity as a site of intervention, their reports are interrupted by alternative claims that make visible other aspects of women's lives and other entry points into a development regime. Women who were targeted for family planning did not represent themselves solely as reproductive subjects, and their concerns about reproduction were often at odds with the anxieties of the family planner.

Some women questioned the need to limit their childbearing, and thus challenged the basis of a development logic that made fertility reduction essential to economic growth. Dhanvanthi Rama Rau reported on these challenges when describing her attempts to persuade "village women" to adopt contraception; they refused, arguing that children were necessary in every household because they could tend the fields and help with domestic work. Moreover, they insisted, children were an absolute necessity to their parents in old age.[34] These claims resonate with the findings of many feminist critics of population control, who have since shown that the economic value of children within agrarian households was a crucial factor in driving families' childbearing decisions. Since children in these households produced more than they consumed from an early age, and since adult children provided the only available form of care and support for the elderly, large families were a rational choice for many agrarian households. In some cases, they were foundational to the household's survival.[35] Rama Rau herself seemed somewhat persuaded by these women's "reasoned and thoughtful" comments. She admits that her "only answer to these arguments was that spacing children would result in healthier mothers and children, and such large families would no longer be necessary."[36] Yet these assertions about an imagined future of healthy mothers and small families, as even Rama Rau acknowledged, had limited bearing on women's choices in the present, where they confronted high rates of child mortality and an absence of social welfare supports for the elderly.

In urban contexts as well, family planners were confounded by women who rejected the connection between large families and poverty. For instance, Visalakshi Narayanswamy, a family planning worker in Tamil Nadu, reported on three days spent in Madurai, where she led a disappointingly small meeting of "only" a dozen people in an industrial workers' neighborhood. There, one woman "proudly declared that she was not in favour of Family Planning, as all the members of her family were working and earning enough to maintain a whole family."[37] The unnamed woman's comments turned the economic logic of family planning on its head: if family planning was meant to limit the number of children to suit a family's budget, then a sufficiently large income would eliminate the need to curtail reproduction. The suggestion here is that the family's earning capacities transcended the need for reproductive control. If family planning were solely a requirement for the "poor," the Madurai worker refused this label and asserted her right to have as many children as she desired.

Many of the voices that emerge through these records suggest a profound valuing of children that disrupts the rhetoric of family planning as a technology of economic development. We find traces of this in the reports of "rumors" that family planning would render people completely unable to conceive. Such rumors halted S. K. Khan's efforts in Mahomedpur, discussed above. Similarly, researchers conducting a study of family planning in Bombay found that "some men and women were prejudiced against the social workers as they thought them to be the agents for stopping children from coming into the world and thereby going against God's wish."[38] Family planners dismissed these "rumors" as examples of ignorance and superstition; in the words of one report from Kerala, people who were most in need of fertility limitation had "peculiar notions about children given to them by the grace of Allah."[39] Such "peculiar" beliefs prevented the spread of the supposedly more rational claims of the family planner. Yet, read against the grain, perhaps the persistence of rumors that family planning workers had the power to prevent childbearing entirely suggests the importance accorded to children, and an accompanying concern about infertility. Rather than viewing the rumors as ignorance or irrationality, I read them alongside the challenges that rural women posed to Rama Rau. If children were absolutely essential to the well-being of their parents and households, then limiting or curtailing childbirth may have appeared to be the less "rational" outcome. The problem was not too many children—as family planning programs maintained—but rather their absence.

Consequently, visitors to clinics and attendees at public meetings often asked about fertility problems. According to Prem Lata Gupta, for instance, family planning meetings sometimes attracted "women who do not have children" who "ask if there is medicine for this also, and are directed to the Hyderabad Family Welfare Center." Indeed, she advised, "it appeals more to our women if you speak to them of a Family Welfare Programme and not merely about Family Planning."[40] Gupta was not alone in this observation; despite family planning workers' commitments to teaching women how to limit their children, women themselves called for assistance in increasing their fertility or supporting the children they already had. Thus, a study of family planning programs in Bombay concluded that people were uninterested in family planning on its own and would not attend clinics. However, family planners got around this problem by offering milk to children; many mothers came to the clinic for the milk, and then family planning workers tried to "motivate" them to adopt birth control. A children's health clinic was also an inducement, since the study's authors concluded, apparently without irony, that "women are more interested in talking to people who help their child." Similarly, a "sterility clinic" had helped to "eradicate the idea that family planning merely means the prevention of births."[41]

Within these texts, programs to feed children, provide health care, and treat infertility appear merely as inducements to persuade women to regulate their reproduction. These priorities reflected the government's organization of its own family planning programs, which privileged contraception and sterilization over expenditures for maternal and child health or nutrition. Yet, even while biological reproduction and its control remained the official focus of family planning, women themselves broadened their concerns about "reproduction" far beyond these categories. As we have seen, they sought the means to combat infertility and to promote the survival, health, and welfare of their existing children. They challenged the notion that fewer children equaled greater prosperity and valued children for their economic and emotional support within families. Among the most powerful of these challenges were comments that Hem Sanwal reported from the village of Gomet in Aligarh District: "The women of this village . . . expressed their desire to have a school for their girls so that in times to come their lot would be better than that of their mothers."[42] The women's desires gesture toward a reproductive future that exceeds the more circumscribed horizons of family planning discourse. Women's call for the resources to educate their daughters offers a vision of their reproductive responsibilities, of motherhood and parenting, and of development, that sets aside the demographic rationalities of the state. It refuses the family planner's claim that women's fertility determines their futures. It also refuses to stake claim to national development through reproductive regulation; women's childbearing does not determine their entrance into economic or political life. The call for a girls' school instead envisions a future in which the daughters of Gomet are not only reproductive subjects.

Sacrificing Women in a "War" on Population

A building sense of crisis—namely continued population growth, shortfalls in food, and national security concerns—fueled India's population control programs during the 1960s. In the face of these crises, Indian planners increased their efforts to regulate reproduction, and women's bodies became the terrain to enact planned development. The government introduced numerical targets of contraceptive "acceptors" that individual states were pushed to achieve. It also began to use incentives, typically cash payments, to induce acceptance of sterilization or long-acting contraception. The growing urgency of Indian family planning aligned with rising fears in the West, especially in the United States, about a "population bomb" that threatened planetary survival. Panic about "explosive" population growth in Asian, Latin American, and African countries targeted poor women's reproduction as the source of global crisis. In India, this severed even the tenuous, bifurcated citizenship claims that had marked poor women's relationship to the state after independence. Subaltern women were no longer represented as potential citizens responsible for controlling their reproduction in service of the nation, nor even as the recipients of social welfare. Instead, the rhetoric of the population bomb positioned women's bodies themselves as bombs to be defused. These changes in family planning programs also changed the nature of the historical archive. The more individualized reports of family planners that I examined in the previous section, which recounted the experiences of volunteers and paid workers, gave way to an emphasis on demonstrating aggregate results. The focus turned away from the potential connections—however tense—forged between the family planner and her targets, and toward documenting the "births averted" through contraceptive use.

I trace these changes to cracks in India's development regime that began to emerge in the 1960s. The Third Five Year Plan (1961–65) and subsequent annual plans (1966–69) grappled with the limitations of economic growth. Though industrial and agricultural production had increased during the first two Plans, the NPC raised concerns that production had not kept pace with need, had not met rising expectations, and was not sufficient for a growing population. Perhaps disillusioned by the unfulfilled promises of independence—Nehru's "tryst with destiny"—ordinary people expressed frustration with the slow pace of change. Some turned to the ballot box, and in 1967, voters in Tamil Nadu handed the Congress Party its first statewide defeat in the two decades since independence. In that same year, peasants and Adivasis in Naxalbari, West Bengal, rose in open rebellion against the government, launching an insurrection that would soon spread across districts in several states. This mood of rebellion seemed to echo far beyond India's borders, as popular dissatisfaction with the status quo upended politics around the world in the late 1960s. In this context, population growth came to be blamed for the failures and slow pace of economic development.

Population anxieties gained focus and momentum once again after a decennial census. The census of 1961 documented a population increase of 21 percent over the decade since 1951, a higher rate than demographers had predicted. Meanwhile, an increasing body of evidence suggested that Indian family planning efforts had not succeeded in controlling population. One notable and highly publicized failure was the Harvard-directed Khanna study. With the support of substantial funding and numerous personnel, the Khanna study had begun in 1953 with the goal of educating villagers in Punjab about family planning and providing them with contraceptive methods. By 1960, when the study concluded, it was apparent that the targeted villagers—who had been meeting regularly with study personnel for years—remained unconvinced, uninterested, or actively opposed to curtailing their reproduction.[43] These failures raised questions about what kind of family planning program might be effective in curbing population growth. If a program as well funded and intensive as the Khanna study was unsuccessful, in other words, what options might Indian family planners have?

Two wars on India's borders heightened these population anxieties. India's defeat in the Sino-Indian War of 1962 raised questions about the nation's security, the preparedness of its military, and the "quality" of its soldiers. Anxieties about security increased in 1965, when India and Pakistan fought a war that began in Kashmir and soon extended to the border areas of Punjab. The rhetoric of militarization that accompanied these conflicts transformed the language of family planning as well. Government officials proclaimed that, as part of strengthening the nation, population control efforts must be put on a "war footing." For instance, Lieutenant Colonel B. L. Raina of the Army Medical Corps—who, as head of the Central Family Planning Board, coordinated the government's family planning programs—regularly invoked the language of battlefield casualties in the "war" on population. Speaking at a 1966 seminar at AIWC headquarters, he argued, "If the programme of family planning is to be implemented on war footing—which has become the cry of the day—we will have to accept the risks and wastages."[44] Though Raina did not specify who would bear these risks and whose lives might be rendered "wastage," it was impoverished women whose bodies were targeted by these intensified population control campaigns. Sushila Nayar, an AIWC member and a Gandhian who served as minister for health and family planning from 1962 to 1967, similarly made the bodies of poor women the site for wartime sacrifice. As she argued before an assembly of scientists and family planners, "If [this] is a programme on war footing an occasional casualty should not scare you away. We accept that. At the same time if we can avoid that casualty we would like to do so."[45]

In Nayar's and Raina's terms, women's bodies might need to be sacrificed to win the war against population growth. Women appear here less as the reproductive subjects of development than as soldiers within a militarized family planning regime. Perhaps not coincidentally, the border state of Punjab, at the frontier of military conflict with Pakistan, soon became a center of the "war" on population as well. Among the most striking juxtapositions of this twinned conflict was a report from the Bharatiya Grameen Mahila Sangh, an organization that offered civil defense training for women in border states alongside a hundred "Family Planning Orientation Camps" that aimed to "motivate" women to use IUDs or be sterilized.[46]

Adding to these anxieties was a crisis in food production.[47] Consecutive years of monsoon failure during the mid-1960s led to food shortfalls and raised the prospect of starvation for millions of people. The Indian government looked internationally for food aid. The United States offered support but linked its provision of food to Indian commitments to population control.[48] The explicit connections made by Americans between food aid and reproductive regulation reshaped the discourses of family planning. In Nayar's terms, India's dependence on food shipments from abroad meant that population control was no longer solely a question of national economic development, as family planners had been arguing since the 1940s. It was now also a matter of national "self-respect": "It is very humiliating to have to ask for aid of any kind, and when the giver is reluctant or shows hesitation it makes the aid all the more humiliating and galling. As a self-respecting nation it is absolutely necessary for us to be self-reliant and to be able to do away with this type of assistance and situations which make us feel small or humiliated in any way. . . . It is our duty to decrease reproduction to make the nation self-respecting and self-reliant."[49] For Nayar, women's wartime sacrifice—via regulating reproduction—was critical to this drive toward national self-reliance. Indeed, she suggested, it was women's responsibility to make their bodies available via IUD insertions and sterilizations. Women's fertility thus became both cause and solution for India's myriad failures of development—from wars to the "humiliating" request for international aid.

This representation of Indian women's bodies as wartime targets to be sacrificed for national need aligned with transnational representations of a planetary population "explosion" caused by the reproduction of women in the "Third World." Population control discourses in the West adopted the imagery of a literal explosion to argue that family planning was an urgent priority to combat a dangerous population emergency. For example, one striking image of the "population bomb" published in the United States in 1960 shows an exploding earth whose overcrowded inhabitants are, quite literally, falling off the planet (figure 4.1).[50] As it had in the past, India served as a case study for these Western representations of (over)population. Commentators suggested that the country's current-day conditions presaged how the entire world would look if nothing was done. American author Paul R. Ehrlich's best-selling book *The Population Bomb* (1968) encapsulated these fears in its famous opening scene, which described the author's visit "one stinking hot night" to a crowded Delhi street full of "people, people, people, people" in a "scene [of] hellish aspect."[51] As Matthew Connelly argues, Ehrlich's imagery fueled American concern about population growth in India and simultaneously played upon American anxieties about domestic crime, contagion, and migration, without explicitly naming these factors.[52] The discourse of a worldwide population explosion thus contributed to a racial politics that was at once localized and globalized; it drew upon fears of population growth in the "Third World" alongside poverty and racial anxieties in the "First World."

Feminist critics of population control have made visible the antiwomen underpinnings of this discourse and have challenged the neo-Malthusian assumptions that blame reproduction, rather than unequal distribution of

FIGURE 4.1. This striking image shows an exploding earth whose inhabitants are falling off the overcrowded planet. Courtesy of Rockefeller Archive Center.

Voluntary
HUMAN STERILIZATION
Is it an Answer to the
POPULATION BOMB?

resources, for poverty and hunger. They have shown, moreover, that black and brown women—Asian, Latin American, African, and racial minorities in the US—were the ones blamed for bringing the world to the brink of a supposed population explosion and targeted for the most invasive methods of reproductive regulation.[53] This politics of blame was often explicit in population control imagery, as in a set of images produced by the IPPF. Among these was "A Child's Reproach," in which an impoverished, brown-skinned child gazes balefully at the viewer. Another shows an "Unplanned Family," composed of a dark-skinned mother and three children. Meanwhile, the "planned families" were depicted as white, including two in images titled "Reverence for Life" and "Wanted," both showing a white mother caressing a white infant.[54] This imagery suggested that the "unplanned" reproduction of brown bodies threatened the supposedly "planned" reproduction of white populations. It mobilized a claim about differential fertility whereby the supposed overreproduction of Asians, Africans, and Latin Americans threatened to displace their white American and European counterparts.

Such a politics hearkened back toward debates about eugenics, migration restrictions, and a global color line, discussed in chapter 2. It also gestured forward, toward a future of American imperial hegemony that seemed threatened by decolonization and the rise of a "Third World."

These gendered, classed, and racialized anxieties of the "population bomb" provided the context for increasingly intensive campaigns to curb global population growth, and India emerged as a key test case. Foreign donors poured into India, bringing demographers and other social scientists with their own sprawling bureaucracies and networks for population control. Private US funds—in large measure from the Ford Foundation—had provided support for Indian family planning programs beginning in the 1950s. By the last years of that decade, Ford officials were working closely with the Indian government, often joining planning meetings at the Central Family Planning Board and the Health Ministry. Ford funds also launched pilot projects and paid for consultants whose ideas were widely adopted by government programs.[55] Eventually, the Ford Foundation was joined by the US government itself. In 1966, in the wake of the Indo-Pakistan War and the US president's insistence that food aid be tied to population control, the United States Agency for International Development (USAID) replaced Ford as the largest foreign donor to India's family planning programs. Even at the height of USAID and Ford support, foreign funds were never more than 10 percent of India's total health budget, but as Mohan Rao argues, these funders exercised disproportionate influence on the shape of family planning campaigns.[56] Although the fears of brown bodies obviously held little resonance in an Indian context, racialized fears of differential fertility aligned with long-standing Indian elite anxieties about the overreproduction of poor, lower-caste, and Muslim populations.

These national and transnational anxieties about population growth were apparent in the Indian government's Third Five Year Plan (1961–65). Family planning policy moved away from an earlier focus on clinics and toward an extension approach that aimed to "motivate" people to use birth control. The program's ambitious goal was to reduce the birthrate from forty per thousand to just twenty-five per thousand by 1973. The twin crises of war and monsoon failure led to the temporary abandonment of Five Year Plans in favor of annual plans for the years 1966 through 1969. In each year, family planning expenditures continued to increase. Increased funds prompted a huge expansion of the family planning bureaucracy, but, as in the past, this expansion was not linked to health care overall but more narrowly to family planning. Thus, for instance, Primary Health Centers—which were meant to be the rural population's first point of contact for health care—received more resources, but these were required to be spent on family planning, not on other services, including maternal and child health. In 1966, following a UN recommendation, the Directorate of Family Planning was relieved of responsibilities for maternal and child health and nutrition so that field-workers could focus solely on birth control.[57]

The expansion of family planning at the expense of health care and the continued underfunding of health services became a deep and enduring feature of India's population control regime. These imbalances in funding reflected at a policy level what we have seen rhetorically in claims about the population explosion; women's reproduction was held responsible for crisis, and their bodies were targets to be sacrificed in an attempt to defuse the population "bomb." Yet even as population control intensified, critiques of these policies also began to emerge. Notably, the landmark *Towards Equality: Report of the Committee on the Status of Women in India* (1974), which was commissioned by the government and authored by prominent women academics, questioned the state's focus on population control at the expense of maternal and child health and refused to make reproductive regulation an important feature of their investigation.[58] These early reservations were an important precursor for the more robust feminist critiques of population control that would develop in later decades.

Contexts for population anxieties also began to shift as the global "Green Revolution" changed the long-standing equation between population and food. For a century of Indian history, as we have seen, concerns about population had been directly linked to fears of food shortfall and famine. However, with the Green Revolution, new, scientifically developed hybrid varieties of wheat and rice vastly increased crop yields and transformed agriculture. The first hybrid wheat seeds arrived in India in 1963, and the government encouraged imports of hybrid seeds during the food crisis of 1965 to 1967. The results were dramatic. Within five years, Indian wheat harvests had increased by 150 percent and rice by over 30 percent. Quelling some of Health Minister Sushila Nayar's fears about national "self-respect" and "self-sufficiency," the country's reliance on food imports decreased rapidly, and by the late 1970s, Indian farmers had planted the world's largest area of high-yield crops.[59] This dramatic increase in food production suggested that perhaps the earth could feed a larger population than had been imagined before. However, although Green Revolution technology increased the amount of food grown, it did not solve the problem of hunger, which, as we have seen, was rooted not only in agrarian production but also in the unequal distribution of land and resources. In fact, the Green Revolution exacerbated these inequalities, both regionally within India and between wealthier and poorer farmers. In retrospect, the Green Revolution also incurred tremendous environmental costs. Neither hybrid seed nor associated social and economic changes would be a panacea for Indian development.

Perhaps most surprisingly for a history of reproduction, however, the Green Revolution's vastly increased crop yields did not overturn the Malthusian premise that underpinned population control programs. Despite an occasional claim that "development was the best contraceptive," the changing balance between food and population did not lead planners to question the need to regulate reproduction. The system of targets and incentives seemed to continue unchanged, and women's fertility remained the site of intervention. Indeed, as I discuss later in the chapter, during the period of Emergency rule (1975–77) some of the Indian government's most draconian population controls developed concurrently with the greatest gains of the Green Revolution.

"This simple device can and will change the history of world": IUDs and Struggles to Control the Uterus

By the 1960s, a growing consensus within the transnational population establishment determined that the planetary "population bomb" could not be defused by existing contraceptive technologies alone. Contraceptives in use during the 1950s and early 1960s were largely barrier methods (such as pessaries or condoms) or spermicides (such as vaginal foam tablets). They required couples to make a conscious and repeated choice during each sexual encounter. Family planners dreamed of something different: a birth control method that was highly effective, did not require continuous decision-making by couples, and was inexpensive and simple enough to be used widely across the "Third World." The birth control pill was a landmark new contraceptive technology that seemed to meet some of these needs. "The pill" was a hormonal rather than a barrier method, and it worked by inhibiting ovulation and thickening cervical mucus, preventing fertilization from taking place. Approved for the US market in 1960, the pill proved highly effective in preventing pregnancy and promised an entirely new paradigm for birth control. However, it did not fully meet the requirements envisioned for large-scale population control because taking the pill was a daily decision made by individual women. As two Indian family planning consultants noted, "In India the lack of general motivation makes it hazardous to entrust the pill to our women at this stage." Thus, while "the decision to take 'The Pill' is left to the individual user in most developed Western Societies," such individual decision-making was neither possible nor desirable in an Indian context.[60] Moreover, the high cost of the pill discouraged its widespread adoption by government-funded programs.

The intrauterine contraceptive device (IUD or IUCD) seemed to overcome these limitations of the birth control pill. The device is a loop or ring inserted into the uterus by a medical professional. After insertion, it can prevent conception for years. Contraception thus does not hinge on a woman's daily decision; her initiative is limited to the moment when she has the device inserted, and removal requires further medical assistance. By its very design, the IUD could narrow a woman's day-to-day control over her reproduction while widening that of medical professionals. This alignment between the design features of the IUD and the goals of population controllers was not coincidental: it was designed with these goals in mind. The Population Council, an organization founded by John D. Rockefeller III with the goal of controlling global population growth, made its first grants for IUD research in 1959 to two doctors, Jack Lippes and Lazar Margulies, who designed and tested various forms of the device.[61] In 1965, with backing from the Population Council, Lippes's design, known as the "Lippes loop" or simply the "loop," became the contraceptive device of choice for India's newly launched extended family planning program. Both in its design and in its implementation, the IUD exemplifies the links between Western fears of a "Third World" population explosion and Indian anxieties about population and development, which together determined the course of Indian population control in the 1960s.

At its inception, as Chikako Takeshita has argued, the IUD "disindividualized" its users. That is, its creators did not imagine the woman who used the IUD as an individual deciding to control her reproduction; rather, "Third World" women en masse were the "implied users" of this new technology.[62] We may trace this construction of the IUD's users to some of the initial scientific debates about the device, most notably in a "fact-finding" conference in New York sponsored by the Population Council in 1962 to promote IUD research. At the conference, Alan Guttmacher—an obstetrician-gynecologist who was president of the IPPF's World Population division and who would later lead IPPF's American affiliate, the Planned Parenthood Federation of America (PPFA)—emerged as an eager proponent of the IUD. As Guttmacher remarked to the assembled gathering of health professionals, he had recently visited India and Southeast Asia, where he learned something about population control: "The reason the restraint of population growth in these areas is moving so slowly is the fact that the methods which we offer are Western methods, methods poorly suited to their culture and to the control of mass-population growth. Our methods are largely birth control for the individual, not birth control for a nation. Therefore, I felt very strongly that new methods must be offered and, if the new methods are good and proper, results will be astounding."[63] The IUD, Guttmacher suggested, offered this "birth control for a nation."

The emphasis on mass population control deprioritized the reproductive health needs of individual women users. Speaking after Guttmacher, Dr. Robert Wilson made this point explicit:

> The traditional medical training is toward a single individual. We are concerned with whether an individual develops infection, or whether she has her baby safely, as one person to another. We are less concerned, by training and tradition, about groups of people, and about the welfare of the world in general. This is something that certainly has to be considered in any discussion of world-wide population control. We have to stop functioning like doctors, thinking about the one patient with pelvic inflammatory disease; or the one patient, who might develop this or that, or the other complication from an intra-uterine device; and think of the need for this in general.[64]

For Wilson, contraception that focused on individual outcomes might never meet the goals of global population control. He thus transformed the calculus of risk. The risk to individual women patients should not be weighed against the benefits to the patient herself but rather to the supposed benefits of controlling population on a mass scale. Thus, Wilson acknowledged, the IUD might occasionally be inserted into the "wrong patient," who would suffer complications. Nevertheless, he suggested to his audience, "perhaps the individual patient is expendable in the general scheme of things, particularly if the infection she acquires is sterilizing but not lethal."[65] Speaking after Wilson, Dr. Mary Calderone of the PPFA agreed. The risks to individual women, she suggested, must be accepted as "the realities of mass application of any medical technique."[66]

These "disindividualized" users of the IUD—whose health or fertility might be sacrificed in service of population control—were assumed to be poor women in the "Third World" or racial minorities within Western nations. In early clinical trials, Puerto Rico stood in for the former. For instance, a presentation by Adaline Satterthwaite and Clarence Gamble about their work in Humacao, Puerto Rico, discussed their trials with 125 women. Only in one case, they noted, did pain require removal of the device. In this instance, a physician removed the spiral-shaped IUD that was initially inserted: "The spiral was removed and shown to the patient and the loop inserted immediately after that. *The patient did not know that the loop had been inserted* and did not complain of any pain." Satterthwaite and Gamble represented this deception as a clever workaround to the problems engendered by what they decided was a patient's unfounded anxiety. These results led to their recommendation that the device "may prove a highly satisfactory method for widespread population control in overpopulated countries."[67] Other clinicians aimed for the mass application of IUDs for racial minorities and poor populations in the United Kingdom and the mainland United States. Dr. Don Jessen's study at Chicago's Wesley Memorial Hospital inserted IUDs into 121 patients selected from among the "indigent population," of whom there were "109 Negro, 1 Oriental, and 11 white." Jessen's results were mixed, and in a rare dissent, he did not recommend the device for use among poor patients "unless close medical supervision is possible."[68] By contrast, Margaret Jackson of the United Kingdom noted that she had greater success with 192 women who were "highly fertile" and were "problem patients and mothers of problem families."[69]

Debates about the IUD's design and use reflected these population control priorities. For example, a core question discussed during the New York conference was whether IUDs should have a "tail" that would extend outside the uterus. The potential disadvantage of a "tail" was an increased risk of infection. Its potential benefit would be to enable women themselves to check whether the IUD was in place or whether it had been involuntarily expelled. However, clinicians from Puerto Rico and India insisted that women would be unable or unwilling to examine themselves intravaginally to check for the "tail." Consequently, Guttmacher concluded, the fact that "women in undeveloped areas would be unwilling to examine themselves is a strong argument against the addition of a tail."[70] Another scientific debate centered on the need to take detailed medical histories from potential users. Such histories might screen out women with pelvic inflammatory disease (PID), who should not have IUDs inserted. However, as Bombay gynecologist and founding FPAI member Dr. V. N. Shirodkar remarked, it was difficult in India to obtain accurate patient histories of PID.[71] Consequently, Guttmacher suggested that "underdeveloped countries" needed fewer restrictions on insertion so as not to "lose sight of our goal—to apply this method to large populations." Guttmacher also pushed for insertions as soon as possible after a woman delivered a child, presumably in hopes that this would increase insertion rates. As he reminded his audience, "If we can insert early, it has great advantage. These remarks do not concern the 'carriage trade.' I am talking primarily about clinic patients."[72] That is, the safeguards about postpartum insertion and detailed medical histories that might be deemed necessary for privileged patients in Western countries did not hold for impoverished "clinic patients" or the women of Puerto Rico and India, whose bodies needed to be made available for population control.

A few years later, when the Population Council sponsored a second conference on the IUD, these assumptions about disindividualized users and mass population control had taken firm hold. The vice president of the Population Council, Bernard Berelson, announced with excitement that the IUD was now a "truly revolutionary development in enabling mankind to deal with the major world problem of undue population growth. . . . This simple device can and will change the history of the world."[73] Among the audience members listening to Berelson's claims was B. L. Raina of the Indian government's Central Family Planning Board. Raina was attending the conference with a collaborator, M. W. Freymann of the Ford Foundation, to present a paper on "Intra-uterine Contraception in India." In tones more measured than Berelson's apocryphal claims, Raina agreed that the IUD offered a welcome expansion of India's "contraceptive armamentarium."[74]

The Indian government's decision to focus on the "Lippes loop" IUD was taken in some haste. Only a few clinical trials were held within the country before the determination was made to use it on a mass scale.[75] Within the Indian population control establishment, the rapid push for the IUD came from a frustration with existing birth control technologies, none of which seemed to meet an "emergency" need to curb population growth. As Sushila Nayar noted, for instance, "conventional contraceptives" required "very strong motivation and persistence," and birth control pills were costly, had a high dropout rate, and required a thorough medical exam that Indian medical services would be unable to provide on a mass scale. Moreover, people were reluctant to be sterilized unless they had many children, "which means that so far as population control is concerned much damage has already been done." The IUD thus offered a technical fix, according to Nayar: "The contraceptive that does not need that persistence and which can be used even after the first child is the loop and that is why we have been trying to push forward this program of the loop."[76] The Population Council, the IUD's chief promoter, encouraged this point of view. The organization supplied India with one million devices in order to move the program forward quickly. Meanwhile, the Ford Foundation funded an IUD factory to ensure that India had its own national supply.[77] The Ford Foundation also conducted a pilot study using Lippes loops in the Hooghly District of West Bengal, and this became the model for expanding the program across India.[78] Soon after, the government was poised to introduce the IUD, or the "loop," as it came to be known among the millions of women who used it.

Once the device was adopted, there was a relentless push to locate IUD "acceptors" and increase the rate of insertions. Though there were almost no IUD insertions prior to March 1965, a total of 800,000 were completed during the 1965–66 Plan year.[79] Targets for IUD usage were set at the national, state, and district levels; these ranged from an ambitious twenty insertions per thousand population in urban areas to ten per thousand in rural India. If achieved, this would have resulted in four million Indian women using the device.[80] When these targets proved difficult to achieve, the Indian government adopted the model of some state governments—and the recommendation of Ford, UN, World Bank, and IPPF consultants—to introduce incentive payments.

In October 1966, the Health Ministry announced that states would receive eleven rupees for each IUD insertion, which they could distribute among patients, staff who performed the insertions, and "motivators" who recruited and brought in patients.[81] The inclusion of motivators, who were not necessarily state employees and had no special training or qualifications, helped to vastly expand the network of people involved in the state's family planning program. A woman might receive an IUD and then become a motivator to bring in other women. Alternately, her husband or other family members might receive the payment for motivation; others in the community, both kin and nonkin, government employees and private citizens, might supplement their earnings by identifying and persuading IUD "acceptors." Motivators typically brought their acceptors to IUD "camps," which were multiday events that aimed to bring together large numbers of acceptors and insert devices as rapidly as possible. Where there were not adequate numbers of doctors to do the insertions, states organized mobile squads to visit underserved areas. Meanwhile, propaganda efforts—radio programs, family planning exhibitions, films, theater—all aimed to persuade people of the benefits of the "loop."[82] By July 1968, the minister for family planning, Govind Narain, reported that over 2.5 million women had been fitted with IUDs.[83]

The technological shift represented by the IUD and its implied users led to several changes in family planning. As we have seen, the first two Five Year Plans situated birth control within a category of "women's welfare," then delegated such welfare work in large measure to women's voluntary organizations. By the mid-1960s, however, the state was more directly involved, and the IUD campaign became increasingly separated, both in rhetoric and in policy, from any claims about the "welfare" of women. Voluntary organizations, in turn, shifted their activities to participate in extended family planning, whether by supporting publicity efforts or by arranging clinical services themselves. Both the FPAI and the AIWC, for instance, were proponents of the IUD. As Rama Rau proclaimed, the IUD was among "the methods likely to bring the quickest and most satisfactory results in the emergency the country faces."[84] AIWC president K. Lakshmi Raghuramiah announced with satisfaction that "loop-camps have become very very familiar to our members. We have enough grounds to claim that we have played a great part in making women Family Planning conscious."[85] In 1966, for example, the Bombay branch's Skippo mobile clinic had "motivated" ninety-one women and fitted them with IUDs while also supporting efforts at a loop camp. In Mangalore in the same year, the Bhagini Samaj began rural IUD insertions, and its mobile unit had worked with the Public Health Department to conduct loop camps across rural parts of the district, where they completed 788 insertions. They concluded optimistically that the "loop is catching the attention of the people and the response is encouraging."[86] In the following years, branches in Kodaikanal and Malabar similarly began to focus on IUDs in their mobile vans.[87]

The numbers reported by voluntary organizations represented only a small fraction of the several million IUD insertions performed during this period. Yet the reports' accounting suggests how thoroughly the earlier claim that birth control was a component of women's welfare had now become folded into a relentless drive to document numbers—numbers of loop camps held, IUDs inserted, incentives provided. Numbers had long been the vocabulary of debate on population; now they were also the language of birth control. Success or failure was measured by numbers, and both state agencies and voluntary organizations aimed to measure up. If the IUD's designers had imagined a disindividualized user whose uterus might be defused by the device before it exploded with children, its proponents in India strove to create exactly such a user. They aimed to bring in women en masse, "motivate" them to use the IUD, and then insert the device into as many women as possible. The quest to scale up use of the loop thus became a race of the numbers against time, to inoculate as many women as possible against the threat of reproduction.

At the intersection of all this were the millions of women into whose uteruses the Lippes Loop was inserted. Their bodies bore the brunt of the undue haste that marked the launch of IUDs on a "war footing." We may find evidence of this haste at all stages of the process. The initial devices themselves—supplied by the Population Council—arrived unsterilized and with only one inserter per twenty devices. The responsibility to sterilize the IUDs properly thus fell on medical personnel, but conditions were often inadequate within the large-scale camps and mobile vans that conducted the bulk of insertions. Moreover, medical personnel were poorly trained in insertion and removal of the device, and the limited number of doctors available increased the pressure to perform insertions as rapidly as possible. Many women received little or no follow-up after an insertion, and complaints of pain, excessive bleeding, or other complications were often ignored.[88] As news of these problems began to spread, the IUD fell rapidly out of favor, and women refused in large numbers to be inserted with the "loop." The result was a dramatic decline in insertions from 1967 onward.[89]

Whereas the technological promise of the IUD had been to circumvent the question of women's "motivation," officials found that, instead, women refused the loop outright. As insertions fell, officials at the highest levels ascribed women's refusal to their supposed irrationality, which made them victim to "rumors" about the IUD. Narain, the minister for family planning, blamed rumors that loops caused cancer or death, claiming that "village *dais* and other persons who stand to gain from illegal abortions or sale of oral contraceptives were the chief sources of such distorted statements."[90] The Bombay gynecologist B. N. Purandare agreed that ordinary women were susceptible to "rumor," given their supposedly irrational beliefs and lack of education. He insisted that women targeted for IUDs had to be disabused of the beliefs that they were "committing sin by its use, of creation of the wrath of God, of going against nature, of danger of developing cancer, of injury to herself and her husband and of many other silly notions rampant among the uneducated women folk." For Purandare these ideas represented a serious setback to the IUD program, and he blamed women even while acknowledging that some of them faced complications after insertion, such as bleeding, pain and cramping, and dysmenorrhea.[91]

Once they imagined women as irrational and prone to rumor, IUD proponents could justify multiple methods of persuasion and even coercion. For example, Population Council consultant Harry Levin sidestepped questions about why women might choose or refuse an IUD. He suggested instead providing a "gift" to women who obtained the device or persuaded others to be fitted. In his terms, "Things like ball point pens and small plastic gadgets and notebooks have proven very effective in other areas when used as rewards to encourage insertions."[92] Levin's startling comment, in which a plastic gadget might be traded for a decision with vast implications for women's health and reproduction, reveals how the IUD's implied users entered into population control discourse. Rather than framing the issue in terms of why a woman might seek contraception or why an IUD might offer an acceptable method of birth control for some women, Levin imagines an Indian woman user who is swayed by access to a ballpoint pen. Certainly there is no discourse of citizenship here, nor of welfare or development. Rather, Indian women must be fitted with IUDs despite themselves. Levin's hopes, voiced in the early stages of the IUD program in 1965, would come to some fruition after 1966, when the government approved cash incentives for IUD "motivators." Though cash was likely more useful to women than Levin's plastic gadgets, the underlying implication still holds. Women were not trusted to choose birth control, and thus incentives would become the basis of the program.

Although the government insisted that the program was entirely voluntary, histories of its inner workings show that it was potentially coercive. Evidence from drought-stricken regions in Bihar, Madhya Pradesh, and Orissa, for example, suggests that starving women might have "chosen" an IUD as an alternative to hunger.[93] Paying an incentive to motivators also opened up avenues for coercion, as those with social or economic power might exert their influence to compel others to "choose" an IUD. Such effects have been well documented for family planning campaigns in later decades.[94] Cases in which women were denied removal of an IUD are another example of coercion; these women sometimes sought removal from private doctors or attempted to remove it with the assistance of a *dai* or family member.

More direct instances of coercion are rarely visible in the historical archive, given that family planners were invested in claims of voluntarism. However, one example comes from a physician working among women employed in tea estates in Assam. Dr. L. C. R. Emmet, chief medical officer of the Mariani Medical Association, took the opportunity to impose IUDs on women who had been married at ages below the legal limit. When three young women under age thirteen miscarried, Emmet claimed, "their husbands were given the opportunity to either induce their wives to volunteer for the IUCD, or be trotted down to the local Police Station. Needless to say, they chose the former and easier course of action."[95] Emmet's curious formulation, whereby he compelled husbands to "induce" the women to "volunteer," points to the coercive underpinnings of his IUD campaign. His assumption that an IUD insertion was "easier" for husbands further discounts the experiences of the young women. As in the case of the acceptors of Levin's plastic gadgets, women are not represented as making reasoned decisions about IUDs but are assumed to be irrational subjects who have to be persuaded, bribed, or coerced into insertion by any available means. For such imagined users of the IUD, the line between coercion and consent was porous and, in this case, was disregarded entirely.

Even IUD promoters who were more sympathetic toward the loop's users operated within this paradigm, whereby women's bodies and uteruses were put in service of another's reason. The rationality of the population controller, in other words, trumped the supposed irrationality of the IUD's implied user, rendering her into a body that was more or less available for an insertion. This was the case for Kumudini Dandekar, a feminist demographer and critic of some population control certitudes, who conducted a study with fellow demographer Surekha Nigam to assess why IUD insertions fell so sharply a few years into the program.[96] They were primarily concerned with "the capacity of the women to tolerate the device in spite of bleeding and similar accompanying discomfort." Basing their conclusion on a study of 2,100 loop adopters in rural Maharashtra, they claimed that despite bleeding, most "women bore the device patiently."[97] This emphasis on women's bodily abilities to "bear" the device—a language that recurs repeatedly across the scientific discourse—reinforces the turn away from any comprehensive analysis of women's interests, choices, or reasons for controlling their reproduction. In its place, women's bodily sacrifice became the very basis upon which the IUD program was built.

Sterilization and States of Emergency

Like the IUD, surgical sterilization became a key contraceptive technology to put India's family planning program on a "war footing." From a population control perspective, surgical sterilization was highly effective at preventing conception, was controlled by medical providers, and required patients to make only a one-time decision. Unlike the IUD, surgical sterilization was a permanent rather than temporary measure, and it was available to both men and women. Vasectomy for men was the medically simpler procedure, but tubectomy or tubal ligation for women also became part of the government's family planning program. The inclusion of men as targets of family planning marked a shift from earlier technologies and programs, which had focused on women and their bodies as reproductive threats to the nation. This attention to men even reshaped the gender politics of population control for a brief period during Emergency rule, from 1975 to 1977. After the Emergency, for reasons I discuss below, vasectomy was marked as an "excess" of Indian population control, while the program for female sterilization, and its regulation of women's bodies, was left intact.

Sterilization first became widespread in the southern states, where it was a mainstay of family planning even before the Indian government adopted it on a national level. In Madras State (later Tamil Nadu), the emphasis on sterilization was due in large measure to R. A. Gopalaswami, who served as independent India's first census commissioner and then worked for the Madras government. In his 1951 census report castigating "improvident maternity," Gopalaswami had argued strongly for a national population control policy, and in Madras he aimed to put this into effect through sterilization. As he explained, "Mechanical and chemical contraceptive appliances" were useful for "sections of the population who can be largely left to themselves." These were middle-class couples, Gopalaswami implied, who might decide to reduce their childbearing for reasons of family economy or national development. However, "from the point of view of the large mass of the people who will not space their pregnancies or limit their number except as a result of Governmental action, reliance should be placed primarily on natural methods for securing the former and on surgical methods for securing the latter."[98] In other words, surgical sterilization was the technology of choice to impose the state's will upon the reproductive capacities of the poor and marginalized. Nonpermanent methods, by contrast, were a luxury of the middle classes. The government of Madras introduced sterilization in its *Family Planning Manual* and noted that both vasectomy and female sterilization methods (recommended in the first twenty-four hours after delivery) were equally important to the state's program.[99] The Madras government also became the first in India to offer cash incentives for sterilization, with thirty rupees for men or women who underwent the procedure and ten rupees for the "motivator" who brought them to the clinic.[100]

With the intensification of family planning regimes during the 1960s, the central government joined states like Madras, Mysore, and Kerala in promoting sterilization for both men and women. The number of these surgeries grew rapidly. Government figures, though potentially imprecise, still indicate the scope of the increase. From just over 7,000 sterilizations of men and women in 1956, for instance, there were nearly 270,000 in 1964 and 1.8 million in 1967 through 1968.[101] The number of men increased still further with the inauguration of mass vasectomy camps, which eventually became a defining feature of the family planning program. The first of these camps was organized by S. S. Krishnakumar, the district collector of Ernakulam, Kerala, in December 1970. The camp aimed to bring together medical personnel and a large number of patients in a "festive atmosphere" in order to convince men to obtain vasectomies. The first Ernakulam camp provided transport to patients, was publicized widely in advance, and offered vasectomy "acceptors" a cash incentive alongside gifts. The result, as reported by the government, was more than 15,000 vasectomies in one month. A second camp in July 1971 resulted in more than 63,000 vasectomies, representing a staggering 42 percent of all such procedures performed in Kerala that year. Others adopted Krishnakumar's approach, holding camps at a variety of venues, including even Bombay's Victoria Terminus rail station.[102]

Supporters of mass vasectomy camps promoted the procedure's cost and efficiency. In contrast to female sterilization, vasectomies did not require hospitalization, used only a local anesthetic, and could be done relatively quickly. The main difficulty was thus not in the procedure itself, according to family planning proponents, but in convincing men to "volunteer" for it. Doctors, social workers, and government bureaucrats lamented public perceptions of the surgery, especially notions that it might lead to impotence or was akin to castration. They hoped that publicizing vasectomy camps might assuage these fears; the government also paid "motivators" to persuade men to agree to the procedure and bring them to the camps.

Whereas promoters of mass vasectomy camps touted them as purely voluntary events that destigmatized surgical sterilization, scholars have noted their coercive structures and effects. For impoverished populations, cash incentives were large enough to shape decisions about "consenting" to the procedure, especially when patients were uninformed about alternatives. The vast majority of camp attendees marked their occupation as laborers, most with monthly incomes of under 100 rupees; incentives at camps ranged from 70 to 150 rupees. Moreover, increased numbers at the camps tended to coincide with periods of agricultural crisis and scarcity; this indicates that men were more likely to "accept" vasectomy when other means of supporting themselves and their families had failed. Meanwhile, when government budget shortfalls led to the withdrawal of incentives in the mid-1970s, vasectomy adoptions fell sharply, again suggesting that the incentive was responsible for men's "choices" about the surgery. These implicit structures of coercion were reinforced in some cases by more explicit measures, such as at one camp in Uttar Pradesh for which the district collector arranged for police vehicles to locate and transport vasectomy acceptors.[103] In short, the mass vasectomy camps exactly echoed the call of population controllers like Gopalaswami to make surgical sterilization the primary method to control the reproduction of the masses. In the words of one physician in West Bengal, temporary contraceptive measures could be used by the "educated community" but "sterilization would be ideal for the illiterate."[104]

Vasectomy campaigns departed from previous family planning programs to target men's reproductivity as a source of national danger and a site for medical intervention. Family planning had already reduced subaltern women's bodies to their reproductive rather than productive functions. Moreover, the state's development regime had historically prioritized men's productive labor in providing access to agricultural resources and technologies, while ignoring women's contributions to agrarian production.[105] However, the new campaigns highlighted men's reproduction as an obstacle to national development, and with vasectomy, the state aimed for new kinds of control over men's reproduction. This shift from production to reproduction—from agricultural extension to family planning—was not easy, as one Ford Foundation consultant noted. Despite family planners' best efforts, he wrote glumly, "it is considerably easier to demonstrate the benefits of fertilizer than of vasectomy."[106] Perhaps it is unsurprising, then, that the targets of the vasectomy camps were those men least likely to have benefited from agricultural extension and rural development. These were the landless and land-poor, which meant they were more likely to be lower-caste, Adivasi, and Dalit populations that agrarian development efforts overlooked. In the absence of substantive land redistribution, their sterilization was touted as a route toward alleviating poverty. In the process, their bodies were subject to the kinds of reproductive control that had hitherto been reserved for women.

Despite this attention to men, however, we must remember that female sterilization continued uninterrupted throughout the late 1960s and 1970s. Although vasectomy was the simpler and cheaper procedure, family planners insisted that female sterilization was necessary as well, especially after the failure of the IUD campaign. But the ratio of procedures for men and women changed over time. When the government first began keeping records in the mid-1950s, female sterilizations accounted for about two-thirds of all sterilizations performed. With the rapid rise in vasectomies in the 1960s, this proportion fell. Though absolute numbers of sterilizations increased, women were receiving fewer of them in comparison to men, down to just 10 percent of such surgeries in 1967 to 1968.[107]

The campaign for sterilization acquired new urgency when Prime Minister Indira Gandhi suspended parliamentary democracy and declared a state of emergency in June 1975. She was responding to growing economic crises and rising social unrest, the latter spearheaded by Jayaprakash Narayan's anticorruption movement and call for "total revolution." Her position became even more precarious when, in June 1975, the Allahabad High Court found Gandhi guilty of malpractice in the 1971 elections. JP, as he was known to his followers, called for the prime minister's resignation, and the opposition staged a mass rally in New Delhi on June 25. Just one day later, Gandhi claimed there was a threat to India's "internal stability" and instituted the Emergency. Under Emergency rule, the government declared public meetings and strikes to be illegal, imposed press censorship, suspended the right of habeas corpus, and amended the Maintenance of Internal Security Act (MISA) to allow the detention of political prisoners without charge. Thousands of people were subsequently arrested. Within a month, Gandhi announced a "Twenty-Point Program" that claimed to tackle economic crises by controlling prices and increasing production. Soon thereafter, Gandhi's son and close associate Sanjay Gandhi created a "Four-Point Program" (later Five-Point) that explicitly included family planning among its development goals. Though he had no official government position, he became the unofficial leader of the government's population control efforts, which he combined with a drive for urban slum clearance.[108]

In popular imagination, the Emergency is inseparable from state-sponsored sterilization, so much so that the period is known in Hindi as *nasbandi ka vakt* (the time of sterilization).[109] Yet as we have seen, sterilization did not begin under the Emergency but already had a history in India's family planning program. The system of targets and incentives—and their underlying coerciveness—had begun a decade earlier, as had the attempt to introduce the procedure on a mass scale. Moreover, the notion that sterilization was a necessary fix for the country's disenfranchised, alongside the claim that temporary birth control measures were a luxury of the middle classes, circulated openly within the state bureaucracy. The state's intervention into the reproductivity of its citizens and the claim that such intervention alleviated poverty and promoted national development—an economization of reproduction—were established facts well before Sanjay Gandhi's

Four-Point Program. In short, virtually all the systems and institutions of sterilization that underlay *nasbandi ka vakt* already existed before Emergency rule.

Given these continuities, what were the potential ruptures that linked the Emergency so intimately to sterilization, such that Emergency time itself became marked as the period of *nasbandi*? There was undoubtedly an intensification of existing policies. For instance, in April 1976, nearly one year into Emergency rule, the minister for health and family planning, Karan Singh, announced a National Population Policy (NPP) that established new targets and further increased incentives for sterilization. The NPP sought to downplay any coercive intent, as Ashwini Tambe notes, by adding the presumably less controversial goal of raising the age of marriage as a way to reduce fertility rates.[110] Yet there were potentially coercive measures aplenty. For instance, the NPP proposed freezing states' representation in Parliament based on 1971 census figures, thus rewarding states that slowed population growth with greater representation and instituting political penalties for those whose population grew more rapidly. At the same time, it explicitly enabled states to pass legislation for compulsory sterilization.[111] Maharashtra soon complied with a measure calling for the compulsory sterilization of couples with three or more children; however, before this policy could be approved at the central level, the Emergency had ended.[112] Thus, although coercive practices had existed implicitly before, the doors were now open to more explicit acts of coercion. Finally, we must remember, the coercive effects of Emergency-era sterilization policies operated within a larger system of repression. The imprisonment of Gandhi's political opponents and the suspension of civil liberties and press freedoms were part of the political environment in which the Ministry of Family Planning pursued its sterilization targets.

This environment shaped how the government enforced its sterilization policies. State employees were pressed to meet their targets for motivating private citizens to be sterilized, and thus sterilization became a condition for continued employment or promotion. However, it did not need to be the employee who was sterilized: workers could produce "sterilization certificates" proving that they had "motivated" others for vasectomy or tubectomy. This process of "motivating" another person to be sterilized encompassed all manner of coercive methods. In her study of the Emergency in one Delhi neighborhood, anthropologist Emma Tarlo unearths a number of strategies to obtain such certificates. One schoolteacher, for instance, announced that students whose parents refused to turn over sterilization certificates would fail their exams. Housing officials demanded sterilization certificates to allot land to people whose homes had been demolished during the Emergency drive for "slum clearance." Sterilization certificates became a currency for obtaining state services such as health care, food rations, and electricity or water connections. To meet such demands, middlemen developed a thriving trade in such certificates—obtaining them through coercion and selling them to others for a price. Consequently, Tarlo concludes, during the Emergency ordinary citizens became newly enmeshed in the drive for sterilization, either as bodies to be sterilized or as agents in expanding the state's reach to ever more "targets" for the surgeries. She describes this as a "forcible deal" struck by the government with its own citizens, whereby "in theory, everyone was under pressure [for sterilization]. In practice, that pressure accumulated downwards" in such a way that only those at the very bottom rungs of society, those who had nothing to offer but their own bodies, underwent the surgery.[113] In this sense, following Tarlo, the pressure for sterilization during the Emergency percolated from the highest echelons of power down toward those living on the margins of society—urban slum dwellers and the landless poor. As each layer of the family planning bureaucracy transferred the burden of the surgery to a more vulnerable level, it was finally only the bodies of the poor that could satisfy the voracious demands for sterilization that kept the system running.

Emergency-era sterilization targets applied to both women and men, but it was the latter whose bodies were targeted most intensively as the numbers surged. Thus, during 1975–76, when Emergency family planning measures were being put into place, government figures reported over 2.6 million sterilizations, of which just over half (53.9 percent) were vasectomies.[114] The numbers grew rapidly when the NPP and Emergency measures were in full swing, during 1976–77. As nongovernmental organizations like the FPAI continued to work closely with the state, sterilizations totaled a staggering 8.2 million.[115] Equally significant was the shift in proportion between men and women; vasectomies totaled three-fourths of all surgical sterilizations, with tubectomies representing just 25 percent of procedures.[116] Documentation of the Emergency's family planning programs, which is sparse in the archives, rarely discusses this shift from women toward men. We are left only to speculate about the "efficiency," cost, and speed of this procedure in comparison with tubectomies. In this sense, the procedure aligned with the urgency behind the NPP. Perhaps, then, male sterilization was well suited to a state of emergency, representing both national crisis and solution.

The Emergency came to an end in January 1977, when Indira Gandhi announced elections, released political prisoners, and rolled back some of the government's authoritarian measures. Elections, held in March of that year, led to a massive defeat for Gandhi, who lost even her parliamentary seat, and for the Congress Party, which lost its majority. The victorious Janata Alliance, a coalition of Gandhi's opponents, came to power. Since that momentous defeat—the first faced by Congress at the national level since independence—scholars have tried to explain the Emergency in relation to the history of democracy in India, and of population control transnationally. Connecting the two, Matthew Connelly argues that the elections of 1977 represented a repudiation of population control at the ballot box. "People voting, one by one," challenged the ideological underpinnings of the state's drive to control population in the mass.[117]

Certainly, the rejection of sterilization played an important role in the election campaign, but to represent 1977 as a democratic repudiation of population control overstates the case. During the campaign, opposition parties and the media highlighted instances of horrific sterilization abuse; indeed, the Congress suffered its worst defeats in the states that Indira and Sanjay Gandhi had targeted most intensively for population control. However, these electoral defeats were temporary, as Congress and Gandhi returned to power just three short years later, in 1980. In 1983, she received the United Nations Population Award, signaling the support of transnational population control networks. Consequently, some historians emphasize the continuities that make the Emergency less an aberration and more a product of failures in Indian democracy. According to Gyan Prakash, Indian political democracy never addressed the country's lack of social transformation—its ongoing inequalities and entrenched hierarchies. The Emergency was a "last-ditch attempt to salvage with exceptional means the global and elite-driven projects of modernization" that did not have popular support, or popular interests, at heart.[118] But while the means were exceptional, the underlying norms of governance and political power were continuous with the years before, and after, Emergency rule. Understanding this period purely as aberration masks continuities in state policy regarding poverty and population.[119] Indeed, as this chapter suggests, although the Emergency was a distinct moment in the histories of both democracy and population control, *nasbandi ka vakt* would have been impossible without the institutions and ideologies that had already made (women's) reproductive bodies available for coercive control by the state. Moreover, Emergency's end in 1977 did not signal the end of the government's coercive reproductive and population policies.

Yet, in the immediate aftermath of Emergency rule, there was much at stake in marking those years as aberration. In the heady days after the Janata victory, journalists, activists, and politicians suggested that the Emergency was a period of "excess." It represented a moment when the government had overstepped its bounds, and Gandhi's defeat in 1977 marked a reassertion of these boundaries. This narrative of excess and aberration framed the inquiries of the Shah Commission, the Janata government's only official investigation of the Emergency. The Shah Commission report, as Rebecca Williams argues, contrasted the Emergency with an implicit "normal" functioning of the state but never questioned this normality. In the realm of population control, the commission's narrative of the normal assumed that the program had been entirely voluntary prior to the Emergency and did not challenge the system of targets and incentives that had underpinned coercion since the 1960s.[120] Perhaps most importantly, the Shah Commission did not question the reigning ideologies of population control, which insisted that sterilization of the poor on a mass scale was a necessary component of family planning and that population control was necessary for poverty alleviation and economic development. Thus, the underlying systems of coercion within India's family planning program remained unscathed while the commission excoriated the most egregious examples of repression during the Emergency years. The central question—for the commission as for the Janata government—became how to continue India's population control program while rejecting the "excesses" of the Emergency years.

The Janata government answered this question, I argue, by making male sterilization the site and symbol of Emergency "excess." That is, in the post-Emergency era, vasectomy itself stood in for the terror and repression of population control. We may trace this narrative in the Shah Commission report, which highlighted violent examples of coerced vasectomy, most notoriously in the Dujana House neighborhood in the old city of Delhi. Journalists understandably emphasized horrific instances of forced sterilization in trying to reckon with the violence of the Emergency. Even decades later, as Tarlo notes, these narratives of the most explicit forms of force and coercion circulate in popular understanding of the period.[121] But in the process, I suggest, the Emergency's attention to the male body was marked as the "abnormal excess" that enabled the state's "normal" targeting of female bodies to continue unquestioned. Women's bodies did not figure as central in narratives about the Emergency's excesses, even though more than two million women were sterilized and women alongside men were ensnared in the government's "forcible deal" to either undergo the surgery or produce a sterilization certificate. Rather, even as the Emergency's "excess" was understood to include only the most explicit acts of force in population control, post-Emergency critiques narrowed their attention to the targeting of male bodies as the sites of regulation.

Thus, rather than challenging the entire apparatus of coercive incentives and targets, or of the mass camps that prioritized numbers over safety and informed consent, the Emergency's aftermath witnessed a renewed commitment to reproductive regulation as a component of India's development regime. But this time, there was one important difference: vasectomy was sidelined, so sterilization patients were increasingly women. Once again, the numbers help to tell this story. In the immediate aftermath of the Emergency, sterilizations overall fell sharply, from more than eight million annually to less than a million in 1977–78. In that year, women accounted for over 80 percent of all such surgeries, in contrast to the Emergency period, when vasectomies exceeded tubectomies by three- and fourfold.[122] In other words, though the "time of sterilization" supposedly ended with the elections of 1977, women continued to be sterilized, while men's sterilizations decreased. Moreover, the effects of these Emergency years and the "abnormalization" of male sterilization have had long-lasting effects. Since the Emergency, Indian men have had low rates of sterilization, compared both to women and to worldwide averages.[123] Meanwhile, female sterilization has become the most common form of contraception among women in India.[124] This, too, is a legacy of the Emergency, which marked the reproductive regulation of male bodies as an excess of state power while continuing to intervene in the reproductive bodies and lives of its women citizens.

Conclusion

In one scene of Deepa Dhanraj's 1991 documentary film *Something Like a War*, women are lined up for sterilization. A surgeon, while conducting the procedure, describes to the filmmaker the speed and efficiency of his techniques for laparoscopic sterilization, which enable him to "finish this operation in forty-five seconds." Meanwhile, the camera lingers on the face of his patient, who is writhing in pain while her mouth is held shut by a medical attendant. The camera then pans out across the clinic, where we see dozens of patients in states of bodily pain and suffering as they prepare for or recover from the surgery. Juxtaposing these images with archival footage of Indian family planning propaganda, the film suggests that India's "war" against population was in fact "something like a war" against women. Yet despite this powerful critique, women do not appear only as victims in the film. Dhanraj's camera also dwells on an extended conversation among women—of varying age, caste, class, and religious backgrounds—about sexuality, reproduction, childbearing, and their families. This conversation offers an understanding of reproduction that transcends the official family planning discourse. The women's words connect their reproductivity not to population or economy but to their desires, fears, and experiences in multiple, intimate ways.[125] We may find accounts of the connections between reproduction and women's experiences in ethnographic research as well, as in Cecilia Van Hollen's study of the routine insertion of IUDs in postpartum women in Madras public hospitals during the mid-1990s. Van Hollen documents that insertion occurs both with and without a patient's consent and that women sometimes resort to private clinics for IUD removal. As Van Hollen notes, the state's mandate to insert IUDs postpartum can be at odds with women's own understanding of their bodies. Those who do not want or like the IUD suggest that the device "does not agree" with their bodies.[126] Taken together, both film and ethnography suggest that women assign multiple meanings to their reproduction that contradict the state's claims about population and their fertility.

Reproduction, moreover, never exists in isolation but is enmeshed in a wider net of social, economic, and political relationships. Here again, ethnography is revealing. Emma Tarlo's research on the Emergency, discussed above, shows that although the stated purpose of sterilization was to control fertility and defuse the "population bomb," this was not how or why patients encountered the surgeon's knife. Rather, sterilization became the only means for people to access what they needed to survive, from housing and employment to hospital treatment and education. Thus, "for many of those at the bottom end of the socio-economic heap, life in Delhi without a sterilization certificate became untenable, if not impossible."[127] Narratives of life during the Emergency, therefore, were dominated by an "idiom of survival" in which one's reproductive capacity became something to exchange when one had nothing else to give. This suggests the vast distances between the official discourses of the Emergency and the narratives of *nasbandi ka vakt* as people understood and experienced it.

REGULATING REPRODUCTION 165

Such evidence of experience is more difficult to access from the historical archive, which tends not to preserve—or ever record—voices that are so at odds with the state's discourse and imagining. Drawing upon ethnography and documentary film can thus remind the historian that there are entire lifeworlds not accounted for in the archives. At the very least, we must leave a place in our historical accounts for these alternative understandings, and I return to that issue in the epilogue of this book. For now, we might remember that, despite the family planning program's attempts to make women's reproductive bodies a terrain for development, women themselves did not passively accept these interventions into their bodies and lives. They questioned the claims of "service" rendered by the middle-class family planner and evaded or rejected interventions that positioned their fertility as responsible for a population explosion. On occasion, they demanded something different or more—treatments for infertility, food and milk for their children, education for their girls. Never simply the disindividualized and docile users imagined by family planners, women assigned meaning to their reproduction that far exceeded population controllers' more limited imagination.

CHAPTER 5

HETEROSEXUALITY AND THE HAPPY FAMILY

IN 1964, THE INDIAN MINISTRY OF INFORMATION AND BROAD-
casting issued a pamphlet in several languages titled *Methods of Family
Planning*.[1] True to its title, the *Methods* pamphlet outlined several contraceptive options, but its main concern was with what family planners termed
"motivation." It aimed to convince its readers—imagined as the literate
Indian public—to limit their number of children. "Remember!" the text
admonished its audience in one striking image, "A small family is a happy
family" (figure 5.1). The "happy family" pictured includes a husband and
wife and their two children, a boy and a girl. The husband, seated on a
chair, instructs his wife, who is seated more submissively on the floor, in
family planning methods. Their son sits in front of his father while reading a
book; the daughter plays behind her mother. All are well dressed and smiling. Hovering in the background of this domestic scene, evoking both
prosperity and a desire for modern consumption, is a transistor radio.

The image situates birth control firmly within the boundaries of the heterosexual nuclear family. Women's use of contraception is associated not
with sexual freedom but with instruction by husbands in how to plan small
families. These small families are happy ones, suggesting that affective experience is connected to number. The small family's happiness is also linked
to its modest prosperity, suggested by the radio, and its upward mobility,
suggested by the educated son. Use birth control to limit your number of
children, the text implies, and you too may be able to educate your children
and engage in "modern" forms of consumption for your home. This seductive promise, which links heterosexual conjugality and reproductive regulation to emotional fulfillment and material prosperity, circulated widely
across Indian family planning discourse. It recurred in government and
commercially published texts, was repeated in the exhortations of population

REMEMBER !

A SMALL FAMILY IS A HAPPY FAMILY

Designed and produced by the Directorate of Advertising and Visual Publicity,
Ministry of I. & B. Govt. of India for the Ministry of Health (D.G.H.S.)
and printed by M/s Zodiac Press, Delhi-6.
6/8/64-PI   English-10,000.   September '64.

FIGURE 5.1. This representation of a husband, wife, and
two children promotes the
idea that small families are
both happy and prosperous.
Courtesy of Rockefeller
Archive Center.

controllers, and appeared in film, radio, and other media. This vision of
the small and happy family was the cornerstone of Indian family planning's quest to "modernize" the family in the service of national development goals. It brought sexuality together with planning, affect with economy,
and marriage with population control.

This representation of the small family as happy, as I argue in this chapter, established a heterosexual norm at the center of national planned development. An appropriate heterosexuality, in other words, would produce
the small and happy family necessary to meet the nation's economic needs.
Of course, normative heterosexuality has a long and complex history; it did
not originate in discourses about small families. However, the small family
configured heterosexuality, and attached it to nation and state, in specific
ways. This family centered upon a heterosexual conjugal couple that ratio-
nalized its sexualities, reordered its affective relationships, and economized
its behaviors. Husbands and wives, family planners argued, could use contraception to express a "natural" sexual desire that was marked as distinct
both from Indian tradition and from Gandhian models of marital celibacy.

This "modern" family also shifted its emotional attachments. Parents were now to find joy in having a small number of children, whom they could provide not only with increased love and affection but also with consumer goods. Happiness would derive from fulfilling this consumer desire while preparing one's children for a future of upward mobility and increased economic prosperity. Above all, the small and happy family was characterized by its commitment to planning itself: planning when to engage in sexual intimacy, planning how many children to have and at what intervals, and ultimately, planning for the future. This plan-oriented heterosexuality both legitimized, and was legitimized by, national development planning. As the Five Year Plans held up a specific heteronormative ideal, in other words, normative claims about sexuality and family helped to promote the act of national planning itself.

The small family thus connected heterosexuality and economic planning in ways that might be familiar to readers of Foucault, for whom a "socialization of procreative behavior" in modern European history hinges upon economic and political rationalities. As he argues in *The History of Sexuality*, the "Malthusian couple" was a privileged object of knowledge within modern sexual discourses whose behaviors were regulated by "an economic socialization via all the incitements and restrictions, the 'social' and fiscal measures brought to bear on the fertility of couples, [and] a political socialization achieved through the 'responsibilization' of couples with regard to the social body as a whole."[2] The "Malthusian couple" was thus expected to align its reproductive sexuality to meet economic need for the benefit of "the social body." One means of this alignment was birth control; thus, contraception became a mechanism to put sexuality into the realm of economy—a key component of "transforming sex into discourse."[3] Scholars have discussed the salience of Foucault's argument for understanding family planning and the governance of population in several national contexts.[4] My chapter builds upon this research, which incorporates a history of reproductive regulation into a history of sexuality.[5]

Departing from the chronological parameters of the previous chapters, this chapter examines representations of the small family from the 1920s, when such images and discourses began to appear in print media, to the 1960s and 1970s, when a small-family norm became yoked to discourses of population control. Throughout these decades, debates about sexuality, about emotion and affect, and about the rationalities of planning proliferated alongside claims about the value of small and happy families. Some of these debates circulated regionally within India, whereas others—especially those in English—aspired to national prominence from the 1920s onward. A range of writers and thinkers, from social reformers and sexologists to advertisers of birth control and sex tonics, made claims about the benefits of contraceptive use—and in the process reimagined both family and sexuality. After 1952, when the Indian government committed itself to population control, the small family became a bedrock of national development planning and a key feature of the state's family planning propaganda. These familial images circulated transnationally as well. Networks like the IPPF and the Population Council actively promoted small families across Latin America, Africa, and Asia and viewed India as a test case to develop promotional materials for other countries.[6] As a result, the image of the small family in the Indian government's *Methods of Family Planning* might have looked familiar to a viewership across the "Third World." For family planners, the small-family norm was both a universal ideal and a key component of national progress.

To investigate the proliferating image of the small and happy family, this chapter examines a wide variety of texts, including transnationally circulating films and posters, state-sponsored propaganda campaigns, and commercially published books and pamphlets. This includes substantial material in Tamil, which circulated among literate (and in some cases, nonliterate) Tamil-speaking populations in Madras Presidency, later Tamil Nadu. I also include texts and films in English, produced both in India and abroad, that aimed for a national circulation. My focus is limited to materials that explicitly advocate contraception, sterilization, or other methods of family planning rather than works on reproductive sexuality more generally. Given the vast quantity of materials produced, alongside their somewhat sporadic and random collection within archives in India, the United Kingdom, and the United States, I do not claim that my sources are comprehensive or necessarily representative. However, taken together, they suggest how a wide range of Indian writers, illustrators, and government bureaucrats, alongside foreign communications experts, made the small and happy family central to their claims about modernizing sexuality and developing the economy. I read them to ask how a history of heterosexuality might be written into the history of Indian population control and development more broadly.

This chapter builds upon scholarship in feminist and queer studies of South Asia, which illuminates the connections between an Indian sexual modernity and projects of nationalism, social reform, and neoliberal capitalism.[7] Temporally, much of this research centers either on the late colonial decades or on the postliberalization years of the 1990s on.[8] We are thus left with a chronological and theoretical gap in the scholarship, a space of silence about the sexual politics of India's family planning regime in the mid-twentieth century, when the Five-Year Plans held sway over state-led development planning. Yet during this period, I argue, public discourses about small, happy families transformed the terms by which both sexuality and economy were understood. To investigate this history, I first turn briefly to its contexts in twentieth-century print culture. The chapter then considers the heteronormative ideal of the small family in relation to its sexualities, its economic rationalities, and its commitments to planning. The final section examines the small and happy family as a point of tension between the universalizing ambitions of population control and the specific anxieties engendered by national difference.

Small Families in Print Culture

During the early twentieth century, visions of the modern family using birth control were intimately linked to a proliferating culture of print. Increasing numbers of publishing houses and printing presses produced material in English and in Indian languages for a growing reading public.[9] Although literacy rates were low, representing just over 12 percent of the Indian population in 1941, these literate classes became the readership for newspapers, magazines, books, and pamphlets that circulated in urban centers and in smaller towns.[10] This surge in popular publishing, in India as elsewhere in the colonized world, was part of a growing culture of print capitalism that underpinned the rise of nationalism.[11] But national identities were not the only modes of identification forged by the new markets for print, nor did print materials displace older modes of communication or community.[12] Rather, while commercial publishing used nationalist ideologies as a legitimating paradigm, the new newspapers and books also engaged with topics that were not always, or necessarily, tied to the production of national subjects. Moreover, markets in print were also linked to other markets, specifically to a growing consumer economy, whose products began to be advertised in newspapers and magazines.

Birth control was among the topics addressed within this new market for print. Unlike in Britain or the United States, colonial law in India did not explicitly prohibit the dissemination of birth control information, and such material was part of a thriving marketplace of "contraceptive commercialism" during the 1920s and 1930s.[13] Thus, as one contemporary observer in Madras noted in 1931, "Books on the subject [of birth control] are to be found in any bookstall or publisher's list and whether they are read as mild pornography or for serious guidance, it is unlikely that they can fail to exert some influence."[14] As this quote suggests, the print culture of birth control skirted the boundaries of respectable and nonrespectable sexualities— suggestive at once of a titillating "pornography" and of "serious guidance" for married couples.

This boundary was an important one for publishers, since although contraceptive information was not forbidden, colonial authorities some- times did prosecute sexually explicit texts on the grounds of obscenity. To avoid prosecution, as Charu Gupta notes in her study of Hindi sex manuals, authors and publishers "camouflaged themselves with the lan- guage of sexual science" while simultaneously highlighting erotic ele- ments through color pictures and in book advertisements.[15] Indeed, the birth control manual perfectly allowed this combination of a science of sex with its eroticization. Such manuals implicitly disavowed nonnorma- tive sexualities in favor of heterosexual marriage and reproduction, while claiming to reveal the "truth" of sex through the scientific investigation of reproductive anatomy and physiology. Thus, the title of one popular Tamil birth control manual, *Ilvazhkkaiyin irakaciyankal* (Mysteries of wedded life), served as both invitation and admonition to readers while situating birth control as a necessary component of modern marriage and family life.[16]

While the commercial publication of birth control manuals continued to thrive after independence, the media landscape shifted with the Indian government's official commitment to family planning. The state entered into existing markets in print by publishing pamphlets and books and also uti- lized newer media such as film and radio to spread its family planning message. State involvement rendered birth control information part of a technocratic field of "communications," to be practiced by experts and stud- ied for its effectiveness in persuading couples to use contraception. State- sponsored family planning communication became one component of a larger drive to marshal media in service of education and information to serve the state's development goals.[17]

Working with commercial advertisers and with voluntary organizations like the FPAI, the Indian government during the 1950s, 1960s, and 1970s launched media campaigns, promoted films, designed posters, sponsored radio programs, and in multiple other ways sought to fill public spaces with family planning messaging.[18] Thus, by 1968, about six hundred family planning programs were broadcast on the radio each month.[19] All movie theaters in the country were expected to screen family planning films in advance of features, and five hundred audiovisual vans brought media to rural areas. Ten thousand billboards and fifty thousand bus boards were part of this proliferation of imagery as well.[20] The state's massive intervention did not exhaust the spaces of sexuality discourses—which, as Sanjay Srivastava notes, also developed outside the realms of state control and regulation.[21] However, the government's entrance into the field of family planning radically shifted the terms of "contraceptive commercialism" that characterized the interwar years, edging it away from the liminal spaces between respectable and nonrespectable sexualities and more firmly into the field of development. That is, family planning messaging represented itself as a kind of public service. Postcolonial family planning manuals drew from the ideological and material resources of the state and claimed to uphold the ideals of the Five Year Plans.

Even while the government of India thus became a purveyor of birth control discourse, foreign funders were also eager to be involved in India's family planning experiments. For example, the Ford Foundation made its first population control grant to investigate "how to communicate and educate people about family planning."[22] This became a momentous beginning to Ford's many efforts in developing family planning propaganda in support of a "small-family norm." Foreign funders like Ford worked alongside the government of India to produce a range of media, such as flip books to be used by family planning extension workers, posters to be hung on clinic walls advertising their services, and pamphlets that "motivators" could share with their clients. Sometimes the messaging was more outlandish. Locomotive engines, for instance, were painted with family planning messaging. Even an elephant was pressed into service, and it traveled to villages dispensing government-subsidized contraceptives and pamphlets with its trunk.[23] Some of the Indian family planning program's most iconic messaging was produced in this period of the mid-1960s, notably the inverted red triangle and the stylized "four faces" of husband and wife with son and daughter. In sum, the contexts for visioning the small and happy family—rendered modern through its size and use of birth control—changed significantly over time. Yet across these changes, as we shall see below, the normative ideal of the small family promised its adherents a better future—characterized by modern sexualities, economic prosperity, and a commitment to planning.

Sexuality and the Small Family

The questions of how to modernize sex and the appropriate relationship between sexuality and modernity occupied public discourse across the twentieth century. For family planners, any claims about modernizing sexuality had to grapple with Gandhian thought, which famously rejected birth control in favor of a "married *brahmacharya*," which Gandhi defined as follows: "When a man has completely conquered his animality, involuntary incontinence becomes impossible, and the desire for sexual gratification for its own sake ceases altogether. Sexual union then takes place only when there is a desire for offspring. This is the meaning of what has been described as 'Married Brahmacharya.'"[24] Gandhi's claims drew upon classical Indian thought that marked *brahmacharya* as both a lifelong celibacy observed by ascetics and a stage of life practiced by young men. It was linked to notions about the conservation of semen, a practice thought to give spiritual power. Gandhi was one among many nineteenth- and early twentieth-century leaders who, as Shrikant Botre and Douglas Haynes note, "espoused brahmacharya as a vehicle for renewing Indian masculinity and militancy."[25] At the same time, Gandhi drew women into the practice, noting in his famous debate with Margaret Sanger that woman was not "prey to sexual desire to the same extent as man. It is easier for her than for man to exercise self-restraint."[26] By suggesting that husbands and wives could practice *brahmacharya* through a control and transcendence of sexual desire, Gandhi opened up the practice to a much larger group of people and offered an alternative to contraception. Thus, rather than recommending controlling reproduction via birth control, he called for an "education of the passions," which would enable married couples to limit their children while also gaining spiritual strength for the national struggle.[27]

Supporters of family planning, however, rejected these Gandhian notions of *brahmacharya* as outmoded and unscientific and claimed instead to offer a modern science of sex. Indian eugenicists and sexologists such as R. D. Karve, A. P. Pillay, and N. S. Phadke were at the forefront of this modern revisioning of sexuality, which they claimed was in line with the "natural" functions of the human body. In a quest to modernize sexual ideology and practice within India, they engaged with transnationally circulating sexology research that challenged existing social and sexual norms.[28] In particular, they attacked *brahmacharya* as an unnatural practice that caused physical and psychological damage.[29] In some cases, as Ishita Pande demonstrates, promoters of sexual science developed a "chronological view of *brahmacharya*" that marked it as a life stage before marriage that "ensured the preservation of semen and strength for conjugal sex." This notion of *brahmacharya* as a kind of adolescence helped to situate sex—alongside work—within modernized clock time, linking sexuality to the chronological rhythms of contemporary capitalism.[30] Naturalizing sexual activity as part of a life stage that followed *brahmacharya* also opened space for discussion of birth control within heterosexual marriage.

Birth control was an essential technology in the modernization of sexuality, sexologists argued, because it enabled the expression of sexual desire within marriage while meeting economic imperatives to control reproduction. This argument became the basis for contraceptive advocacy during the interwar decades and gathered increasing momentum in the context of economic depression. For instance, an advertisement for Contrafant tablets pulls together twin motives of sexuality and economy to suggest that "the necessity of preserving the health and beauty of women and the increasing economic depression requires every man to adopt methods of birth control" (figure 5.2).[31] Here, contraception is represented as a rational choice made by men to limit reproduction without limiting sexual expression when faced with economic constraints. At the same time, the pills promise to promote the "health and beauty of women," perhaps gesturing toward pleasurable sexuality within heterosexual marriage. Contrafant, in short, was invoking a modernized sexuality that was at once pleasurable and subject to economic needs and rationalities.

Like the advertisers of Contrafant, many authors of birth control manuals in the interwar period similarly positioned contraception as a sexual solution to economic scarcity and crisis. One example is the Tamil manual *Karppatci, allatu cuvatina karppam* (Contraception, or control over pregnancy). Like writers of many other such manuals in the 1920s and 1930s, the anonymous author begins with a justification for writing about birth control—and, by extension, sexuality. Although many readers might assume that discussing sexuality was "vulgar or disgusting," in fact sexual intercourse was a natural, even "divine" aspect of human experience. This attitude toward sexuality was not new, the author hastens to add, but had been recognized by long-standing Tamil tradition. However, in recent times, married couples had lost touch with this divinity because of concern that their expression of desire would lead to the birth of many children and consequently the impoverishment of their families. The manual thus offers birth control as a solution to the problem of sex in an era of scarcity. Contraception

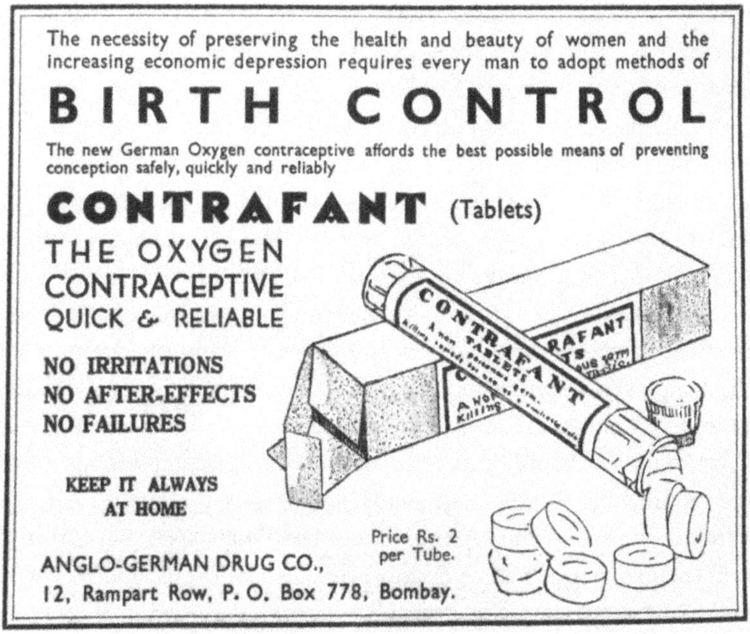

FIGURE 5.2. This advertisement links sexuality and economy to promote Contrafant contraceptive tablets. Courtesy of the Wellcome Library.

would enable husbands and wives to experience the "domestic pleasure" (*inpam*) that came from sexual intimacy while also allowing them "to have fewer healthy children who can be cared for properly."[32] Birth control would bring together traditional Tamil appreciation for reproductive sexuality within marriage and the insights of Western scientific research on preventing conception. Readers would thus be able to link a timeless and natural experience of sexuality to a distinctly modern approach to both reproduction and economic life.

The pseudonymous author Devidasan makes a similar argument about birth control, natural sexuality, and modern life in the Tamil birth control manual *Karppatatai* (Birth control, 1929). According to Devidasan, heterosexual expression was a natural part of human relationships: "Men and women were created to live together and their body structures were also made for the same purpose. It is very necessary for man and woman to have intercourse after they attain puberty."[33] Implicitly disavowing nonheterosexual intimacies, Devidasan identifies marriage as the necessary institution to contain this sexual expression, noting that anyone who "wants to enjoy conjugal happiness should get married." Thanks to birth control, however, this "natural" (hetero)sexuality need not result in uncontrolled reproduction. *Karppatatai* develops this argument most dramatically in an illustration within the book. The drawing depicts a woman standing on the edge of a cliff over an ocean marked "poverty." Menacing her in the foreground is a demonic figure representing "wrong customs and habits." Threatened by these "wrong customs"—presumably conventional sexual norms involving marriage and widowhood—she risks a plunge into poverty. The woman's only salvation is an airplane marked "birth control" that has landed nearby.[34] Associated with that other quintessential modern technology, the airplane, birth control saves women from the demonic customs that prevent the expression of a natural sexuality and from the poverty that results from unregulated reproduction.

Both manuals, published just a few years apart, make monogamous marriage the linchpin of their arguments about modern sexuality and birth control. For instance, *Karppatatai* locates all sexual expression within the marital relationship, which Devidasan argues is good for the body, the mind, and the "development of the soul."[35] He supports these claims through references to Western sexual science, noting research from various European countries suggesting that abstinence leads to physical and mental debility and even early death. Rendering *brahmacharya* a life stage to adopt until marriage, he insists it is "against nature and human disposition to remain abstinent after marriage. . . . The feeling of love for each other is very natural and marriage is meant to enjoy that feeling." Sexual expression, in turn, strengthens the marital relationship: "There is natural and mutual attraction between male and female. . . . [Sex] strengthens love in the process."[36] *Karppatatai* thus evidences an openness to discourse about sexual desire but also regulates sexual expression more closely in terms of time and life stage, such that a temporary period of *brahmacharya* gives way to normative heterosexual intimacy. The anonymous author of *Karppatci* makes a similar claim, noting that heterosexual marriage is the locus of human sexual expression.

These arguments about modernizing sexuality via birth control transformed the terms of public discussion about marriage during the 1920s and 1930s. Marriage reformers in the nineteenth and early twentieth centuries privileged romantic love as a force to improve marital relationships. A few decades later, in the context of growing movements for eugenics and a science of sexuality, they increasingly looked toward sex as the impetus for change. As J. Devika observes, reformers began to insist that sexual pleasure was necessary to sustain monogamous marriage; sexual satisfaction became a measure of marital success.[37] This argument created space for the supporters of birth control, who claimed that contraception could enforce heterosexual monogamy by locating the pleasures of sexual intimacy within marriage itself. Birth control thus became the bedrock both of modernizing marriage and of scientizing sex.

With the establishment of state-directed population control after 1952, family planners began to advocate what they termed a "small-family norm" as a sign of these modern marital, sexual, and scientific ideals. They claimed that small families were attuned to both the economic needs of the nation and the "natural" bodily and sexual needs of its citizens. Family planning manuals published during the 1950s and 1960s thus began to cast the small family as a site of aspiration. Families who had a small number of children, they suggested, had successfully reconciled otherwise competing claims between the expression of sexual desire, which was necessary for a happy marriage, and the need to limit children, which was necessary for economic progress at the familial and national levels. Whether published commercially or by the government, family planning manuals during the first few Five Year Plans tended to follow a similar pattern to make their case for the small family. They often begin with a discussion of reproductive physiology, followed by a social and economic argument about the need to control reproduction. Having situated the question of modern sexuality this way, they offer birth control as a solution to the problem of aligning sexuality with economy. They typically conclude with a description about various contraceptive methods.[38]

This growing dominance of a small-family norm in Indian family planning contributed to a centering of heterosexuality that Nivedita Menon identifies as critical to modern nation-building projects. In her terms, the nationalist production of the "naturally heterosexual, properly bi-gendered (unambiguously male *or* female) population of citizens" went hand in hand with the "delegitimation of homosexual desire."[39] In India as in other national contexts, the production of heterosexuality thus depended upon marking homosexuality as "deviant."[40] Normative heterosexuality was produced upon this foundational distinction from the homosexual; the small-family norm, I argue, was a key site for its elaboration. That is, proponents of the small family insisted that not any and all heterosexual desires represented a modernized, nation-building sexuality. Rather, they valorized the regulated reproductive sexuality of the married couple, while rendering all behaviors and intimacies outside of this norm both antinational and antimodern. Representations of the small family thus became co-constitutive with discourses of normative heterosexuality. The small-family norm helped to elevate heterosexuality as serving the interests of national development. At the same time, the turn to national development—as expressed in heterosexual monogamous marriage—helped to separate discussion of sex and birth control from its associations with obscenity and situate it more respectably within nation and family. In this sense, the small-family norm shaped the contours of a modern, respectable, and nationalized heterosexuality in the twentieth century.

Menon notes further that nationalist respectability went hand in hand with a process of desexualization, particularly for women. Postcolonial discourses marginalized women's desire, rendering them "respectably desexualized."[41] While this was certainly true in many cases, attention to family planning complicates this history. By the 1960s, through its programs of population control, the Indian state had emerged as a chief purveyor of sexual discourse. Rather than desexualizing its citizens to render them respectable, family planning discourse aimed to produce a specific sexual subjectivity that could align "natural" behaviors with national planning goals. Thus, the promise of the small family was not that it offered a desexualized and therefore respectable form of conjugality. Rather, it reinvigorated conjugality by rendering sexual desire respectable only within heterosexual marriage. This was the promise offered by the government's *Methods of Family Planning* (1964), discussed at the start of this chapter, which informed its readers that after vasectomy, "men enjoy sex just as they did before."[42] Similarly, the author of a commercially published volume, *Katal rakaciyam* (Secrets of love, 1960), assured his audience that the best methods of contraception, including vasectomy, would not diminish male pleasure.[43] In both these cases, husbands are the subjects of heterosexual desire within the small family, and wives are rendered the objects of their passions. This was, indeed, the most common framework of sexual discourse within my archive of midcentury family planning manuals.

Nevertheless, a few texts did address female desire explicitly. Among several Tamil examples is the oeuvre of T. S. Janakakumari, a woman author who published prolifically on subjects of birth control, sexuality, and fertility. Her 1959 book *Kuzhantai ventam enral?* (What if you don't want children?) begins with the assertion that "in today's conditions, it is enough for everyone to have three or four well-educated children."[44] The book rehearses the statistics of Indian population growth, infant mortality, and familial poverty to argue that birth control is immediately necessary for the country. Having established this rationale for contraception, Janakakumari devotes most of the book to explaining the male and female reproductive systems. She describes how conception occurs and how it can be avoided via the rhythm method, various barrier methods, medicinal means, and surgical sterilization. The text is addressed to both women and men, and its discussion of female anatomy explicitly includes mention of female sexual arousal. Similarly, in her *Kuzhantai ventum* (You want a child, 1960), which was addressed to couples concerned about infertility, Janakakumari stressed the "human instinct" of heterosexual desire among women alongside men. Of course, this desire is always contained within marriage and is "central to the marital relationship."[45] In Janakakumari's work, therefore, both men and women appear as desiring subjects, and their desires are best understood within a framework of knowledge about reproductive anatomy and physiology. Having thus rooted sexuality in biology, Janakakumari suggests that it finds social expression via heterosexual monogamous marriage.

Another example of attention to female sexuality comes from Dr. K. Satyavati's *Family Planning (Birth Control).*[46] Written in English by a "lady doctor" identified as a "sterility and fertility specialist," *Family Planning* opens with a neo-Malthusian view of population, then turns to sexuality. Like other manuals of the time, the text is premised on the notion that heterosexual desire is a natural, universal physiological response among all people. *Family Planning* naturalizes female sexuality in particular through reference to women's reproductive anatomy and physiology. Unusually among the texts I have considered from this period, *Family Planning* even mentions female orgasm and sexual satisfaction. However, Satyavati's acknowledgment of female desire is not by itself a critique of patriarchal sexual norms; there is no liberatory history of sexuality that can be read from *Family Planning*'s attention to orgasm. Instead, the text valorizes marital heterosexuality as both natural and pleasurable through its condemnation of women's sexual expression outside marriage. For instance, when discussing sterilization methods, Satyavati insists that a wife who undergoes tubectomy to meet familial and national economic goals stands in stark contrast to "widows and prostitutes" who do so for other reasons. In Satyavati's terms: "Sometimes widows and prostitutes want to get themselves sterilized for enjoying sexual relations safely. Such people cannot be entertained."[47] In other words, sterilization for controlling reproduction within marriage is admirable; the same procedure for sexual pleasure outside marriage is not. The text's insistence on the naturalness of female sexual expression thus collapses when confronted by the social constraints of widowhood or the long-standing division of women into "wives" and "prostitutes." Her support for female sterilization hinges on this distinction. Sterilized wives stand as exemplars of sexual modernity who enjoy both sexual pleasure and the benefits of national development. This modernizing sexuality left little room for the "widows" and "prostitutes" who peopled its margins, an implicit threat to the married heterosexual couple.

Economy, Prosperity, and the Small Family

The small and happy family, envisioned as modern through its sexuality and reproductive regulation, stood in contrast to large families, imagined as poor, sad, and backward. The association of large families with poverty has a long Malthusian genealogy, as we have seen. Malthus himself made this connection, as did his late nineteenth-century disciples, including Annie Besant and the Madras Malthusian League. Less explicitly Malthusian thinkers in the late nineteenth century—including M. G. Ranade and Behramji Malabari, discussed in chapter 1—warned of the risks large families posed to the nation and its economy. By the interwar decades, birth control discourses consolidated these claims into visual images of large and small families. In contraceptive manuals and birth control advertising, the large and poor family came to represent a dystopian vision. Marked as the opposite of the modern and well-regulated small-family norm, large families with multiple children signaled both sexual and economic disorder. With uncontrolled bodies and finances, the large family exhibited not modernizing progress but rather its aimless and timeless lack. By contrast, the small family measured its progress in clock time and life stage, signaling its happiness through its economies of both sex and finance. With the advent of state-sponsored family planning, images of the small family consolidated a range of discourses about family life into representations of parents and their two or three young children. Yet, as we shall see, this image of the small and prosperous family did not necessarily resonate with its intended audience, who may have understood both "family" and "prosperity" differently.

During the interwar decades, in the age of eugenics and concerns about the health of the Indian "race," birth control activists highlighted physical weakness alongside the poverty of large families. Consider, for instance, the birth control manual *Karppatci, allatu cuvatina karppam* (Contraception, or control over pregnancy, 1931), discussed above. The book's cover image is a drawing of a husband and wife, obviously poor and hungry, surrounded by their numerous children. Their poverty, which is evident from their torn clothing, thin bodies, and sorrowful expressions, stems from their "excess" of children, who huddle sadly around parents incapable of providing for their needs. Thus, from the outset, the reader of *Karppatci* encounters birth control as a remedy for familial poverty and bodily decline. The written text continues this theme, recommending that readers use birth control to "reduce the financial difficulties of the family, and to keep the mother in good health so she can care for the family properly and maintain feelings of affection [*anpu*] toward the husband." Birth control would thus ameliorate "poverty, disease, and suffering . . . the most important goal is to have fewer children who can be properly cared for."[48]

Many texts and images made explicit comparisons between the large and impoverished family and its smaller, more prosperous counterpart. This approach became increasingly common in both state-produced and commercially published texts after the First Five Year Plan. The Tamil pamphlet *Pale Tankam: Kutumpak kattupatu virivakkappattatu* (Well done Thangam: Family planning explained), for example, offers a visual contrast between planned and unplanned families (figure 5.3).[49] The drawing of the planned family with few children shows a husband leaving the home on a bicycle, presumably on his way to salaried employment. His wife stands by with an older daughter and younger son, both of whom carry books and are headed to school. All are well dressed. The husband's dhoti, the wife's sari and the flowers in her hair, the children's school uniforms, and the family's tile-roof house all indicate prosperity and intergenerational upward mobility. Members of the family each have distinct responsibilities based on age and gender, which are also linked to a specific organization of time. We glimpse this family, apparently in the morning, as they head off to their respective occupations. The unplanned large family, by contrast, has five children, all of whom are apparently boys. The mother comforts one crying child while others play in the dirt. The children do not wear school uniforms, and the mother's clothing indicates her poverty. The husband is seated on the verandah, presumably without salaried employment, and their house has a thatched (not tiled) roof. The organization of time and labor that drives the small family seems absent here; this glimpse of their lives could have occurred at any moment and indicates their aimless lack of modern progress.

Thus, the small family, which uses family planning, is clearly poised to benefit from a modern economy. Its modest prosperity, as Nilanjana Chatterjee and Nancy E. Riley note, does not imply a Westernized or wealthy lifestyle but rather highlights the developmental promises of the Five Year Plans.[50] The larger family, marked as unplanned, remains outside this

குறைந்த குழந்தைகள் :
வளர்ப்பது எளிது.

நிறையக் குழந்தைகள் ;
வளர்ப்பதில் தொல்லை

FIGURE 5.3. The visual contrast between small and large families is emphasized in the Tamil captions. On the left: "Few children: raising them is easy." On the right: "Many children: raising them is a torment." Reproduced from the original held by the Roja Muthiah Research Library Collection.

promise of modernity and progress. Contraceptive advertisers adopted this kind of contrasting image to market the economic rationalities of birth control. One example among many is an advertisement for Planitab Contraceptive Ovules, which appeared in the souvenir volume of the FPAI's fifth All India Family Planning Conference in 1964. The text proclaims, "It is the number that upsets your budget" (figure 5.4).[51] The references to numbers and budgets evoke broader national population trends, but the imagery also links to individual families. Viewers see a drawing of a wife facing her husband while he gazes upward, preoccupied by "fooding [sic], clothing, education, housing, etc., etc." Meanwhile, in a separate drawing, we see contrasting visions of a happy family with two children and a squabbling family with many children. Planitab is offered as the solution to the husband's worries and preoccupations about the material necessities of daily life and is "reliable, simple, [and] inexpensive." Contraception is thus one purchase a married couple can make in the present in order to

FIGURE 5.4. Like many advertisements for contraceptives during the 1950s and 1960s, this one for Planitab highlights the expense of large families. Courtesy of the National Archives and Records Administration.

enable a lifetime of future material consumption. By adopting economic rationality to plan their reproduction, the advertisement suggests, all families can become prosperous in a modernizing India. Such comparisons circulated in films as well. For instance, the Indian government production *Three Families* (1963) features a large family, a family with two children, and a couple that decides in favor of family planning. The FPAI sponsored a similar film, *Enough's Enough* (1973), which emphasizes the disadvantages faced by a large family in comparison with a small one in terms of food, discretionary spending, and living space.[52]

Texts like these highlighted the happiness, alongside the prosperity, that families might achieve through their small size. For instance, an advertisement for Volpar contraceptive paste and foaming tablets, directed at physicians, raised an alarm about large numbers. Underneath a graph with a sharp upward trajectory outlined by the text, "How many mouths to feed" is the following conclusion: "An increasing number of patients agree that the planned family is the most likely to be the happy family in the twentieth century economy."[53] Another advertisement, this one for Protecto Jelly, envisioned what this familial happiness might look like (figure 5.5). Viewers see a well-dressed and smiling husband and wife, both facing a laughing infant, whom the mother carries. Their two older children—a boy and a

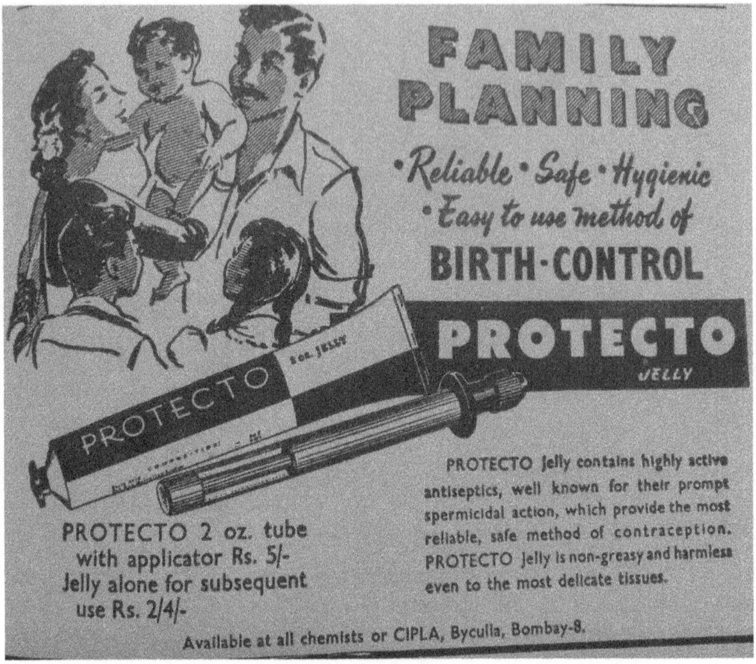

FIGURE 5.5. This advertisement for Protecto Jelly envisions what familial happiness may look like. Courtesy of the Wellcome Library.

girl—face away from the viewer toward their baby sibling and parents. Together, this family forms a social unit entirely sufficient unto itself; all members gaze happily at each other in a circle of emotional fulfillment and joy. Accompanying text urges readers to use Protecto as a "reliable, safe, hygienic, easy to use method of birth-control."[54]

The comparison between small/prosperous and large/poor families challenged conventional understandings of children and wealth; it introduced different economic rationalities to underpin its heteronormative ideal. Children, especially sons, had conventionally been a marker of prosperity, and we find traces of this popular mentality in proverbs, song, and classical literature. Moreover, for poor families, having many children could be a strategy of economic survival, since both boys and girls contributed to the family's support from a young age. By contrast, the small-family ideal imagined children not as economic assets but as liabilities. These children did not work in the fields, care for their younger siblings, or perform household labor. They attended school. However, for many poor families, this vision of a middle-class, school-going childhood may have been unattainable or even undesirable, regardless of their size. Many villages lacked even a primary school, and children's access to education was mediated more by class, caste, and gender than by the size of their families. Consequently, family planners' assertion that prosperity followed the *small* family—one that by definition was "poor" in children—was at odds with popular understanding. For some people, the dissonance between these representations of small and large families and their own experiences may have made family planning discourses unintelligible. According to one study that investigated a family planning poster campaign, for instance, many in the targeted audience identified with the image of the large family with undernourished children. Perhaps they saw themselves more in that representation than in the images of a smaller and wealthier family.[55]

The image of the small family may have differed from many people's experience in another way, insofar as it assumed a nuclear family structure composed of husband, wife, and their minor children. This unit was the basis of a proliferating visual imagery across urban and rural landscapes, such as one Tamil poster proclaiming that "a small family is a happy family" that hung outside the doors to the government's Family Planning Center in Vellore during the mid-1960s.[56] In the genre of Indian calendar art, a husband and wife, marked as Hindu and modestly prosperous, stand side by side facing the viewer. A young son stands in front of his parents, while the wife holds her baby daughter; both children gaze out to the viewer. This vision of the small family displaced other notions of family composition and familial relationships that may have privileged multigenerational households composed of extended kin. Relegating these other family forms to the realm of "tradition" and nostalgia, representations of the small family erased other household members—grandparents, uncles and aunts, other kin—to imagine a domestic life centered on the relationships between the conjugal couple and their young children. This small-family norm also ignored families and households whose composition was not patrilineal, thus contributing to a broader marginalization of heterogeneous family forms as a condition of "modern" family life.[57] Happiness and prosperity were not be found within these extended and variable kin networks, family planners implied, but within the warm affective bonds of a smaller group. In particular, they were rooted in the attachments—both emotional and sexual—between husband and wife.[58]

The children of the small family were invariably represented as one boy and one girl; if a third child was present, as in the advertisement for Protecto, it was typically a baby of indeterminate gender. On the one hand, this vision of a small planned family implied that the gender of the child was less relevant than the number. In a social context of widespread son preference and disparate sex ratios in some regions, perhaps this claim suggested, subversively, that a daughter—equally with a son—was also a descendant and heir. Given the history of debate about the childhood of girls in modern India,[59] this proliferating imagery may have helped to counter a long-standing demographic and representational absence of the girl child. Indeed, some designers of such images noted that specifying only two or three children was a "bold and risky step" since it pushed against Indian traditions that valued sons, regardless of the number of children; they took the risk because they feared the demographic consequences of a fourth child.[60]

On occasion, state-sponsored publications acknowledged the demographic impact of son preference, noting that it might lead to large families since parents would have multiple children in hopes of bearing sons.[61] However, representations of the small family generally sidestepped any direct confrontation with son preference and the devaluing of girl children. The state discourses of family planning during the 1950s and 1960s did not challenge the patriarchal ideologies and institutions that encouraged parents to value sons over daughters. In the imagery of the small family, son preference was not even explicitly mentioned, let alone questioned or rejected. Moreover, within the archives, I have not found a single representation of a small family from this period that includes children of only one gender. Thus, family planners avoided asking whether a family composed of parents and their two *daughters* was also a small and happy family. This unasked question, and its implied refusal to engage with the ideological and economic structures that underpinned gender disparities, lurked behind the image of the small, happy family.

Planning Families for the Future

Underpinning the small family's economic rationality and sexual modernity was a commitment to planning itself. Planning signaled the small family's orientation toward an imagined future, marked as wealthier, more modern, and more joyous than the present. In this sense, the discourse of the small family was deeply embedded in, and contributed to, a larger narrative about national development, which claimed that the future would be better than the past and present through the mechanism of planning. While the Five Year Plans signaled this orientation toward future progress on the national and global stage, the individual family's planning signaled a future orientation on the part of ordinary citizens. Planning, moreover, implied a specific relationship to time and a willingness to defer present desires to meet future needs. In other words, the discourses of family planning promised a better future to those families who delayed or prevented childbearing in the present. Significantly, this "better future" was invariably defined in and through consumption. Family planning discourses oriented the small family toward markets, suggesting that reproductive regulation would eventually allow access to the pleasures of consumer capitalism. With market-based consumption thus imagined as a sign of modernizing progress, planning one's children became the necessary precondition for entry into more prosperous futures.

Government family planning manuals called upon citizens to plan their family lives as a service to the nation. For example, the Madras government's official *Family Planning Manual* (1956) called for readers to remember that "family planning is *no longer* a matter of purely private interest to married couples. The welfare of the nation as a whole will be promoted or retarded by what every married couple does or fails to do about family planning."[62] The suggestion of "no longer" implies that, although the decision to use contraception may once have concerned only husbands and wives, it was now vital for national development. As the text argues, this urgency was due to an imbalance between birth and death in India, resulting in population growth and causing food shortages, rationing, and unemployment. Under these circumstances, it was a patriotic duty to regulate reproduction: "Whether you do or fail to do your duty is not merely a matter of concern to you and your children. It is a matter of vital concern to that larger family to which we all belong—'The Indian Nation.'"[63]

The Madras government's Tamil handbook *Kutumpa kattupatu titta kaiputtakam* (Family planning instructional handbook, 1962) takes these claims further. Since the country was unable to "grow food crops corresponding to the ever-increasing population," citizens needed to recalibrate the balance by regulating their reproduction: "By controlling the population explosion, each couple is contributing to the welfare of the country, and to implementing national development schemes, thereby discharging their duties for their country."[64] Family planning is thus the sign of responsible citizenship, a "duty" that citizens owe to the nation in the wake of independence. However, this position of the responsible citizen-planner was not equally available to everyone; heterosexual monogamy was its necessary precondition. Husbands in particular were the rational agents of planning. Addressing them directly, the manual exhorts men "to make every effort to ensure that your wife gets pregnant only after a minimum period of three years after the birth of your first child; you should plan things accordingly."[65] The husband's plans within the space of the home thus paralleled the Five Year Plans within the space of the nation.

Even more than in the exhortations of government manuals, the call to plan for the future unfolded most fully in stories about families. Didactic in their approach, these narratives invited readers to imagine the life course of a single family over time. The texts were relatively formulaic and tended to revolve around similar plot points. Beginning with a couple's marriage or birth of the first child and continuing through to a decision about whether or not to use contraception, the stories concluded with a vision of the family's prosperous or impoverished future. These narratives about family life echoed the message about small/prosperous and large/poor families discussed above. But unlike an image—which usually pictured a family at one moment in time—stories about families explored the relationship between past, present, and future. Asserting that choices in the present moment affected future happiness, these stories valorized husbands and wives who weighed the present delights of many children against a future of scarcity or plenty. With a more explicit focus on change over time, these narratives crafted a more thorough commitment to the future.

One example of these narratives is a didactic Tamil short story mentioned above, *Pale Tankam: Kutumpak kattupatu virivakkappattatu* (Well done Thangam: Family planning explained, 1961). Written by Ca. Pasyam, the story was published commercially as a short pamphlet—but, as we shall see, its themes adhere closely to the government-sponsored family planning manuals of that era. *Pale Tankam* narrates the early married life of Thangam and Murugan, whose names mark them as Hindu (likely caste Hindu). Pasyam represents them as ideal subjects and agents of national development. Murugan is a salaried worker in a bicycle factory, signaling his position in the modern industrial sector rather than in a "traditional" occupation in agricultural labor. His wife, Thangam, is described as beautiful, literate, and good at managing household expenditures. She is an educated housewife and companion to Murugan. The two newlyweds live blissfully together, since "Thangam was Murugan's life's breath [*uyir*]."[66]

When Thangam becomes pregnant, she and Murugan have a sober discussion about the shape of their future family. Murugan, as the gentle pedagogue, suggests to Thangam that having only a few children will benefit both the children themselves and the couple's own loving relationship.

Contrasting his goals with an impoverished neighboring couple that has many children, Murugan suggests that "we should always live together as one. Let's have just one or two children. Only then will we be able to pay attention to them and raise them well."[67] He goes on to enumerate the same reasons for family planning that were common to public discourse in this period: having fewer children would be good for both infant and maternal health; it would enable the family to be prosperous; it would contribute to national development. Murugan also teaches his wife about government programs that offer free sterilizations at state-operated family planning centers.

Throughout, Thangam is positioned as a somewhat recalcitrant subject. With visions of a large family, she has doubts about each of Murugan's arguments. Nevertheless, he insists that family planning will be good for couples, families, and the nation: "Each family should plan their size to having one or two children based on their income. Only then can the family prosper. . . . Husband and wife will live without fights. Each couple should plan their family for the betterment and growth of the nation."[68] Thangam finally agrees to this alignment of familial happiness, economic rationality, and future-oriented planning. At the end of the story, Thangam and Murugan become so confident of their choices that they persuade their prolific neighbor, Velayuthan, to inquire with a doctor about birth control methods. Their conclusions are summed up in an illustration captioned, "Family planning is important for implementing the Five Year Plan for national development" (figure 5.6).[69] The image shows a well-dressed family composed of husband, wife, daughter, and son; in the background is their tiled-roof house and fertile agricultural land.

In *Pale Tankam*, family planning and national planning thus occur in tandem, merging sexual with economic rationalities to produce a better future. For Thangam and Murugan, a modernized sexuality enables a modern economy; their careful sexual and economic planning enables their future prosperity. This was the seductive promise of the small-family ideal. Moreover, like other texts, *Pale Tankam* makes Murugan the chief agent of such planning; Thangam's role is to understand and acquiesce. Murugan's reward for enacting this patriarchal authority is not only a grateful and loving wife but a future with a tiled-roof house, plenty to eat, and happy children. *Pale Tankam* does not dwell on this future, perhaps leaving readers to imagine the joy and wealth that may flow from the couple's decision to limit childbearing.

நாடு செழிக்க ஐந்தாண்டுத் திட்டங்கள் வெற்றிபெற
குடும்பக் கட்டுப்பாடு அவசியம்.

FIGURE 5.6. "Family planning is necessary for implementing the Five Year Plan for national development." Reproduced from the original held by the Roja Muthiah Research Library Collection.

Another narrative, the English-language *We Two Our Two*, makes these futures more explicit. This is an illustrated comic book published by the Central Board for Workers' Education (India) and financed by the UN Fund for Population Activities. Intended for an Indian working-class audience, the book was likely published in the late 1960s. *We Two Our Two* explores the pleasures and rationalities of consumption-oriented family planning. The color-illustrated comic book tells the story of Ram, the first-person narrator, and his wife, Rashmi. When the narrative opens, Ram has just completed a training course and secured employment in his town's textile mill. The accompanying image—the first in the book—shows Ram touching his widowed mother's feet and receiving her blessing upon obtaining a position in the industrial workforce. We see Ram and his mother inside their home, a bare but clean room furnished only with a table and single chair. Through an open door, the viewer glimpses a factory with smokestacks, signaling Ram's future employment. Soon thereafter, Ram marries Rashmi, described as a "coy little girl from a neighboring village."[70]

Rashmi gives birth to their first child, a son; signaling the modernity of the couple's choices, the birth takes place in the hospital. Ram's mother welcomes her grandchild with the words, "This is the will of God!" As the child grows, Rashmi "thought of lending her helping hand to our income" and takes up a "small job" in a local welfare center, while Ram's widowed mother cares for their son. Soon, Rashmi becomes pregnant again, leaves her job, and gives birth to a daughter. With two children and only one income, Ram and Rashmi struggle to manage their finances; in order to buy milk for their daughter, they are forced to forgo small luxuries, such as toys for their son. One night, Rashmi shares her worries that a possible third child may shatter their dreams: "What about our ambition of having our own small house? Shall we never be able to save for the future?"[71] She is concerned, as well, that they will be unable to provide three children with nutritious food, take care of their health needs, and send them to school. Thus, although Ram and Rashmi are presented as an ideal working-class couple, their finances do not allow for a third child. Even Ram's steady employment in Indian industry and Rashmi's "supplemental" income through welfare work can barely support two children.

As Ram soon recognizes, family planning offers a solution to the family's financial precarity. In a visit to his union office, he encounters his friend Rahim, who introduces him to the idea that couples can plan their children. Ram is marked as Hindu, and it is significant that he learns of family planning through the Muslim Rahim. In keeping with the text's broader claims that all Indian workers need to practice family planning, Rahim emerges as an elder confidant, already experienced in life and ready to guide the Hindu protagonist. There is no discussion by either Ram or Rahim about religious objections to family planning. The decision is entirely economic, and planning is framed as a universal and modern common sense across religious boundaries. In the meantime, Rashmi has also learned of family planning from a neighbor and suggests to Ram that "our future is in our own hands." This is the moment that Ram and Rashmi make an explicit commitment to the family's future as a reason and impetus for family planning. Ready to seize their destiny, they visit a family welfare clinic, where they learn of methods from a doctor. The image accompanying this text highlights an IUD alongside various foams and creams. Ram and Rashmi decide to adopt family planning methods. Although Ram's mother has been an important figure in their story so far, they do not consult her. Rather, the choice involves only the conjugal couple, represented as the sole agents of planning. They "organize better our privacy" by hanging a curtain between themselves and their children's sleeping mats, and "make changes . . . to adopt family planning."[72] Without referencing sexuality explicitly, the text nevertheless suggests that the reorganization of sexual intimacy—an essential component of the logic of planning—represents the couple's commitment to the future of their family.

The benefits from Ram and Rashmi's decision to align their family's finances with its reproductive futures are immediate. Rashmi is less tired, and the children thrive. Soon, the family can engage in discretionary spending and begin consuming modern commodities. On Ram's birthday, he "had a surprise when Rashmi presented me [with] a small transistor radio." The accompanying image suggests the significance of this gift. Ram is surrounded by his joyful wife and children, all looking happily at the radio, which occupies the center of the drawing. Meanwhile, Ram is able to purchase an even bigger gift: "On the next anniversary of our marriage I told her about my acquiring a small house through the trade union housing cooperative society." On the advice of Rahim, Ram also purchases an insurance policy that will provide for his daughter's marriage. One of the final images of the text shows Ram and Rashmi as a happy, companionate, and prosperous couple drinking tea together in a new home. In the background, we see the material evidence of their financial success. A stove, a water drum, the teapot and cups, and pots and dishes populate their kitchen. The transistor radio occupies pride of place on a counter (figure 5.7).[73] The image seems full of these modern conveniences, in contrast to the bare room that held Ram and his mother's lives at the start of the text. Via limiting their family when young, the Ram and Rashmi in middle age can now provide for their children, consume modern products in their household, and enjoy leisure time in each other's company.

We Two Our Two offers a vision of the prosperous working-class family that entirely sidesteps fundamental social or economic transformation. Though Ram is employed in the industrial workforce—arguably the most "modern" of occupations in postcolonial India—his wages alone are insufficient to maintain his family. When faced with a tight budget after the birth of his daughter, Ram never raises the question of higher wages. Though he is portrayed as a union member, the union offers no support in this regard either; it serves only as a welfare organization, enabling Ram to purchase a house and insurance. If the working classes have no power over their wages in *We Two Our Two*, what can they control? For this text, the answer is deceptively simple: workers can plan their own reproduction

FIGURE 5.7. According to *We Two Our Two*, family planning enables Ram and Rashmi's prosperity and leisure time. Courtesy of the Ward M. Canaday Center for Special Collections, University of Toledo.

in accordance with their financial goals. The visit to the doctor, the reorganization of Ram and Rashmi's sleeping arrangements, and their decision to buy a house, radio, and tea set instead of having more children all signal their commitment to rationalizing their reproductive sexuality and financial decisions in the present to usher in a more prosperous future. More than Ram's employment, it is this planned alignment of reproduction with finance that produces the family's modest prosperity at the end of the text.

Ram and Rashmi's economization of their family life, which weighs each reproductive decision in light of its future financial costs, marks their commitment to planning and to future prosperity more broadly. Foregoing reproduction enables the family's entrance into a world of market-based consumption, companionship, and joy. On one level, this vision of a future-oriented small family was central to the imagination of a specifically Indian modernity, especially during the reign of developmentalist ideologies in the mid-twentieth century. Ram and Rashmi thus emerge as ideal citizens who plan with an eye toward progress. On another level, *We Two Our Two* also participated in a transnationally circulating discourse that valorized small families as a necessary step toward modernity in Asia, Africa, and Latin America, to which I turn next.

Universalizing the Small Family

During the 1960s, in light of fears about a planetary "population bomb," discourses of the small family were not only national but also aspired to global circulation and relevance. Population controllers claimed that the future of the planet hinged upon millions of people around the world adopting a small-family norm and limiting their childbearing. The image of the small, planned family thus became ubiquitous. In many countries, as Matthew Connelly notes, "posters, films, flip charts, and folk performances depicted the 'unplanned' family as unclean, unhealthy, violent, and ugly."[74] Meanwhile, the planned family was not only small but more beautiful. Surrounded by consumer goods, this family benefited from better housing, health care, and education. Consequently, the image of the small family we see in texts like *We Two Our Two* represented a distinctively "Indian" small family, but one that also resembled the aspirations of family planners in many other parts of the world. Moreover, beyond its seemingly endless repetition across population control programs globally, the discourse of the small family also claimed a universalizing impulse. Supposedly relevant across national boundaries and achievable by anyone, the small family functioned as a universal sign of modernity and progress and signaled that a population had conformed to global norms. Yet, as this section will show, these universalizing aspirations of the small-family norm also grappled with national, racial, and class difference and were haunted by fears of failure. While maintaining that everyone would benefit from limiting their families, family planners worried that the rationalities of planning were not, in fact, understood by all people. Pushing for the economization of family life, they also despaired that some people could not translate relations of kinship and affect into economies of consumption and future planning. These anxieties shaped the attempt to universalize small-family norms in the era of the population bomb.

The animated film *Family Planning* (1968), a Disney Studios venture with the Population Council, made these universalizing ambitions explicit.[75] According to the Population Council, the impetus behind *Family Planning* was to create a "universal film on a topic of universal concern," and a color cartoon was "one of the most familiar, most popular, and most effective materials for mass exposure." The ten-minute film was the most expensive of the kind for its time and aspired to reach "men and women of reproductive age in the developing countries of Asia, Africa, and Latin America."[76]

To this end, it was translated into twenty-five languages, including Hindi, Urdu, Bengali, and Tamil.[77] In hopes of appealing to people across the "Third World," the Population Council and Disney sought characters that would resonate with all viewers.

The film introduced as its protagonist a "common man," described by the Population Council as a "composite of men from major regions of the world."[78] Despite this claim to represent all people, one critic notes that the result was a "curious ethnic mix: [the common man] speaks with a Yiddish inflection, looks Italian, and has an Indian wife dressed in a sari."[79] The common man and his wife are introduced to family planning with the help of Disney's cartoon character Donald Duck, whose charts help to explain the problem of population growth and who offers birth control as a solution. An authoritative narrative voiceover explains that family planning is a "new kind of personal freedom" and offers guidance to the common man and his wife. The film follows them as they envision their future as taking two paths, and the resulting narratives may be familiar to us by now. The large family is poor and hungry. By contrast, the small family engages in the pleasures of consumption, from abundant food at family meals to a transistor radio for the family's enjoyment. Eventually, the common man and his wife are persuaded to choose their family's future prosperity by adopting family planning methods. As the narrator concludes, "Every couple has the opportunity to help build a better life not just for themselves, but for people everywhere. And all of us have a responsibility toward the family of man, including you."

While the narrative voiceover thus claims a universal applicability, we have seen that the Population Council aimed for an audience of Asians, Latin Americans, and Africans. The film itself marks its characters as not white and not North American or European. The common man's difference from "First World" audiences is also measured by gender norms; throughout the film, his wife is too shy to ask questions of the narrator and whispers her queries to her husband instead. Moreover, the common man's prosperity is measured by a radio, not a television, suggesting his distance from the wealth and consumption practices of US families. In this sense, the film modeled a vision for "modern" families in the Global South, a vision of modernity that gestured toward universality but was also marked by its difference. While every family could plan for its future by planning reproduction, these futures themselves diverged. The prosperity of the small family, held out as a seductive promise to couples everywhere, hinged on national and class difference. The "common man" in the "developing" world could aspire, at best, to a radio. As Donald Duck explains in the film, an error of planning—an extra child—could erase even this goal. Thus, while all people (or men, in the language of the film) were expected to orient themselves to future consumption and to a market economy, only some men could experience their full rewards. The others must content themselves with a more modest prosperity, a difference that is ever present but never addressed within transnational discourses of the small family.

Despite appeals like *Family Planning*, population controllers were concerned that the rationalities of planning would not, in fact, translate to the "Third World" in general or to India in particular. They feared that failure would be the inevitable result of their efforts. Specifically, organizations like the IPPF, the Ford Foundation, and the Population Council expressed anxiety that the small-family norm was too novel and too "modern" to bridge the differences between India and the West. Even as they aimed to jump-start a demographic transition through a reorganization of family life, they worried that Indian families were simply too different—too backward, too mired in tradition—to adopt this ideal. Two Ford Foundation consultants summed up these fears in 1971, nearly two decades after the organization had begun funding family planning in India: "Family Planning in India is still somewhat of an alien creed. This is because a small family is not entirely a question of numbers; it carries with it a particular way of life which includes the diminishing authority of the wider kin group with a corresponding increase in the authority of the immediate parents; emancipation of women from the drudgery of child-bearing accompanied very often with their social employment and consequent financial independence and greater scope for companionship between man and wife."[80] However, the consultants lamented, the conditions that provoked such changes in the West were lacking in India, where "concepts such as 'emancipation of the individual'" were making only "hesitant progress."[81] Perhaps India, then, would always lag behind the West's march toward modernizing families, sexualities, reproduction, and economies. For transnational population controllers, the small family, while repeated across India's print and visual landscape, still seemed elusive.

Within family planning communications—a technocratic field devoted to population control messaging that emerged in the 1960s—debates ensued about whether Indians could truly be convinced through "rational" argument to adopt a small-family norm. These debates grew especially fraught by the middle of the decade when, as we have seen, the Indian government put family planning on a "war footing." Two of the leading communications experts working in family planning at the time, Deep K. Tyagi and Frank Wilder, raised these concerns explicitly. Tyagi was assistant commissioner for media in the Indian government's Department of Family Planning; he worked closely with Wilder, who was hired by the Ford Foundation as consultant to the government of India in mass communication for family planning. Together, Tyagi and Wilder pioneered some of India's most iconic family planning imagery. They developed the symbol of the inverted red triangle, which would eventually mark all of the state's family planning efforts, from signs posted on dispensaries to the armbands of family planning extension workers.

The team also produced the famous "four faces" symbol, which represents the "stylized front-view faces of a smiling mother and father, a son and a daughter."[82] Accompanying text usually included the message "Have only two or three children . . . that's plenty!" (figure 5.8).[83] The "four faces" relied upon the small-family norm; the image represented the ideal members of a properly constituted small family. At the same time, as Tyagi and Wilder argued, the four-faces symbol sidestepped the aspirational claims of other

FIGURE 5.8. This message from the Indian government's Department of Family Planning exhorts its audience to "Have only two or three children . . . that's plenty! Follow your doctor's advice." Courtesy of the Ward M. Canaday Center for Special Collections, University of Toledo.

images. Rather than figuring the small family as a site of desire in a rational economization of family life, it represented an explicit call to limit childbearing: "Does the small-family-happy-family message transmit the specific action to be taken? Can fertility programs succeed if people are left to 'Have Only Those Children You Can Afford?' And are these not rather elusive concepts for a villager whose personal aspirations do not parallel those of the educated program administrator or the foreign communications advisor?"[84] Tyagi and Wilder aimed to move away from "elusive concepts" that idealized the small family toward a "direct exhortation to have a specific number of children." More complex messages, including those that asked people to plan their families or explained various contraceptive options, were liable to be misunderstood. These messages missed their mark, Tyagi and Wilder insisted, due to the "great intellectual distance between message-maker and audience. . . . By definition, the message can be got across only within the audience's frame of reference."[85] Defending this approach to US readers, Wilder added that the "massed human misery on a Calcutta street" made it impossible for the Indian government to spend time educating people in general about the need for family planning or its various goals and methods. Rather, he called for a "forceful message" such as "You Don't Need Another Child Now" or "Postpone the Next Pregnancy, and Never Have a Fourth."[86]

Tyagi and Wilder's more "forceful" messages turned away from evoking the small family as a vehicle of upward mobility for all Indians. This message was deemed irrelevant—or wasteful of time—for an audience marked as irreducibly different from the middle-class Indian bureaucrats or the foreign consultants who developed the government's family planning propaganda. The middle classes, it was assumed, were already aware of the need to regulate their fertility, but the masses of rural and urban poor would not, or could not, follow the same logic. They would not be seduced by the promise of middle-class lifestyles, and the idea that small families were necessarily happier and more prosperous was simply outside their "frame of reference." This distinction echoed what we have seen already in the implementation of family planning programs, discussed in chapter 4. Population controllers insisted that temporary methods—condoms, diaphragms, pills—were best suited to the middle classes, which were presumed capable of choosing them. For the masses of ordinary people, however, population controllers pushed permanent methods like surgical sterilization. Similarly, as population control entered a "war footing" in the mid-1960s, the small-family ideal was entrusted only to some. They might occupy the position of the citizen-planner, capable of inhabiting the economic and (hetero)sexual rationalities that focused on the future. For the rest, whom transnational population controllers represented as Indians-in-the-mass, family planning became a state-sponsored injunction. Thus, even as the small-family norm was held forth as a universal ideal, it was marked by national, race, class, and caste difference. "Have only two or three children . . . that's plenty!" offered this vocabulary of distinction; it marked the vast difference between those who could be persuaded to choose to have a few children and those who must be told to do so.

Conclusion

The small family represented a seductive and aspirational ideal. It promised a life of happiness and prosperity to those who adopted its normative sexualities and economic rationalities. By reorganizing bodies and lives, the small-family norm offered nothing less than a modern family alongside a modern Indian future. Consequently, the discourse of the small family was far more than just a call for reproductive regulation. It also required transformations on multiple levels, from reorganizing time to rethinking kinship to reorienting toward consumption and markets. It called forth new logics that put heterosexuality in service of familial well-being and national development and imagined a global economy composed of such rational subjects. Yet, although they yoked the conjugal couple to a vision of the future that they claimed was universally applicable, representations of the small family were also troubled by questions of difference and haunted by fears of failure. Family planners expressed concern that subjects marked as too different from the planner would never adopt these new rationalities of family life.

The small-family ideal thus marks a point where the history of heterosexuality intersects with the history of development. In the era of the Five Year Plans, national development required particular kinds of subjects, whose sexuality was expressed through heterosexual monogamy in marriage and whose economic rationality was expressed through the use of birth control. These ideal subjects of development were, at base, committed to planning for the future by aligning their reproduction with an imagined national and familial futurity. Scholarship in queer studies has theorized these connections that link reproduction to heterosexuality and imagined futures, arguing that heterosexuality becomes normalized because of its supposed contributions to reproducing the future. Homosexuality is marked as "deviant" because of its supposed failure to do so.[87] Within this heteronormative ideal, the figure of "the Child"—as abstraction—represents a "reproductive futurism," which, in Lee Edelman's terms, justifies the abjection of the queer subject as incapable of working toward the future. In other words, the figure of the child emerges as "the emblem of futurity's unquestioned value," such that all those who do not participate in heteronormative reproduction are marked as opposed to the future itself.[88] The discourse of reproductive futurism that Edelman identifies is, arguably, the product of specific Western and modern contexts.[89] However, as Eithne Luibhéid suggests, as an analytic framework it may be expanded to include not only queer but also other marginalized subjects and historicized beyond a general abstraction of "the Child" to account for how systems of racism, geopolitical inequalities, and gender violence position different subjects differently in relation to an imagined futurity.[90] For Luibhéid, therefore, Edelman's "reproductive futurism" is manifest differentially across time, place, and history. It can illuminate the heteronormative politics underpinning claims to the future at specific moments, within specific systems.

The discourse of the small and happy family, as I have argued, relies upon a set of claims about heteronormative reproduction and the future. As in the case of texts like *We Two Our Two*, reproduction is exclusively responsible for creating the future envisioned by the Five Year Plans. Rather than socioeconomic transformation, the text calls for regulation of reproduction; appropriate reproduction breeds appropriate futures. This discourse of the small and happy family thus leads us to ask: what constitutes reproductive futurism in an antinatal regime? In other words, how might the future be imagined when it is secured not through valorizing reproduction but through limiting and even demonizing it? Within the population control mandates of the Five Year Plans, whose reproduction is understood to produce the future, and whose is seen as opposed to futurity itself? As we have seen throughout this book, the call to limit reproduction was always differential. Modes of reproductive stratification fueled the drive to curtail the childbearing of some people, not of others. As upper-caste and middle-class Indians aimed to differentiate their own sexual-reproductive practices and futures from those marked as lower caste or class, Western population controllers stigmatized Indian reproduction itself as incapable of working toward the future. The vision of the small and happy family aimed to contain these tensions, gesturing toward a prosperous future secured by having only two (or perhaps three) children. However, despite its claim of universality—everyone could be part of a small and happy family—this vision of the future was always limited. Only some people were rendered capable of receiving its affective and financial benefits, while others were subjected to exclusion in its name.

EPILOGUE

Family planning is a critical, human rights-based, and cost effective approach to climate change adaptation and resilience building.

—INTERNATIONAL PLANNED PARENTHOOD FEDERATION
and the Population Sustainability Network, 2016

Family planning is considered universally as the smartest development investment. For India to realize its sustainable development goals and economic aspirations, it is important to ensure that people have informed access to contraception and quality family planning services.

—NITI AAYOG, 2019

Nowadays, expenses are high. When we had children, it was less difficult. The way things are now, it's not possible to keep them in school and marry them off. They shouldn't experience the difficulties that we faced. For [my daughters] one or two children are enough, and then they should get the operation.

—DEVI, AGRICULTURAL LABORER IN TAMIL NADU, 2014

EACH OF THESE EPIGRAPHS FRAMES REPRODUCTION, AT LEAST IN part, as an economic concern. The report from the International Planned Parenthood Federation (IPPF) and the Population Sustainability Network (PSN) begins from the premise that controlling population growth is a means to control greenhouse gas emissions. If fewer people equal less pollution, then contraception becomes a "cost effective" way to prevent births and combat climate change.[1] NITI Aayog, a policy-making body that replaced India's National Planning Commission, represents family planning as a "development investment" that allows the country to pursue economic growth. It is both a universal strategy—relevant to all countries—and a specific Indian need.[2] For Devi, who shared her story in an oral history interview conducted as part of the research for this book, family planning is a kind of economic decision because of the costs of raising children. She will advise her daughters to get "the operation"—tubal ligation—so that they can manage the costs of schooling and marriage.[3] These varied connections between reproduction and economy should be familiar, given the tangled histories of marriage reform and famine, of eugenics and migration, of birth control and national sovereignty, and of population control and postcolonial development examined in this book. Yet the epigraphs also outline the shifting contours of this long-familiar connection and situate reproduction in the context of changing global, national, and personal crises. The epilogue examines these points of continuity and change.

Within transnational population control networks, and in Global North countries, family planning has recently gained new visibility in the context of climate change. Reducing population growth in the present, the logic goes, is a means toward reducing greenhouse gas emissions in the future. Repurposing 1960s models that calculated the number of "births averted" by contraceptive use in a quest to defuse the "population bomb," the new discourse views "averted lives" as "averted emissions."[4] The IPPF and PSN report outlines this argument, suggesting that eliminating the global "unmet need" for family planning could achieve 16–29 percent of the emissions reductions required to reach targets under the Paris Agreement on climate. Moreover, the document argues that contraception is among the cheapest ways to meet these targets, calculating that "emissions averted through investments in family planning would cost about $4.50 per ton of carbon dioxide, compared with more expensive options such as solar power ($30 per ton) or carbon capture and storage from new coal plants ($60 per ton)."[5] The Sierra Club, an environmentalist organization, makes the point even more directly: "A concerted, worldwide family-planning campaign can be just as effective at reducing carbon output as conserving electricity, trapping carbon, or using alternative fuels."[6] Reducing population growth through contraception, in short, becomes a key mechanism to address climate change.

Certainly, population size impacts the environment. However, feminist scholars have identified problems with the simple equivalence between averted births and averted emissions. As Jade Sasser reminds us, there has never been a "single, evidence-based model that has successfully calculated or predicted the global environmental impact of human numbers *alone*."[7] We have seen throughout this book that numbers acquire meanings within specific contexts; it is impossible to abstract the impact of these numbers from the social, political, economic, and environmental contexts in which they are embedded. Thus, for instance, transnational family planning networks tend to target women in sub-Saharan Africa, where fertility rates are higher than in most of the world. However, per capita emissions rates in the region are among the very lowest globally.[8] Meanwhile, industrialized countries, which encompass just 20 percent of the world's population, are responsible for 80 percent of accumulated carbon dioxide in the atmosphere.[9] Claiming that family planning is a "cost effective" means to fight climate change ignores these disparities between who is responsible for emissions and who is rendered responsible for addressing them. The accompanying rhetoric that it is "easier" to institute family planning in sub-Saharan Africa than it is to require change in consumption patterns in the Global North, or to curb industrial emissions, similarly refuses to ask for whom is it "easy," and who will pay the cost. Consequently, as Betsy Hartmann argues, focusing on family planning as a solution to climate change shifts attention away from the root causes of environmental degradation.[10] Disregarding the role of fossil fuel industries and the biggest emitters of greenhouse gases, discourses that equate births and emissions blame women in the Global South for planetary crisis and offer family planning as a solution.

This idea that family planning can solve planetary crises is not new; it has been part of contraceptive advocacy since at least the mid-twentieth century. As we have seen, the IPPF made a similar link at the very moment of its founding in Bombay in 1952. Dhanvanthi Rama Rau and Margaret Sanger came together to advance a neo-Malthusian argument connecting family planning to global population crisis, while sidelining a competing agenda about contraception and sex education. This choice by Rama Rau and Sanger was, in part, strategic. By connecting their cause to an emergent global problem, they brought new attention and resources to birth control; this contributed to the vast expansion of family planning programs during the 1950s and 1960s. Now, decades later, as we face the material impacts of climate change, the IPPF and PSN may similarly be making a strategic connection between births and emissions. Their report thus notes that highlighting the impact of family planning on climate change "could lead to significant programmatic and funding opportunities" for the IPPF's national affiliates as countries strive to meet their targets under the Paris Agreement.[11] Pivoting toward climate, in other words, may allow organizations like the Family Planning Association of India to tap into the development dollars directed to climate change adaptation and mitigation.

Whether strategic or not, however, such decisions have consequences. There is clearly an ongoing need for contraceptive access, and there is still a long road ahead to ensure sexual and reproductive health care on an equitable basis for all people. Linking to climate change may well allow increased resources to flow in this direction. However, when family planning is posed as a solution to climate change, it risks the same pitfalls we have seen in decades past, when it was posed as a panacea for economic development. In both cases, family planning is not geared toward reproductive autonomy for persons who may become pregnant. Instead, it becomes a means toward a different end—defusing the "population bomb" or mitigating climate change. Moreover, people, through their reproductive capacities, become the means toward this end, rather than ends in themselves. In the mid-twentieth century, this logic drove family planners' assertions that birth control offered a mechanism to solve the problems of poverty without contesting underlying inequality. This was a seductive logic for some, since it avoided structural change in favor of a supposedly easier intervention in the fertility of poor women. But this logic also opened the door to coercion and abuse, as women's bodies and lives came to be sacrificed to prevent a "population explosion" or promote economic development. Ultimately, this neither served women nor addressed poverty. Similarly, the notion that family planning can solve the growing climate crisis offers its own seductions, implying that global warming can be stopped by curtailing the fertility of poor women, rather than through structural changes that address greenhouse gas emissions. As in the past, this is only an empty promise, one that neither increases reproductive freedom nor guards against the dangers of a warming planet.

Even as family planning has been repurposed as a climate change solution in transnational contexts, it remains a linchpin of development discourse in contemporary India. Development policy is no longer outlined in Five Year Plans, since the government dismantled the National Planning Commission and ended centralized planning in 2017. The policy board NITI Aayog serves as a partial replacement for the NPC, but it is an advisory body that does not grant funding; its three-year action plans are recommendations only, and not binding. In 2019, NITI Aayog called attention to population, as noted in the epigraph. The policy board promoted family planning for "population stabilization" in service of the country's "sustainable development."[12] The reference to sustainability alludes to climate change, now increasingly part of development discourses, thus bringing climate into the long-standing nexus between population and national economic development. Although NITI Aayog's call echoes Indian development planning from an earlier era, it confronts a demographic landscape that has changed substantially. For the last several decades, Indian women have been giving birth to fewer children than they did before. As of 2018, the total fertility rate—a calculation of the average number of children born per woman—was 2.2. This figure approaches a replacement rate and is below the global average. Despite regional variations in this number, which ranges from 1.6 in some states to 3.3 in others, there is no current "explosion" of population growth in India.[13] Indian population is continuing to increase, but this is due to the large number of people who are currently within childbearing age; it does not portend significant population growth in the future. To this extent, the "population stabilization" that NITI Aayog calls for already exists.

Nevertheless, the framework of crisis pervades contemporary reference to population. There are some changes to the terms—NITI Aayog thus calls for "stabilization," not control, and emphasizes "informed" contraceptive access with "quality" family planning services. The shift in language is due, in large measure, to transnational feminist organizing that successfully challenged the underlying logics of population control and called for a reconceptualization of population policy worldwide. These feminist efforts culminated in 1994, at the Cairo Conference on Population and Development, sponsored by the United Nations. The conference's Program of Action marked a radical departure from earlier policies; it asserted that reproductive rights were universal, highlighted women's empowerment, and called upon governments to abandon targets and quotas in their population policies.[14] These were important changes, and they signaled the promise of a sexual and reproductive rights agenda that centered women. However, feminists at the time voiced concern that the Program of Action did not go far enough in rejecting the core premises of population control.[15] In hindsight, we know that the declarations at Cairo ran headlong into rising neoliberal ideologies that promoted market-based solutions and encouraged the privatization of health care globally.[16] In that context, the goals of the Program of Action still remain largely unfulfilled.

In response to the Cairo declaration, the Indian government abandoned its population targets, but it maintained an assumption that population posed a crisis for development. Consequently, the state supports a "two-child norm" that is enforced through policies that serve as both carrot and stick.[17] Meanwhile, the government's continued underinvestment in health-care, including in maternal and child health, becomes plain in its family planning programs. For instance, between 2003 and 2012, an average of twelve women died per month due to botched surgical sterilization proce-dures across the country.[18] Occasionally, there have been catastrophic fail-ures, as in the case of a sterilization camp in Chattisgarh in 2014, when thirteen patients died after a surgeon operated on eighty-three women in a single day using the same unsterilized gloves, syringes, and sutures, spend-ing just three minutes per patient.[19] While this case was exceptional in its high death rate, it reflects a disregard for poor women's health, rights, and well-being that is widespread among the sterilization camps that are still a mainstay of Indian population programs.

If the actual workings of the Indian family planning system employ a model of population crisis, so also does the government's rhetoric. In his 2019 Independence Day speech, for instance, Prime Minister Narendra Modi announced his concern about the country's "population explosion" due to "uncontrolled population growth." He praised families that regulated their reproduction, and urged others to follow their example: "Before a child arrives into our family we should think—have I prepared myself to fulfill the needs of the child? Or will I leave it dependent on the society?" Those who recognized the need for family limitation, Modi concluded, were con-tributing not only to the "welfare of their family but also to the good of the nation."[20] Modi's words resonate with long-standing Malthusian assump-tions about population and poverty, and they echo, nearly unchanged, the pronouncements of postcolonial India's first population controllers, who insisted that reproductive control was a chief method of promoting national development. Yet at the same time, the long history of representing Indian population as a crisis—and thus as a target of intervention—now shapes new modes of reproductive regulation as well. Alongside the rhetoric of popu-lation control, which we see in Modi's speech, emerging population dis-courses sometimes function without explicitly pathologizing fertility. Beyond reducing numbers, they also aim to promote economic development through a "demographic dividend," which capitalizes on a high ratio of younger workers to older retirees, or to produce a "bio-citizen" who man-ages her own fertility in line with markets.[21]

The question of population and reproduction rears its head in yet another way in contemporary India, in its skewed and worsening sex ratio. As I dis-cussed in chapter 5, the question of son preference was both hinted at and obscured in family planning propaganda that centered the heterosexual happy family. However, the demographic consequences of son preference have grown increasingly clear in the decades that followed. Currently, the sex ratio (expressed as the proportion of "Females/1000 males") stands at 900 nationally and falls as low as 837 in the state of Haryana.[22] This disparity is due not only to the neglect of girl children but also to the use of technologies to determine the sex of the fetus before birth, followed by the selective abortion of female fetuses.

Feminist activists have called attention to this problem and, in 1994, pushed for legislation to prohibit health-care workers from revealing fetal sex to prospective parents. Today, campaigns against sex selective abortion are an important part of feminist health movements. Nevertheless, the ratio continues to worsen and is now a fact of life even in states where, a few decades ago, this was not a problem. The government has intervened through policies that provide financial incentives to families of daughters. Known as Conditional Cash Transfer (CCT) programs, these policies provide monetary incentives to parents whose daughters meet certain milestones, such as immunizations, schooling, or remaining unmarried until age eighteen.[23] However, although these policies may have offered some benefits to recipients, they are also tied to ongoing legacies of population control. Some state plans, for instance, provide cash incentives only if the parents accept sterilization after two children; others limit incentives to only two daughters and not to a third.[24] In this way, policies that claim to promote the value of girls enact potentially coercive mechanisms of reproductive control against their parents, and in particular, their mothers.

The relationships of mothers and daughters—and the attendant questions of reproduction, population, and economy—emerge differently in Devi's narrative, the third epigraph above. As a mother of four children who works as an agricultural laborer in rural Tamil Nadu, Devi spoke about her difficulties in raising children and her hopes for their future. Her story was among fifteen oral history interviews conducted in the Thiruvallur District as part of my research for this book.[25] The women interviewed ranged in age from about thirty to ninety years, with the majority in their fifties and sixties. Most worked in agricultural labor and were also enrolled in programs under the Mahatma Gandhi National Rural Employment Guarantee Act, which provides one hundred days of wage employment to people willing to do manual work. All fifteen women depended on the public health-care system, which meant they visited Primary Health Centers (PHCs) for their basic health needs, including for reproductive health care, and were sometimes referred to secondary and tertiary centers, such as public hospitals. Some women also used their own funds to access privatized healthcare for themselves or their families. As patients within the public healthcare system, and as poor and working women, they fit the demographic profile most targeted by state-led family planning and population control. The state of Tamil Nadu, in particular, has historically prioritized targeting women like Devi. During the late colonial decades, as we have seen, organizations like the Madras Neo-Malthusian League and the Self Respect movement brought birth control to public attention in Madras Presidency. Since independence, the state of Madras, now Tamil Nadu, has been heralded by the Indian government and international agencies as a "success story" of Indian family planning. Today, the state's total fertility rate, at 1.6, is lower than that of the country as a whole.[26]

In collecting and learning from women's narratives, my first instinct was to seek alternatives to the kinds of economic rationalities that I analyze throughout this book. In an admittedly oversimplified fashion, I initially sought a way out of the reproductive injustices this book has documented; I hoped for ways of thinking and speaking that did not filter reproduction so narrowly through population and economy and that offered different imaginings of reproductive futures. However, upon hearing these stories, and in light of the enduring connections among reproduction, population, and economy that this book documents, I eventually began to approach women's narratives differently. Rather than seeking an imagined alternative that severed reproduction from economic rationalities, I began to ask how women narrated these intersections.

Thus, for instance, our interview questions invited women to speak about their reproductive histories in relation to pregnancy and childbirth; however, our interlocutors tended to focus more on the reproductive labor of raising children and grandchildren. For instance, Devi spoke of this labor in intergenerational terms. Her mother, she said, had eight children, since "there was no family planning back then." She managed to raise them all, but Devi herself made a different decision. After having two sons and two daughters, and despite the opposition of her father-in-law, Devi decided to have the "family planning operation."[27] Her advice for her own daughters, as cited in the epigraph, would be to have just one or two children, in order to be able to pay for their education and their marriage. In this way, Devi represented her reproductive decisions, at least in part, in relation to their economic costs. Surgical sterilization became a technology that would align reproduction with her household's economic capacity, and in this sense, Devi's words seem to fit the mold of the "rational" subject figured by family planning discourses. Like the responsible citizen praised in Modi's Independence Day speech, Devi recounts her reproductive history in terms of her ability to bear the financial costs of raising children. However, her narrative is not exactly in alignment with Modi's call for citizens to contribute to the "welfare of the family but also to the good of the nation." It is less a story about modern and prosperous futures—the seductive ideal of much family planning discourse—than it is one about scarcity and precarity. So that her daughters will not experience "the difficulties that we faced," she will encourage them to have just one or two children.

Many women spoke similarly about the reproductive and economic exigencies of the present, rather than the promise of future prosperity. Darshini, an agricultural laborer and mother of three, for example, decided upon surgical sterilization after her son and two daughters were born. She had considered it even earlier, after the birth of her son and first daughter. But her son fell ill, and fearing she might lose him, she delayed the operation. After her third child, a daughter, she and her husband decided it was time: "Costs are high, and so people like us cannot care for many children. People like us don't have land and all that. Only if we earn that day, do we eat that day."[28] Darshini's family's landlessness, a fact linked to her class and caste position, meant that they were entirely dependent on wages earned from labor, and in these circumstances, she and her husband saw sterilization as a necessity. Like Devi's story, Darshini's narrative models a kind of economic rationality, but it also challenges the promise of small and happy families to narrate stories of difficult survival. It is "people like us," and emphatically not all people, who face these burdens on their reproduction. While national governments and transnational family planning networks have long imagined the small family as a site of desire for all citizens committed to familial and national prosperity, Darshini figures the small family as a necessity of survival for landless laborers. More than achieving the promises of development, it is development's failures—the failure to redistribute land, the failure to provide other sources of employment—that shape Darshini's account of reproduction as a point of intervention into her own economic future.

Kasturi, who was the mother of one son, now deceased, and the grandmother of two children, made explicit this distinction between people who had to limit their childbearing and those who were truly free to choose. The issue, she explained, was money: "That's how the country is. If you don't have money, no one respects you. If you have money, you could have as many daughters as you want and settle all of them in marriages. Those who don't have money are just beggars." Throughout her interview, Kasturi was consumed with worry about supporting her grandchildren, especially her granddaughter. Kasturi helped to pay for her granddaughter's school fees, and the girl was doing well in school. Kasturi also planned to help her daughter-in-law pay for the granddaughter's marriage when the time came. She was deeply concerned about these responsibilities: "Back in the day, it was common to have even seven children without any concerns. But now, everyone says one is enough, or two is enough. Somehow, back then, my mother got four daughters married off. But now, even the guy who delivers the newspaper asks for [a dowry of] eight *savaran* [sixty-four grams of gold]. So nowadays, if you have so many children, how could you manage all this. . . . People who don't have wealth, if they have so many children, how could they do it? I myself, how will I be able to marry off my granddaughter?"[29] Like Darshini, Kasturi ties her narrative about children and grandchildren to economic precarity. As the quotation suggests, this precarity is also gendered. Because of the costs associated with her marriage, Kasturi represents her granddaughter as a tremendous financial responsibility. Since the girl's father is deceased, Kasturi adds, this is a responsibility that falls exclusively to women. While wealthy households can afford to raise girls and "settle all of them in marriages," she and her daughter-in-law confront a present and future of struggle.

These concerns about the costs of raising children and grandchildren echo across the narratives, linking reproductive choices to economic constraints and posing "the operation" as a necessary response to financial precarity. Among all the women interviewed, Veena made this point most explicitly. At the time of her interview, Veena was thirty-three years old and the mother of two children, a son and daughter. Although her husband wanted more children, she dismissed his logic: "Even when there was no food to be had, he thought we should have another child." After giving birth to her first child, a son, Veena was ready for sterilization and obtained a consent form from the hospital, but she was dissuaded from this decision by her aunt. After her daughter was born, she decided to have the operation. When the hospital asked for her husband's signature on the consent form, she recounts, "I said, 'I'm the one who works hard for the kids, and I'm not able to take care of another one' . . . I do everything. So I just decided that two is enough."[30] Her husband, she added, brought some income into the household, but he refused to contribute in any other way. Veena's narrative is a recounting of reproductive, and social reproductive, labor. She connects reproduction and economy through work—and in particular, through the work that women do to bear children, to raise and educate them, to arrange their marriages, and to support their grandchildren. Like the discourses of population control, she is concerned about what children "cost," but hers is not the rationale of "averted births" or, indeed, of "averted emissions." Therefore, Veena's decision to have "the operation" was based not on "the economy" in some abstract sense, but on her experiences of her labor in raising and caring for children. While linking reproduction to economy, she does not employ the justificatory frameworks of national development or global environmental crisis. Rather, her labor justifies these connections and, in her telling, guides her reproductive decisions.

As this book demonstrates, enduring connections among reproduction, population, and economy have shaped over a century of reproductive politics. Colonial officials alongside nationalists, eugenicists alongside postcolonial bureaucrats, transnational population controllers alongside Indian feminists have argued that regulating reproduction was a necessary mechanism to intervene in the population and insisted that limiting the population was essential to economic development. They have blamed reproductive practices for poverty and the failures of development, while hoping that more effective methods of contraception would enable more effective reproductive regulation in the future. These connections have endured even when population growth rates were not increasing, such as in the late nineteenth century or in the contemporary moment, and have redoubled when faced with documented growth in population. They have been part of a specifically Indian story, but Indian developments have come to shape the global and modern history of reproduction as well. We have seen, moreover, that the connections linking reproduction to population and economy have created situations of reproductive injustice—of top-down control of people's reproductive capacities, of a disregard for their bodies and lives, of a demonization of some women's reproduction as the cause of national and planetary catastrophe. This history should make us wary of the ongoing instrumentalization of women's reproduction to serve other ends, whether to shore up state claims about economic progress or to claim action on climate change. Yet this history also shows us how to ask questions and think differently. From the women of Gomet who asked the family planner for schools when they envisioned alternative reproductive futures for their daughters to Veena, who insisted that her work as a mother gave her the right to decide about "the operation," women have challenged the instrumentalization of their bodies. They pose different means of connecting their reproduction to their lives, and to history.

NOTES

INTRODUCTION

1 Dhanvanthi Rama Rau, *An Inheritance: The Memoirs of Dhanvanthi Rama Rau* (London: Heinemann, 1977), 262; Beryl Suitters, *Be Brave and Angry: Chronicles of the International Planned Parenthood Federation* (London: International Planned Parenthood Federation, 1973).

2 *The Third International Conference on Planned Parenthood: Report of the Proceedings* (Bombay: Family Planning Association of India, 1952), 9.

3 *Third International Conference*, 12.

4 Rama Rau, *An Inheritance*, 262.

5 The IPPF's predecessor had worked in four countries: the US, the UK, Sweden, and the Netherlands. Rama Rau, *An Inheritance*, 263. I follow Beryl Suitters in calling the IPPF's predecessor organization the "International Committee for Planned Parenthood." Suitters, *Be Brave and Angry*.

6 Rama Rau, *An Inheritance*, 256; Rama Rau to Margaret Sanger, September 5, 1951, Margaret Sanger Papers, Sophia Smith Collection, Smith College Libraries, Northampton, MA (hereafter cited as MSP), series III (subseries 1—Correspondence).

7 Rama Rau, *An Inheritance*, 257.

8 Government of India, Planning Commission, *The First Five Year Plan* (New Delhi: Government of India, 1953), 522.

9 Michelle Murphy, *The Economization of Life* (Durham, NC: Duke University Press, 2017).

10 For instance, most of the historical research on birth control in South Asia focuses on the 1920s and 1930s: Sarah Hodges, *Contraception, Colonialism and Commerce: Birth Control in South India, 1920–1940* (New York: Routledge, 2016); Sanjam Ahluwalia, *Reproductive Restraints: Birth Control in India, 1877–1947* (Urbana: University of Illinois Press, 2008).

11 For example, Sama: Resource Group for Women and Health, "Population Policies and Two Child Norm," accessed June 1, 2020, www.samawomens health.in/population-policies-and-two-child-norm.

12 Alison Bashford, *Global Population: History, Geopolitics, and Life on Earth* (New York: Columbia University Press, 2014); Matthew Connelly, *Fatal Misconception: The Struggle to Control World Population* (Cambridge, MA: Belknap, 2009); Karl Ittmann, *A Problem of Great Importance: Population, Race and Power in the British Empire* (Berkeley: University of California Press, 2013).

13 For example, Asha Nadkarni, *Eugenic Feminism: Reproductive Nationalism in the United States and India* (Minneapolis: University of Minnesota Press, 2014); Mrinalini Sinha, *Specters of Mother India: The Global Restructuring of an Empire* (Durham, NC: Duke University Press, 2006); Ashwini Tambe, *Defining Girlhood in India: A Transnational History of Sexual Maturity Laws*: Urbana: University of Illinois Press, 2019).

14 Bangladesh has received scholarly attention in studies of transnational population control programs, such as Betsy Hartmann, *Reproductive Rights and Wrongs: The Global Politics of Population Control*, 3rd ed. (Chicago: Haymarket Books, 2016); Murphy, *Economization of Life.*

15 Sarah Hodges, "Towards a History of Reproduction in Modern India," in *Reproductive Health in India: History, Politics, Controversies*, ed. Sarah Hodges (Delhi: Orient Longman, 2006), 2.

16 Linda Gordon, *The Moral Property of Women: A History of Birth Control Politics in America*, 3rd ed. (Urbana: University of Illinois Press, 2002), ix.

17 For an overview of the historiography of reproduction, see Nick Hopwood, Rebecca Flemming, and Lauren Kassell, "Reproduction in History," in *Reproduction: Antiquity to the Present Day*, ed. Nick Hopwood, Rebecca Flemming, and Lauren Kassell (Cambridge: Cambridge University Press, 2018), 3–17.

18 In her ethnographic study, Maya Unnithan takes a similarly expansive view of reproductive politics, which she defines as a concept that "combines the gendered struggles over the body . . . and wo/manhood in the interrelated worlds of families, policymakers, state bureaucrats, legal, medical and health professionals and practitioners, as well as in civil society contexts." *Fertility, Health and Reproductive Politics: Re-imagining Rights in India* (London: Routledge, 2019), 3–4.

19 For example: Laura Briggs, *Reproducing Empire: Race, Sex, Science, and U.S. Imperialism in Puerto Rico* (Berkeley: University of California Press, 2002); Angela Davis, *Women, Race and Class* (New York: Vintage Books, 1983); Elena Gutiérrez, *Fertile Matters: The Politics of Mexican-Origin Women's Reproduction* (Austin: University of Texas Press, 2008); Susanne M. Klausen, *Abortion under Apartheid: Nationalism, Sexuality, and Women's Reproductive Rights in South Africa* (Oxford: Oxford University Press, 2015); Eithne Luibhéid, *Pregnant on Arrival: Making the Illegal Immigrant* (Minneapolis: University of Minnesota Press, 2013); Johanna Schoen, *Choice and Coercion: Birth Control, Sterilization, and Abortion in Public Health and Welfare* (Chapel Hill: University of North Carolina Press, 2005); Andrea Smith, *Conquest: Sexual Violence and American Indian Genocide* (Durham, NC: Duke University Press, 2015); Aiko Takeuchi-Demirci, *Contraceptive Diplomacy: Reproductive Politics and Imperial Ambitions in the United States and Japan* (Redwood City, CA: Stanford University Press, 2018); Lynn Thomas, *Politics of the Womb: Women, Reproduction, and the State in Kenya* (Berkeley: University of California Press, 2003).

20 Takeuchi-Demirci, *Contraceptive Diplomacy*, 13–14.

21 Judith Butler, "Is Kinship Always Already Heterosexual?" *Differences* 13, no. 1 (2002): 14–44; Penelope Deutscher, "Foucault's *History of Sexuality, Volume 1:* Re-reading Its Reproduction," *Theory, Culture and Society* 29, no. 1 (2012): 119–37; Lee Edelman, *No Future: Queer Theory and the Death Drive* (Durham, NC: Duke University Press, 2004), Nook ed.

22 Faye D. Ginsburg and Rayna Rapp, "Introduction: Conceiving the New World Order," in *Conceiving the New World Order: The Global Politics of Reproduction,* ed. Faye D. Ginsburg and Rayna Rapp (Berkeley: University of California Press, 1995), 3. See also Shellee Colen, "'Like a Mother to Them': Stratified Reproduction and West Indian Childcare Workers and Employers in New York," in *Conceiving the New World Order,* 78–102.

23 Angus McClaren questions this assumption in *A History of Contraception: From Antiquity to the Present Day* (Oxford: Basil Blackwell, 1990), 1.

24 Hodges, "History of Reproduction," 16.

25 Ahluwalia, *Reproductive Restraints,* 3.

26 Nadkarni, *Eugenic Feminism,* 4.

27 I follow the terminology of my sources and use both *population control* and *family planning* to refer to top-down systems and policies to regulate reproduction. However, *family planning* has also been used in more grassroots contexts, and my use of terms is context-specific as necessary.

28 For example, Sumit Sarkar and Tanika Sarkar, eds., *Women and Social Reform in Modern India: A Reader* (Bloomington: Indiana University Press, 2008).

29 J. Devika, *Individuals, Householders, Citizens: Family Planning in Kerala* (New Delhi: Zubaan, 2008).

30 Loretta Ross and Rickie Solinger, *Reproductive Justice: An Introduction* (Berkeley: University of California Press, 2017), 9.

31 *Merriam-Webster,* s.v. "population," accessed May 10, 2019, www.merriam -webster.com/dictionary/population.

32 Michel Foucault, *Security, Territory, Population: Lectures at the Collège de France 1977–1978,* ed. Michel Senellart, trans. Graham Burchell (New York: Palgrave Macmillan, 2004), 67–74.

33 Michel Foucault, *The History of Sexuality: An Introduction,* vol. 1, trans. Robert Hurley (New York: Vintage Books, 1990), 139; Foucault, *Security, Territory, Population,* 67.

34 Nadkarni, *Eugenic Feminism,* 13.

35 Foucault, *History of Sexuality,* 139.

36 Ruth Miller, "Rights, Reproduction, Sexuality, and Citizenship in the Ottoman Empire and Turkey," *Signs* 32, no. 2 (2007): 352, 358.

37 Susan Greenhalgh and Edwin Winckler, *Governing China's Population: From Leninist to Neoliberal Biopolitics* (Stanford, CA: Stanford University Press, 2005); Chikako Takeshita, *The Global Biopolitics of the IUD: How Science Constructs Contraceptive Users and Women's Bodies* (Cambridge, MA: MIT Press, 2012).

38 Achille Mbembe, "Necropolitics," trans. Libby Meintjes, *Public Culture* 15, no. 1 (2003): 11–40.

39 Arjun Appadurai, "Number in the Colonial Imagination," in *Orientalism and the Postcolonial Predicament*, ed. Carol A. Breckinridge and Peter van der Veer (Philadelphia: University of Pennsylvania Press, 1993), 318–20. See also U. Kalpagam, *Rule by Numbers: Governmentality in Colonial India* (Lanham, MD: Lexington Books, 2014).

40 T. R. Malthus, *An Essay on the Principle of Population* (Oxford: Oxford University Press, 2004), 15–45.

41 Rahul Nair, "The Discourse on Population in India, 1870–1960" (PhD diss., University of Pennsylvania, 2006), chap. 4. See also Sarah Hodges, "South Asia's Eugenic Past," in *The Oxford Handbook of the History of Eugenics*, ed. Alison Bashford and Philippa Levine (Oxford: Oxford University Press, 2010), 228–42.

42 Nair, "Discourse on Population," chap. 4; Charu Gupta, *Sexuality, Obscenity, Community: Women, Muslims, and the Hindu Public in Colonial India* (London: Palgrave, 2001), chap. 7.

43 Carole McCann, "Malthusian Men and Demographic Transitions: A Case Study of Hegemonic Masculinity in Mid-Twentieth-Century Population Theory," *Frontiers: A Journal of Women Studies* 30, no. 1 (2009): 142–71; Carole McCann, *Figuring the Population Bomb: Gender and Demography in the Mid-Twentieth Century* (Seattle: University of Washington Press, 2017).

44 Mohan Rao, *From Population Control to Reproductive Health: Malthusian Arithmetic* (New Delhi: Sage, 2004).

45 Hartmann, *Reproductive Rights and Wrongs*, 14–15.

46 Mahmood Mamdani, *The Myth of Population Control: Family, Caste and Class in an Indian Village* (New York: Monthly Review Press, 1972).

47 Hartmann, *Reproductive Rights and Wrongs*, chap. 2.

48 Hartmann, *Reproductive Rights and Wrongs*, ix.

49 Patricia Jeffery and Roger Jeffery, *Confronting Saffron Demography: Religion, Fertility, and Women's Status in India* (Gurgaon: Three Essays Collective, 2006).

50 Susan Buck-Morss, "Envisioning Capital: Political Economy on Display," *Critical Inquiry* 21, no. 2 (1995): 434–67.

51 Manu Goswami, *Producing India: From Colonial Economy to National Space* (Chicago: University of Chicago Press, 2004), 215.

52 Goswami, *Producing India*, chap. 7.

53 Ritu Birla, *Stages of Capital: Law, Culture, and Market Governance in Late Colonial India* (Durham, NC: Duke University Press, 2009), 4.

54 Birla, *Stages of Capital*, 3–5; David Ludden, "India's Development Regime," in *Colonialism and Culture*, ed. Nicholas B. Dirks (Ann Arbor: University of Michigan Press, 1992): 247–88.

55 Partha Chatterjee, *The Nation and Its Fragments: Colonial and Postcolonial Histories* (Princeton, NJ: Princeton University Press, 1993); Tanika Sarkar, *Hindu Wife, Hindu Nation: Community, Religion, and Cultural Nationalism* (Bloomington: Indiana University Press, 2002).

56 According to some scholars, the mid-twentieth-century moment represents a true origin point for contemporary conceptions of the economy. Timothy

Mitchell notes that Adam Smith does not refer to "the economy" as a structure or whole, and he traces the "appearance of the idea that the economy exists as a general structure of economic relations" to John Maynard Keynes's *The General Theory of Employment, Interest, and Money* (1936). Timothy Mitchell, "Fixing the Economy," *Cultural Studies* 12, no. 1 (1998), 85. For a critique of this periodization, see Goswami, who locates a longer history of this concept. *Producing India*, 335n10. For my purposes here, it seems clear that there were significant changes in the mid-twentieth century. Perhaps, as Suzanne Bergeron suggests, the shift was from population as the object of governance in the earlier period to the economy as the object in the twentieth century. *Fragments of Development: Nation, Gender, and the Space of Modernity* (Ann Arbor: University of Michigan Press, 2005), 7. Nevertheless, following Goswami, I also see key continuities that make it important to trace the history of the concept from the eighteenth century onward.

57 Murphy, *Economization of Life*, 18–20; Mitchell, "Fixing the Economy," 85.
58 Bergeron, *Fragments of Development*, 6.
59 For discussion of women's labor and the development of capitalist economies, see Silvia Federici, *Caliban and the Witch: Women, the Body and Primitive Accumulation* (New York: Autonomedia, 2004).
60 Shirin M. Rai, "Gender and Development: Theoretical Perspectives," in *The Women, Gender and Development Reader*, 2nd ed., ed. Nalini Visvanathan, Lynn Duggan, Nan Wiegersma, and Laurie Nisonoff (London: Zed Books, 2001), 28–37; Ester Boserup, *Women's Role in Economic Development* (New York: Routledge, 2007).
61 Behramji M. Malabari, *Infant Marriage and Enforced Widowhood in India* (Bombay: Voice of India, 1887), 2.
62 All India Women's Conference, 6th Session (Madras, December 28, 1931–January 1, 1932), All India Women's Conference Papers, Margaret Cousins Library, Sarojini House, New Delhi, 81a.
63 Ross and Solinger, *Reproductive Justice*, 6.

CHAPTER 1: ECONOMIES OF REPRODUCTION IN AN AGE OF EMPIRE

1 Richard Temple to John Strachey, March 11, 1877, Papers of Sir Richard Temple, India Office Records and Private Papers, British Library (hereafter cited as Temple MSS), MSS Eur F86/173.
2 Richard Temple to John Strachey, March 11, 1877, Temple MSS Eur F86/173.
3 The Famine Commission Report estimates five million for areas under crown rule. Other estimates range from four million to over five million. Brahma Nand, ed., *Famines in Colonial India: Some Unofficial Historical Narratives* (New Delhi: Kanishka, 2007), 1; Kate Currie, "British Colonial Policy and Famines: Some Effects and Implications of 'Free Trade' in the Bombay, Bengal and Madras Presidencies, 1860–1900," *South Asia: Journal of South Asian Studies* 14, no. 2 (1991): 32.

4 Annie Besant, *The Law of Population: Its Consequences, and Its Bearing upon Human Conduct and Morals*, in *A Selection of the Social and Political Pamphlets of Annie Besant*, ed. John Saville (New York: Augustus M. Kelley, 1970), 25.

5 Sumit Guha, *Health and Population in South Asia from Earliest Times to the Present* (New Delhi: Permanent Black, 2001), 15.

6 U. Kalpagam, "The Colonial State and Statistical Knowledge," *History of the Human Sciences* 13, no. 2 (2000): 40.

7 Norbert Peabody, "Cents, Sense, Census: Human Inventories in Late Precolonial and Early Colonial India," *Comparative Studies in Society and History* 43, no. 4 (October 2001): 825–37. Sumit Guha, "The Politics of Identity and Enumeration in India, c. 1600–1900," *Comparative Studies in Society and History* 45, no. 1 (2003): 155.

8 Kevin Walby and Michael Haan, "Caste Confusion and Census Enumeration in Colonial India, 1872–1921," *Histoire Sociale/Social History* 45, no. 90 (2012): 306; Peabody, "Cents, Sense, Census," 832–37.

9 Arjun Appadurai, "Number in the Colonial Imagination," in *Orientalism and the Postcolonial Predicament*, ed. Carol A. Breckinridge and Peter van der Veer (Philadelphia: University of Pennsylvania Press, 1993), 321–26.

10 Appadurai, "Number," 317; Ian Hacking, "Biopower and the Avalanche of Printed Numbers," *Humanities in Society* 5, nos. 3–4 (1982): 279–95.

11 Appadurai, "Number," 317.

12 Walby and Haan, "Caste Confusion," 306–10.

13 Appadurai, "Number," 316–17.

14 W. R. Cornish, *Report on the Census of Madras Presidency of 1871*, vol. 1 (Madras: Government Gazette Press, 1874), 10.

15 Guha, "Politics of Identity," 156.

16 Michel Foucault, *The History of Sexuality: An Introduction*, vol. 1, trans. Robert Hurley (New York: Vintage Books, 1990), 25.

17 Foucault, *History of Sexuality*, 26.

18 Famines were not disconnected from the conditions that preceded them. The precise moment when a population living with hunger slipped into "famine" is therefore difficult to pinpoint. In the late nineteenth century, definitions of famine varied, with some focused on widespread hunger within a population and others emphasizing mortality. After the Famine Code of 1880, official designation of an event as "famine" would require an administrative response, which affected when the government declared that a famine was occurring. I follow David Arnold's insistence that famine represents both event and structure. Famines of the late nineteenth century were distinct events that had a beginning and an end, but were also part of, and contributed to, broader structures of scarcity in agrarian society. *Famine: Social Crisis and Historical Change* (Oxford: Basil Blackwell, 1988), 7–8.

19 Nand, *Famines in Colonial India*, 1–2.

20 Mike Davis, *Late Victorian Holocausts: El Niño Famines and the Making of the Third World* (London: Verso, 2002), 287.

21 Amartya Sen, *Poverty and Famine: An Essay on Entitlement and Deprivation* (Oxford: Clarendon, 1981), 58–79.

22 Sumit Sarkar, *Modern India, 1885–1947* (Delhi: Macmillan India, 2002), 30–32; David Washbrook, "The Commercialization of Agriculture in Colonial India: Production, Subsistence and Reproduction in the 'Dry South,' c. 1870–1930," *Modern Asian Studies* 28, no. 1 (1994): 164.

23 David Hall-Matthews, *Peasants, Famine and the State in Colonial Western India* (London: Palgrave Macmillan, 2005), 129–30.

24 Burton Stein, "Introduction," in *The Making of Agrarian Policy in British India 1770–1900*, ed. Burton Stein (Delhi: Oxford University Press, 1992), 17.

25 Hall-Mathews, *Peasants*, 129.

26 Davis, *Late Victorian Holocausts*, 9.

27 Arnold, *Famine*, 125.

28 Davis, *Late Victorian Holocausts*, 15–16.

29 Currie, "British Colonial Policy," 55.

30 Nand, ed., *Famines in Colonial India*, 1; S. Ambirajan, *Classical Political Economy and British Policy in India* (Cambridge: Cambridge University Press, 1978), 79–80.

31 The Bihar famine affected 21.4 million people, and the government spent Rs. 675.9 lakhs on relief. The three previous famines had affected a total of 112 million people, but only Rs. 275.9 lakhs had been spent for relief. Interestingly, Temple managed Bihar relief efforts as well, but he and Viceroy Lord Northbrook were criticized for the expenditure; Temple was instructed to practice greater economy in 1876. Ambirajan, *Classical Political Economy*, 86–92.

32 Arnold, *Famine*, 110.

33 Adam Smith, *An Inquiry into the Nature and Causes of the Wealth of Nations* (London: Methuen, [1776] 1904), bk. 4, chap. 5.44, accessed April 9, 2020, www.econlib.org/LIBRARY/Smith/smWN15.html.

34 Ambirajan, *Classical Political Economy*, 72–80, Davis, *Late Victorian Holocausts*, 31; James Vernon, *Hunger: A Modern History* (Cambridge, MA: Harvard University Press, 2007), 40–53.

35 Davis, *Late Victorian Holocausts*, 284.

36 Currie, "British Colonial Policy," 52.

37 *Dnyan Prakash*, December 4, 1876, Report of the Native Papers Published in the Bombay Presidency, India Office Records and Private Papers, British Library.

38 Davis, *Late Victorian Holocausts*, 38.

39 Hall-Mathews, *Peasants*, 196; William Digby, *The Famine Campaign in Southern India, 1876–1878* (London: Longmans, Green, 1878), 340–44. The strike occurred in some Bombay districts in early 1877, following announcement of the one-pound wage. Approximately 136,000 laborers left the relief camps in protest, and when the Bombay government refused to yield, only about one-quarter of them returned.

40 For example, *Suthasabhimani*, September 1, 1878, Report of the Native Papers Published in the Madras Presidency, India Office Records and Private Papers, British Library.

41 *Paschima Taraka and Kerala Pataka*, October 1, 1878, Report of the Native Papers Published in the Madras Presidency, India Office Records and Private Papers, British Library.

42 Arnold, *Famine*, 96.

43 Hall-Matthews, *Peasants*, 172.

44 For example: Pros. No. 14 (January 5, 1877), Pros. No. 18 (January 13, 1877), Pros. No. 61 (January 20, 1877), Pros. No. 66 (February 10, 1877), Pros. No. 77 (February 5, 1877), Proceedings of the Department of Revenue, Agriculture, and Commerce (Famine Branch), National Archives, New Delhi.

45 Pros. No. 14 (January 5, 1877), Proceedings of the Department of Revenue, Agriculture, and Commerce (Famine Branch), National Archives, New Delhi.

46 "Famine Narrative no. IV," *Quarterly Journal of the Poona Sarvajanik Sabha* 1, no. 4 (1877): 55. In more modern categories, this was less, in caloric terms, than the food given to prisoners at the Buchenwald concentration camp. Davis, *Late Victorian Holocausts*, 38.

47 Surgeon Major W. R. Cornish to J. H. Garstin, Pros. No. 57 (July 1877), Proceedings of the Department of Revenue, Agriculture, and Commerce (Famine Branch), National Archives, New Delhi.

48 Pros. No. 66 (March 3, 1877), Proceedings of the Department of Revenue, Agriculture, and Commerce (Famine Branch), National Archives, New Delhi.

49 Report by W. J. van Someren, Pros. No. 55 (March 24, 1877), Proceedings of the Department of Revenue, Agriculture, and Commerce (Famine Branch), National Archives, New Delhi.

50 For example, "Second Famine Narrative," *Quarterly Journal of the Poona Sarvajanik Sabha* 1, no. 1 (1878): 12–21; "Letter to the Famine Commission Regarding the Famine Mortality in the Bombay Presidency," *Quarterly Journal of the Poona Sarvajanik Sabha* 1, no. 2 (1878): 13.

51 "Famine Narrative no. IV," *Quarterly Journal of the Poona Sarvajanik Sabha*, 1 no. 4 (1878): 64.

52 Richard Temple, "Report of the Mission to the Famine-Stricken Districts of the Madras Presidency in 1877," Pros. No. 19 (June 1877), Proceedings of the Department of Revenue, Agriculture, and Commerce (Famine Branch), Temple MSS Eur F86/178.

53 Pros. No. 17 (January 12, 1877), Proceedings of the Department of Revenue, Agriculture, and Commerce (Famine Branch), National Archives, New Delhi.

54 Pros. No. 27 (January 16, 1877), Proceedings of the Department of Revenue, Agriculture, and Commerce (Famine Branch), National Archives, New Delhi.

55 Pros No. 14 (January 25, 1877), Proceedings of the Department of Revenue, Agriculture, and Commerce (Famine Branch), National Archives, New Delhi.

56 Resolution by the Government of India Department of Revenue, Agriculture, and Commerce, January 16, 1877, Temple MSS Eur F86/177.

57 See, for example, "Second Famine Narrative," *Quarterly Journal of the Poona Sarvajanik Sabha* 1, no. 1 (1878): 13–21.

58 Resolution by the Government of India Department of Revenue, Agriculture, and Commerce, January 16, 1877, Temple MSS Eur F86/177.

59 Lewis McIver, *Imperial Census of 1881: Operations and Results in the Presidency of Madras, Report*, vol. 1 (Madras: Government Press, 1883), 9.

60 Currie, "British Colonial Policy," 25.

61 John C. Caldwell, "Malthus and the Less Developed World: The Pivotal Role of India," *Population and Development Review* 24 (1998): 676–77.

62 John Stuart Mill, *Principles of Political Economy with Some of Their Applications to Social Philosophy* (London: Standard Library, 1848), 252, quoted in Caldwell, "Malthus," 679.

63 Catherine Gallagher, "The Body versus the Social Body in the Works of Thomas Malthus and Henry Mayhew," in *The Making of the Modern Body*, ed. Catherine Gallagher and Thomas Laqueur (Berkeley: University of California Press, 1987), 85.

64 Caldwell, "Malthus," 677.

65 Mervyn Nicholson, "The Eleventh Commandment: Sex and Spirit in Wollstonecraft and Malthus," *Journal of the History of Ideas* 51, no. 3 (July–September 1990): 412.

66 Alison Bashford, *Global Population: History, Geopolitics, and Life on Earth* (New York: Columbia University Press, 2014), 44–52.

67 Viceroy Lytton, in Legislative Council Proceedings, 1877, vol. 16, p. 588, quoted in S. Ambirajan, "Malthusian Population Theory and Indian Famine Policy in the Nineteenth Century," *Population Studies* 30, no. 1 (1976): 6.

68 Indian Famine Commission, *Report of the Indian Famine Commission, Part I, Famine Relief* (London: G. E. Eyre and W. Spottiswoode, 1880), 34.

69 Guha, *Health and Population*, 15.

70 James Caird, *Report to Her Majesty's Secretary of State on the Condition of India* (London: Harrison and Sons, 1879), 14–15, 4, Correspondence of Sir James Caird, 1878–1881, India Office Records and Private Papers, British Library (hereafter cited as Caird MSS), IOR H796.

71 Lord Borthwick to James Caird, November 13, 1880, Caird MSS.

72 For discussion of this scholarship, see Mytheli Sreenivas, "Sexuality and Modern Imperialism," in *A Global History of Sexuality: The Modern Era*, ed. Robert M. Buffington, Eithne Luibhéid, and Donna J. Guy (Hoboken, NJ: Wiley Blackwell, 2014), 57–88.

73 Louis Mallet to James Caird, n.d., Caird MSS.

74 Sir George Couper, confidential memo to Lord Ripon on famine expenses, June 24, 1881, Ripon Papers, Adds. MSS. 43, 615, pp. 27–31, quoted in Ambirajan, "Malthusian Population Theory," 8, 9.

75 Indian Famine Commission, *Report*, 35.

76 "Financial Statement," in Parliamentary Papers, 1881, vol. 68, p. 17, quoted in Sheldon Watts, *Epidemics and History: Disease, Power and Imperialism* (New Haven, CT: Yale University Press, 1997), 203.

77 "Over-Population and Marriage Customs," *Quarterly Journal of the Poona Sarvajanik Sabha* 1, no. 7 (1878): 26. In this passage, as elsewhere in the text, there is a slippage between "Hindu" and "Indian," whereby the prepuberty marriage of upper-caste Hindus stands in for "Indian" conjugality as a whole.

In this conflation, the article anticipates the nationalist politics around the age of consent in the late nineteenth century.

78 T. V. Parvate, *Mahadev Govind Ranade: A Biography* (New York: Asia Publishing House, 1963), 97.

79 "Over-Population and Marriage Customs," 26.

80 Antoinette Burton, "From Child Bride to 'Hindoo Lady': Rukhmabai and the Debate on Sexual Respectability in Imperial Britain," *American Historical Review* 103, no. 4 (October 1998): 1125; Stanley A. Wolpert, *Tilak and Gokhale: Revolution and Reform in the Making of Modern India* (Berkeley: University of California Press, 1962), 46.

81 "Over-Population and Marriage Customs," 24. The author thus calls for a "scheme of colonization, organized and supported by the state, to take off all the surplus population" (30).

82 "Over-Population and Marriage Customs," 25.

83 "Over-Population and Marriage Customs," 29.

84 "Over-Population and Marriage Customs," 27–28.

85 "Over-Population and Marriage Customs," 32.

86 Mahadev Govind Ranade, "Indian Political Economy," in *Ranade's Economic Writings*, ed. Bipan Chandra (New Delhi: Gian Publishing House, 1990), 322–49; Manu Goswami, *Producing India: From Colonial Economy to National Space* (Chicago: University of Chicago Press, 2004), 210–31.

87 Behramji M. Malabari, *Infant Marriage and Enforced Widowhood in India* (Bombay: Voice of India, 1887), 1.

88 Malabari, *Infant Marriage*, 2.

89 Malabari, *Infant Marriage*, 2.

90 Keshavlal Madhavdas, comment in Malabari, *Infant Marriage*, 38–39.

91 Gopalrao Hari Deshmukh, comment in Malabari, *Infant Marriage*, 31.

92 M. G. Ranade, comment in Malabari, *Infant Marriage*, 15.

93 Tanika Sarkar, *Hindu Wife, Hindu Nation: Community, Religion, and Cultural Nationalism* (Bloomington: Indiana University Press, 2002).

94 Dadabhai Naoroji, *Poverty and Un-British Rule in India* (London: Swan Sonnenschein, 1901), 341.

95 Naoroji, *Poverty and Un-British Rule*, 191.

96 Naoroji, *Poverty and Un-British Rule*, 191.

97 This is not to suggest that bodies were unimportant to *Poverty and Un-British Rule*, which employed gothic narratives about healthy and diseased bodies to make its arguments about the drain of wealth. Sukanya Banerjee, *Becoming Imperial Citizens: Indians in the Late-Victorian Empire* (Durham, NC: Duke University Press, 2010), 36–74.

98 *The Queen v. Charles Bradlaugh and Annie Besant (Specially Reported)* (London: Freethought, n.d.), 61.

99 *Queen v. Charles Bradlaugh*, 28.

100 Annie Besant, "The Malthusian League," *National Reformer*, July 15, 1877.

101 Annie Besant, "The Fight Before Us," *National Reformer*, July 29, 1877.

102 Besant, *Law of Population*, 32–37.

103 Anne Taylor, *Annie Besant: A Biography* (Oxford: Oxford University Press, 1992), 121.

104 Norman E. Himes, *Medical History of Contraception* (New York: Gamut, 1963), 249–50.

105 Rosanna Ledbetter, *A History of the Malthusian League, 1877–1927* (Columbus: Ohio State University Press, 1976), 68.

106 Besant, *Law of Population*, 16, 25.

107 Besant, "England, India, and Afghanistan," *National Reformer*, October 20, 1878.

108 Barbara Taylor, *Eve and the New Jerusalem: Socialism and Feminism in the Nineteenth Century* (New York: Pantheon Books, 1983), 53.

109 For discussion of Victorian feminists' refusal to engage with birth control and sexual questions, see Philippa Levine, *Feminist Lives in Victorian England: Private Roles and Public Commitment* (Oxford: Basil Blackwell, 1990), 91–92.

110 Vernon, *Hunger*, 17–40.

111 Mytheli Sreenivas, "Birth Control in the Shadow of Empire: The Trials of Annie Besant, 1877–1878," *Feminist Studies* 41, no. 3 (2015): 525–33.

112 For example, *Madras Mail*, July 12, 1877, July 19, 1877, and March 7, 1878; *Pioneer* (Allahabad), July 13, 1877.

113 *Philosophic Inquirer* (n.d.), quoted in "Neo-Malthusians in Hindostan," *Malthusian* 6 (July 1879): 47.

114 *Malthusian* 6 (July 1879): 131.

115 The League listed fourteen vice presidents in 1880, and Mudaliar was one of four from outside England. He was still listed in 1908 and was the only representative from the British Empire. Ledbetter, *Malthusian League*, 64, 68.

116 Veritas [pseud.], "The Population Question in Hindostan," *Philosophic Inquirer* (n.d.), repr. in *Malthusian* 28 (May 1881): 218.

117 Veritas [pseud.], "The Population Question in Hindostan (Continuation)," *Philosophic Inquirer* (n.d.), repr. in *Malthusian* 30 (July 1881): 233.

118 Ledbetter, *Malthusian League*, 192.

119 S. Anandhi, "Reproductive Bodies and Regulated Sexuality: Birth Control Debates in Early 20th Century Tamil Nadu," in *A Question of Silence? The Sexual Economies of Modern India*, ed. Mary E. John and Janaki Nair (New Delhi: Kali for Women, 1998), 141.

120 Annie Besant, *Theosophy and the Law of Population* (Benaras: Theosophical Publishing Society, 1896), 12, 12, 11.

121 Goswami, *Producing India*, 210.

122 For example, M. G. Ranade, *Essays on Indian Economics: A Collection of Essays and Speeches* (Madras: G. A. Natesan, 1906).

CHAPTER 2: FERTILITY, SOVEREIGNTY, AND THE GLOBAL COLOR LINE

1 *Directory of the City Health and Baby Week*, comp. Corporation of Madras (Madras: Current Thought, n.d.).

2 *Directory*, s.vv. "Rajdosan," and "Jeevamrutam."

3   *Directory*, s.vv. "Maternity and Child Welfare."

4   In addition to age categories up to three years, the "best baby of the whole show" was divided into: "Best Musalman baby; Best Adi Dravida Baby; Best Anglo-Indian Baby; Best Indian Christian Baby; Best European Baby; Best Brahmin Baby; Best Non-Brahmin (Hindu); Best Baby of the Corporation C.W.S.; best twins and triplets." *Directory*, 115.

5   Barbara Ramusack, "Bonnie Babes and Modern Mothers: Baby Weeks in Madras" (paper presented at the 36th Annual Conference on South Asia, University of Wisconsin, Madison, WI, October 2007); Philippa Levine, "Imperial Encounters," in *Reproduction: Antiquity to the Present Day*, ed. Nick Hopwood, Rebecca Flemming, and Lauren Kassell (Cambridge: Cambridge University Press, 2018): 485–98.

6   *Directory*, s.v. "Messages," 5.

7   *Directory*, s.v. "Messages," 7.

8   *Directory*, s.v. "Messages," 7.

9   Katherine Mayo, *Mother India* (New York: Harcourt, Brace, 1927), 22, 94.

10   Mrinalini Sinha, *Specters of Mother India: The Global Restructuring of an Empire* (Durham, NC: Duke University Press, 2006), 2; Mrinalini Sinha, ed. *Mother India: Selections from the Controversial 1927 Text* (Ann Arbor: University of Michigan Press, 2000), 55.

11   Alison Bashford, *Global Population: History, Geopolitics and Life on Earth* (New York: Columbia University Press, 2014), 18.

12   Mayo, *Mother India*, 32.

13   Mayo, *Mother India*, 12.

14   Rahul Nair, "The Construction of a 'Population Problem' in Colonial India 1919–1947," *Journal of Imperial and Commonwealth History* 39, no. 2 (2011): 233–42.

15   Sinha, *Specters of Mother India*, 74.

16   Mayo, *Mother India*, 371.

17   Sinha, *Specters of Mother India*, 66–73, 95–97.

18   Marilyn Lake and Henry Reynolds, *Drawing the Global Color Line: White Men's Countries and the International Challenge of Racial Equality* (Cambridge: Cambridge University Press, 2008).

19   DuBois made this statement at a meeting of the Pan-African Congress in London in 1900 and elaborated further in *The Souls of Black Folk* (1903). Lake and Reynolds, *Global Color Line*, 1–2.

20   Mayo, *Mother India*, 379, 380, 408.

21   Hugh Tinker, *A New System of Slavery: The Export of Indian Labor Overseas, 1830–1920* (London: Oxford University Press, 1974), 367–78.

22   Uma Nehru, *Mother India aur uska jawab* (Allahabad: Hindustan, 1928), 67–68, quoted and translated from Hindi by Sinha, *Specters of Mother India*, 124.

23   Radhakamal Mukherjee, *Migrant Asia* ([Rome?]: Tipografia I. Failly, 1936), 9–10.

24   Mukherjee, *Migrant Asia*, especially chaps. 5–6.

25   I understand this racialization in the context of the book's publication in English and Italian by Corrado Gini, an Italian demographer and eugenicist.

Gini, a supporter of Italian fascism and an associate of Mussolini's, first met Mukherjee at a gathering of the International Union for the Scientific Investigation of Population Problems and provided an introduction to *Migrant Asia*. Bashford, *Global Population*, 141.

26 Mukherjee, *Migrant Asia*, 57.

27 Mukherjee, *Migrant Asia*, 79; Aileen Moreton-Robinson, *The White Possessive: Property, Power, and Indigenous Sovereignty* (Minneapolis: University of Minnesota Press, 2015).

28 Mukherjee, *Migrant Asia*, 15.

29 Radhakamal Mukherjee, *Food Planning for Four Hundred Millions* (London: Macmillan, 1938).

30 Mukherjee, *Food Planning*, 221.

31 Sanjam Ahluwalia includes Mukherjee among a group of Indian eugenicists and neo-Malthusians that linked birth control to the problem of overpopulation and drew upon caste and community tensions in vilifying the reproduction of Muslims and lower castes. *Reproductive Restraints: Birth Control in India, 1877–1947* (Urbana: University of Illinois Press, 2008), chap. 1, especially 39–40. Alison Bashford and Rahul Nair, by contrast, explore the anticolonial aspects of his work. Bashford, *Global Population*, 41–42; Rahul Nair, "The Discourse on Population in India, 1870–1960" (PhD diss., University of Pennsylvania, 2006), 79–85.

32 T. S. Chokkalingam, *Piraja urpattiyaik kattuppatuttutal* [Restraining population growth] (Madras: Tamil Nadu Power, 1925), 4. Unless otherwise noted, all translations from Tamil are my own.

33 P. K. Wattal, *The Population Problem in India: A Census Study* (Bombay: Bennett, Coleman, 1934), 138.

34 Mohandas Gandhi, *Self-Restraint vs. Self-Indulgence*, 3rd ed. (Ahmedabad: Navajivan, 1928), 54, quoted in Joseph S. Alter, *Gandhi's Body: Sex, Diet, and the Politics of Nationalism* (Philadelphia: University of Pennsylvania Press, 2000), 11.

35 Mohandas Gandhi, *The Collected Works of Mahatma Gandhi*, vol. 12 (Delhi: Publication Division, Ministry of Information and Broadcasting, Government of India, 1964), 136, quoted in Alter, *Gandhi's Body*, 11.

36 Indian Legislative Assembly Debates, September 23, 1929, vol. 5, p. 1252.

37 Madras Legislative Council Debates, March 27, 1928, vol. 42, no. 1, pp. 32, 37, 32.

38 Honorary Secretary of the Women's Indian Association and the Chairwoman of the All India Women's Conference to Rai Sahib Harbilas Sarda, December 1927, All India Women's Conference Papers, Nehru Memorial Library, New Delhi (hereafter cited as AIWC Papers), file 5.

39 Honorary Secretary of the Women's Indian Association and the Chairwoman of the All India Women's Conference to Rai Sahib Harbilas Sarda, December 1927, AIWC Papers, file 5.

40 Age of Consent Committee, *Report of the Age of Consent Committee, 1928–1929* (Calcutta: Government of India Central Publication Branch, 1929), 168.

In practice, the new minimum marriage age was difficult to enforce, and the state showed little political will in doing so.

41   Throughout the 1930s, calls for state-supported birth control clinics were debated and rejected in Karachi, Delhi, and Ahmedabad municipalities; in the Madras Legislative Council; and in the United Provinces Legislative Council. Sarah Hodges, *Contraception, Colonialism and Commerce: Birth Control in South India, 1920–1940* (New York: Routledge, 2016), 22–25. At the all-India level, a resolution in the Council of State calling for the government to "take practical steps to check the increase in population in India" failed in 1935. A similar resolution calling for the government to "popularize methods of birth control" in view of the "alarming growth of population" passed by a single vote in 1940. Ahluwalia, *Reproductive Restraints*, 127.

42   Sumit Sarkar, *Modern India, 1885–1947* (New York: St. Martin's, 1989), 257–61.

43   All India Women's Conference, 7th Session (Lucknow, December 28 1932–January 1, 1933), All India Women's Conference Papers, Margaret Cousins Library, Sarojini House, New Delhi (hereafter cited as AIWC Papers, Cousins Library), 90.

44   All India Women's Conference, 7th Session (Lucknow, December 28, 1932–January 1, 1933), AIWC Papers, Cousins Library, 93.

45   Previous Indian censuses had shown that the population had increased by 13.2 percent in 1881–91 and by 7.1 percent in 1901–11. Nair, "Population in India," 7n2.

46   Nair, "Population in India," 178.

47   Government of India, *Census of India, 1931*, vol. 1, 32, quoted in Nair, "Population in India," 184n12.

48   Nair, "Population Problem," 233–39.

49   Philippa Levine and Alison Bashford, "Introduction: Eugenics and the Modern World," in *The Oxford Handbook of the History of Eugenics*, ed. Alison Bashford and Philippa Levine (Oxford: Oxford University Press, 2010), 3.

50   Laura Briggs, *Reproducing Empire: Race, Sex, Science, and U.S. Imperialism in Puerto Rico* (Berkeley: University of California Press, 2002), 99.

51   Sarah Hodges, "South Asia's Eugenic Past," in Bashford and Levine, *History of Eugenics*, 228.

52   All India Women's Conference, 6th Session (Madras, December 28, 1931–January 1, 1932), AIWC Papers, Cousins Library, 81a.

53   All India Women's Conference, 6th Session (Madras, December 28, 1931–January 1, 1932), AIWC Papers, Cousins Library, 83. Reddi remained critical of birth control throughout her political life, but she acknowledged in 1952 that "limitation of the family" could be achieved by birth control only if "self-control" was not possible. Muthulakshmi Reddi, "Message to the Third International Conference of Planned Parenthood," Muthulakshmi Reddi Papers, Nehru Memorial Library, New Delhi, s. 197.

54   All India Women's Conference, 6th Session (Madras, December 28, 1931–January 1, 1932), AIWC Papers, Cousins Library.

55 Barbara Ramusack, "Embattled Advocates: The Debate over Birth Control in India, 1920–1940," *Journal of Women's History* 1, no. 2 (Fall 1989), 41–43.

56 All India Women's Conference, 7th Session (Lucknow, December 28, 1932–January 1, 1933), AIWC Papers, Cousins Library, 95.

57 All India Women's Conference, 7th Session (Lucknow, December 28, 1932–January 1, 1933), AIWC Papers, Cousins Library, 90.

58 Ahluwalia, *Reproductive Restraints*, chap. 3.

59 All India Women's Conference, 6th Session (Madras, December 28, 1931–January 1, 1932), AIWC Papers, Cousins Library, 86.

60 All India Women's Conference, 8th Session (Calcutta, December 24, 1933–January 2, 1934), AIWC Papers, Cousins Library, 137.

61 Sanger first learned of Indian birth control efforts through contact with the men involved in contraceptive advocacy, namely N. S. Phadke, R. D. Karve, and A. P. Pillay. In the mid-1920s, she temporarily had another channel to India via Agnes Smedley, a radical activist who had worked briefly with the birth control movement in New York, and who lived intermittently with the Indian revolutionary Virendranath Chattopadhyay in Berlin. Sanger's link to the AIWC was Margaret Cousins, who had been a founding member of the AIWC, and whom Sanger had met in New York in 1932. Ramusack, "Embattled Advocates," 37–38, 48.

62 Ahluwalia, *Reproductive Restraints*, 59–60.

63 For example, a letter from Sanger on behalf of the US National Committee on Federal Legislation for Birth Control to the Mexican feminist Amalia González Caballero de Castillo Ledón references the AIWC's resolution on birth control. Sanger to González Caballero, August 27, 1936, Archivo Particular Amalia González Caballero, Secretaría de las Relaciones Exteriores, Mexico City, caja 4, expediente 55. My thanks to Katherine Marino for sharing this information with me.

64 Quoted in Sinha, *Specters of Mother India*, 107.

65 Dorothy Roberts, *Killing the Black Body: Race, Reproduction, and the Meaning of Liberty* (New York: Vintage, 1998), chap. 2.

66 Sanger and How-Martyn addressed a combined total of 105 public meetings. Sanger did not limit herself to women's organizations but joined forces with the Madras Neo-Malthusian League, which hosted her visit in that city, as well as with A. P. Pillay's clinic in Bombay. Margaret Sanger, "Newsletter to Friends, March 1936," MSP, series III (subseries 1—Correspondence). For a record of Sanger's conversation with Gandhi, as reported by Sanger's secretary Anna Jane Philips, see "Gandhi and Mrs. Sanger Debate Birth Control," *Asia* (November 1936), 698–703, MSP, series III (subseries 5—Family/Miscellany).

67 Reena Nanda, *Kamaladevi Chattopadhyay: A Biography* (Oxford: Oxford University Press, 2002), 11–17.

68 Kamaladevi Chattopadhyay, "Women's Movement in India," in *The Awakening of Indian Women*, by Kamaladevi Chattopadhyay and others (Madras: Everyman's Press, 1939), 32–33.

69   Chattopadhyay, "Women's Movement in India," 33.

70   Chattopadhyay, "Women's Movement in India," 34–35.

71   Hodges, "South Asia's Eugenic Past," 230.

72   Hodges, "South Asia's Eugenic Past," 229, 236.

73   Statement of object of the journal *Marriage Hygiene* 3, no. 3 (February 1937).

74   Wattal, *Population Problem in India*, 99.

75   "Poverty of Mother India," *Madras Birth Control Bulletin* 1, no. 5 (September–October 1931): 51.

76   The clinic aimed to supply a range of contraceptive methods but promoted the Duofoam powder supplied by Margaret Sanger when she visited Madras. "Birth Control Clinic for Madras City," *Madras Birth Control Bulletin* 8, no. 3 (July–September 1938): 42. The clinic did not develop a large clientele and failed to obtain a grant from the Madras Corporation. Consequently, it closed just six months after its opening. Hodges, *Contraception, Colonialism and Commerce*, 72.

77   Madras Neo-Malthusian League, *The Best Birth Control Methods* (Madras: Madras Neo-Malthusian League, 1929), 1, 7. Translated from Tamil by D. Aravindan.

78   "New Year Greetings," *Madras Birth Control Bulletin* 1, no. 6 (November–December 1931): 61.

79   Murari S. Krishnamurthi Ayyar, *Population and Birth Control in India* (Madras: People's Printing and Publishing House, n.d.), 73.

80   Ahluwalia, *Reproductive Restraints*, 38.

81   Krishnamurthi Ayyar, *Population and Birth Control in India*, 73.

82   P. K. Wattal, "Population Trends in East and West," *Marriage Hygiene* 3, no. 3 (February 1937): 217.

83   Charu Gupta, *Sexuality, Obscenity, Community: Women, Muslims and the Hindu Public in Colonial India* (London: Palgrave, 2001), 298–321.

84   E. V. Ramasami, "Karppatatai" [Birth control], *Kuti Aracu* 5, no. 45 (April 6, 1930): 10.

85   See also V. Geetha and S. V. Rajadurai, *Towards a Non-Brahmin Millennium: From Iyothee Thass to Periyar*, 2nd rev. ed. (Calcutta: Samya, 2008), chap. 10.

86   Uma Ganesan, "Gender and Caste: Self Respect Movement in the Madras Presidency, 1925–1950" (PhD diss., University of Cincinnati, 2011), 132.

87   S. Nilavati, "Kattolikkarum karuttatai etirppum" [Catholics and the opposition to birth control], *Kuti Aracu* 9, no. 22 (November 19, 1933): 4.

88   Indrani Balasubramaniam, "Karppatatai" [Birth control], *Kuti Aracu* 9, no. 18 (October 22, 1933): 5.

89   T. D. Gopal, "Times When Women Should Not Conceive," in *Karppatci, allatu pillai perrai atakki alutal* [Controlling pregnancy, or preventing the birth of children] (Erode: Kuti Aracu Press, 1936), 47. For further discussion of Gopal's writing on birth control in *Kuti Aracu*, see Ganesan, "Gender and Caste," 132–33.

90   Editorial, "Karppatatai" [Birth control], *Kuti Aracu* 6, no. 44 (March 1, 1931): 4.

91 S. Anandhi discusses the uneven feminist consciousness in the Self Respect movement in "The Women's Question in the Dravidian Movement, c. 1925–1948," *Social Scientist* 16, no. 5/6 (1991): 24–41; S. Anandhi, "Reproductive Bodies and Regulated Sexuality: Birth Control Debates in Early 20th Century Tamil Nadu," in *A Question of Silence? The Sexual Economies of Modern India*, ed. Mary E. John and Janaki Nair (New Delhi: Kali for Women, 1998): 139–66.

92 Shailaja Paik, *Dalit Women's Education in Modern India: Double Discrimination* (London: Routledge, 2014), 303. See also M. P. Mangudkar, ed. *Dr. Ambedkar and Family Planning* (Pune: Sangam, 1976).

93 For example, "Opposition to Birth Control," *Kuti Aracu* 11, no. 26 (February 9, 1936): 5.

CHAPTER 3: FEMINISM, NATIONAL DEVELOPMENT, AND TRANSNATIONAL
FAMILY PLANNING

1 Dhanvanthi Rama Rau, *An Inheritance: The Memoirs of Dhanvanthi Rama Rau* (London: Heinemann, 1977), 243.

2 Rama Rau, *An Inheritance*, 243.

3 Beryl Suitters, *Be Brave and Angry: Chronicles of the International Planned Parenthood Federation* (London: International Planned Parenthood Federation, 1973), 56.

4 Following from this argument about co-optation, scholars of Indian feminism have had little to say about the 1940s and 1950s. For example, Radha Kumar, *The History of Doing: An Illustrated Account of Movements for Women's Rights and Feminism in India, 1800–1990* (New Delhi: Kali for Women, 1993); Mary John, "Feminist Perspectives on Family and Marriage: A Historical View," *Economic and Political Weekly* 40, no. 8 (2005): 712–15. However, Mary John questions historiographic assumptions about the "quietism of women's movements post-independence," suggesting that this may have been "more apparent than real." Mary John, "Gender, Development and the Women's Movement: Problems for a History of the Present," in *Signposts: Gender Issues in Post-Independence India*, ed. Rajeswari Sunder Rajan (New Delhi: Kali/ Zubaan, 2000), 108.

5 This assumption underlies accounts of population control that center American and some Indian experts but do not consider women's activities in organizations like the AIWC and FPAI. These accounts also tend to center policy but do not consider its implementation. For example, Gyan Prakash, *Emergency Chronicles: Indira Gandhi and Democracy's Turning Point* (Princeton, NJ: Princeton University Press, 2019), 260–67.

6 Historians of Indian population control have shown the continuities between the 1950s and later periods. For example, Mohan Rao, *From Population Control to Reproductive Health: Malthusian Arithmetic* (New Delhi: Sage, 2004); Matthew Connelly, "Population Control in India: Prologue to the Emergency Period," *Population and Development Review* 32, no. 4

(December 2006): 629–67. However, the particular status of the Emergency (1975–77), as I discuss in chapter 4, tends to overshadow the specifics of earlier decades, especially in mainstream discourse.

7   Of course, not all women's activists supported population control, and leftist and peasant movements raised a postindependence "women's question" in different ways.

8   The question of what motivates historical actors is always complex. Debate about motivation animates feminist scholarship about reproductive politics, most notably in ongoing controversies about whether Margaret Sanger's willingness to connect birth control to racist and eugenicist ideologies came from sincerely held belief or from political expediency. Here, I draw inspiration from Dorothy Roberts's considered analysis of Sanger, which recognizes the difficulties of ascribing motivation while also emphasizing the impact of Sanger's decision to connect birth control to eugenicist motivations. *Killing the Black Body: Race, Reproduction and the Meaning of Liberty* (New York: Vintage, 1998), 79–81. Similarly, I recognize that Indian feminists' motivations may have differed from those of some other development planners, but my emphasis here is on the material and discursive impact of their actions, which helped to make top-down family planning that targeted women central to programs of national development.

9   National Planning Committee, *Woman's Role in Planned Economy (Report of the Sub-committee)* (Bombay: Vora, 1947). The evidence is not definitive, but I follow Nirmala Banerjee in suggesting that "Durgabai Joshi" may be the person known as Durgabai Deshmukh, after she married C. D. Deshmukh in 1953. Nirmala Banerjee, "Whatever Happened to the Dreams of Modernity? The Nehruvian Era and Woman's Position," *Economic and Political Weekly* 33, no. 17 (1998): WS6.

10   Maitrayee Chaudhuri, "Citizens, Workers and Emblems of Culture: An Analysis of the First Plan Document on Women," in *Social Reform, Sexuality and the State*, ed. Patricia Uberoi (New Delhi: Sage, 1998), 213.

11   National Planning Committee, *Woman's Role*, 119. The "joint family" references a unit composed of generations of patrilineal kin, often parents, their adult sons and spouses, and grandchildren.

12   National Planning Committee, *Woman's Role*, 33.

13   National Planning Committee, *Woman's Role*, 174–75.

14   National Planning Committee, *Report of the Sub-committee on Population*, 2nd ed., ed. K. T. Shah (Bombay: Vora, 1949).

15   National Planning Committee, *National Health*, ed. K. T. Shah (Bombay: Vora, 1948), 19.

16   Hansa Mehta, *Roshni* 1, no. 1 (February 1946): 19–20.

17   "Draft of Indian Woman's Charter of Rights and Duties," *Roshni* 1, no. 5 (June 1946): 24.

18   Anasuyabai Kale, "Presidential Address," *Roshni* 3, no. 1 (February 1948): 15.

19   Shareefah Hamid Ali, "Status of Women: Review and Suggested Programme," *Roshni* 8, no. 1 (June 1953): 7.

20 Maitrayee Chaudhuri, "Introduction," in *Feminism in India*, ed. Maitrayee Chaudhuri (London: Zed Books, 2004), xvii–xviii. See also Mary John, "Gender and Development in India," in Chaudhuri, *Feminism in India*, 251.

21 Avabai Wadia, *The Light Is Ours: Memoirs and Movements* (London: International Planned Parenthood Federation, 2001), 124.

22 Wadia, *Light Is Ours*, 127, 124.

23 Emily Rook-Koepsel, "Constructing Women's Citizenship: The Local, National, and Global Civics Lessons of Rajkumari Amrit Kaur," *Journal of Women's History* 27, no. 3 (2015): 154–75.

24 Mithan Lam was involved in the FPAI from its earliest stages, and in addition to being vice president, she served as honorary treasurer. Wadia, *Light Is Ours*, 518, 521. She served as AIWC president from 1961–62.

25 Wadia, *Light Is Ours*, 522.

26 Wadia, *Light Is Ours*, 518.

27 Rama Rau, *An Inheritance*, 246.

28 Wadia, *Light Is Ours*, 496.

29 Rama Rau, *An Inheritance*, 247.

30 Dr. Hem Sanwal to Marie Stopes, May 5, 1953, Marie Stopes Papers, Wellcome Library, London, PP/MCS/A.313, India: various correspondents A–W, c. 1930–1953.

31 Wadia, *Light Is Ours*, 133.

32 Wadia, *Light Is Ours*, 521.

33 Rama Rau, *An Inheritance*, 253, 252.

34 Wadia, *Light Is Ours*, 505.

35 Rama Rau, *An Inheritance*, 253; Wadia, *Light Is Ours*, 505.

36 Rama Rau, *An Inheritance*, 253; Suitters, *Be Brave and Angry*, 45.

37 Alison Bashford, *Global Population: History, Geopolitics, and Life on Earth* (New York: Columbia University Press, 2014), 301–16.

38 Sunil Amrith, *Decolonizing International Health: India and Southeast Asia, 1930–1965* (London: Palgrave Macmillan, 2006), 96–98.

39 Wadia, *Light Is Ours*, 134–35.

40 Rama Rau to Sanger, September 5, 1951, Margaret Sanger Papers, Sophia Smith Collection, Smith College Libraries, Northampton, MA (hereafter cited as MSP), series III (subseries 1—Correspondence).

41 Rama Rau to Sanger, December 11, 1951, MSP, series III (subseries 1—Correspondence).

42 Rama Rau, *An Inheritance*, 260–61.

43 Elfriede Vembu to Sanger, February 21, 1952, MSP, series III (subseries 1—Correspondence).

44 Rama Rau to Sanger, September 27, 1952, MSP, series III (subseries 1—Correspondence).

45 Rama Rau, *An Inheritance*, 261.

46 Wadia, *Light Is Ours*, 127, 135.

47 Suitters, *Be Brave and Angry*, 48.

48   Rama Rau to Sanger, September 27, 1952, MSP, series III (subseries 1—Correspondence).

49   Suitters, *Be Brave and Angry*, 38–42.

50   Rama Rau to Sanger, September 4, 1952. Rama Rau quotes a letter from Dr. Conrad Van Emde Boas to Pillay. MSP, series III, subseries 1—Correspondence. See also Suitters, *Be Brave and Angry*, 48–49.

51   Sanger to Rama Rau, September 5, 1952, MSP, series III, subseries 1—Correspondence. The Dutch delegation was not alone in its critique. The Swedish representative (Elise Ottesen-Jensen), who would become the second IPPF president, was a proponent of sex education and critiqued the neo-Malthusian turn of the movement.

52   Suitters, *Be Brave and Angry*, 50–54.

53   Dhanvanthi Rama Rau, "Introduction," in *The Third International Conference on Planned Parenthood: Report of the Proceedings* (Bombay: Family Planning Association of India, 1952), iii.

54   Sanger and Rama Rau worked alongside a few others in shaping the agenda, including Abraham Stone and C. P. Blacker. Sanger to Rama Rau, July 1, 1952, MSP, series III, subseries 1—Correspondence.

55   Kamaladevi Chattopadhyay, "Address of Welcome," in *Third International Conference*, 7.

56   Chattopadhyay, "Address of Welcome," in *Third International Conference*, 8.

57   S. Chandrasekhar, *Hungry People and Empty Lands: An Essay on Population Problems and International Tensions* (London: G. Allen & Unwin, 1954).

58   Suitters, *Be Brave and Angry*, 56.

59   Government of India, Planning Commission, *The First Five Year Plan* (New Delhi: Government of India, 1953), 523, 88–89.

60   "Resolutions Passed at a Special Standing Committee Meeting in Delhi,", 1944, All India Women's Conference Papers, Nehru Memorial Library, New Delhi, reel 20 (files 315–27).

61   Rama Rau, *An Inheritance*, 211.

62   For example: "Mothers Who Starve," *Roshni* 1, no. 9 (October 1946): 31. On hunger in Indian public debate, see Benjamin R. Siegel, *Hungry Nation: Food, Famine, and the Making of Modern India* (Cambridge: Cambridge University Press, 2018).

63   R. A. Gopalaswami, *Census of India 1951*, vol. 1, part 1-A, *Report* (New Delhi: Government of India, 1953), 3.

64   Gopalaswami, *Census of India 1951*, 87.

65   Nirmala Banerjee estimates the informal sector of the economy provided around 90 percent of total employment in 1951. "The Unorganized Sector and the Planner," in *Economy, Society and Polity: Essays in the Political Economy of Indian Planning in Honour of Professor Bhabatosh Datta*, ed. Amiya Kumar Bagchi (New Delhi: Oxford University Press, 1988), 75. For the implications of planning's focus on the formal sector, see Taylor C. Sherman, "'A New Type of Revolution': Socialist Thought in India, 1940s–1960s," *Postcolonial Studies* 21, no. 4 (2018): 485–504.

66 This national commitment to development also had colonial and transnational roots: David Ludden, "India's Development Regime," in *Colonialism and Culture*, ed. Nicholas B. Dirks (Ann Arbor: University of Michigan Press, 1992): 247–88; Subir Sinha, "Lineages of the Developmentalist State: Transnationality and Village India, 1900–1965," *Comparative Studies in Society and History* 50, no. 1 (2008): 57–90.

67 Chaudhuri, "Introduction," xvii–xviii.

68 Pranav Jani, *Decentering Rushdie: Cosmopolitanism and the Indian Novel in English* (Columbus: Ohio State University Press, 2010), 56.

69 Francine R. Frankel, *India's Political Economy, 1947–2004: The Gradual Revolution*, 2nd ed. (New Delhi: Oxford University Press, 2005), 71–112.

70 Partha Chatterjee, "Development Planning and the Indian State," in *State and Politics in India*, ed. Partha Chatterjee (Delhi: Oxford University Press, 1997), 283–86.

71 Karl Ittmann, *A Problem of Great Importance: Population, Race, and Power in the British Empire, 1918–1973* (Berkeley: University of California Press, 2013), 170.

72 Ittmann, *Problem of Great Importance*, 171.

73 Ittmann, *Problem of Great Importance*, 170.

74 Government of India, *First Five Year Plan*, 522.

75 Sunil Amrith, "Political Culture of Health in India: A Historical Perspective," *Economic and Political Weekly* 42, no. 2 (January 13–19, 2007): 117.

76 Government of India, *First Five Year Plan*, 522.

77 Amrit Kaur to Brock Chisholm, January 25, 1952, WHO Archives, Second Generation files (WHO.2), GH/12, cited in Amrith, *Decolonizing International Health*, 96.

78 Sanjam Ahluwalia and Daksha Parmar, "From Gandhi to Gandhi: Contraceptive Technologies and Sexual Politics in Postcolonial India, 1947–1977," in *Reproductive States: Global Perspectives on the Invention and Implementation of Population Policy*, ed. Rickie Solinger and Mie Nakachi (Oxford: Oxford University Press, 2016), 131–32.

79 Amrith, *Decolonizing International Health*, 96.

80 Amrith, *Decolonizing International Health*, 97.

81 Ahluwalia and Parmar, "From Gandhi to Gandhi," 131–32.

82 Amrith, *Decolonizing International Health*, 97.

83 The opposition came from the Vatican, Roman Catholic–dominated countries, and Communist countries. Bashford, *Global Population*, 361–62.

84 Ahluwalia and Parmar, "From Gandhi to Gandhi," 133.

85 Rama Rau to Sanger, December 11, 1951, MSP, series III, subseries 1—Correspondence; Suitters, *Be Brave and Angry*, 45.

86 Ahluwalia and Parmar, "From Gandhi to Gandhi," 132–33.

87 Stopes was critical of the rhythm method and was in contact with the FPAI about her contraceptive sponges. Marie Stopes to Elfriede Vembu, June 1952, Marie Stopes Papers, Wellcome Library, London, India, Pakistan, Ceylon, Hong Kong Correspondence 1952–54, PP/MCS/A.315.

88 Stone himself shared some of these doubts about the effectiveness of the rhythm method. Stone to Sanger, March 1, 1952, MSP, series III, subseries 1—Correspondence.

89 Rama Rau, *An Inheritance*, 259.

90 Susanne Klausen and Alison Bashford note the strange bedfellows among feminists, eugenicists, and neo-Malthusians in "Fertility Control: Eugenics, Neo-Malthusianism, and Feminism," in *The Oxford Handbook of the History of Eugenics*, ed. Alison Bashford and Philippa Levine (Oxford: Oxford University Press, 2010), 10.

CHAPTER 4: REGULATING REPRODUCTION IN THE ERA OF THE PLANETARY "POPULATION BOMB"

1 Information Service of India, "The Family Planning Program in India," in *The Population Crisis and the Use of World Resources*, ed. Stuart Mudd (Bloomington: Indiana University Press, 1964), 157.

2 S. K. Khan, "Report of Honorary Family Planning Education Leaders, 25 August 1960," All India Women's Conference Papers, Nehru Memorial Library, New Delhi (hereafter cited as AIWC Papers), subject file 430.

3 Gyan Prakash notes the mainstream view of the Emergency as an aberration and highlights the importance of understanding this period within a broader historical sweep. *Emergency Chronicles: Indira Gandhi and Democracy's Turning Point* (Princeton: Princeton University Press, 2019).

4 I use the term *subaltern* to reference nonelite women, who were marked as different from the middle-class family planner by virtue of class, caste, religious, and/or tribal/Adivasi identity.

5 Government of India, Planning Commission, *The First Five Year Plan* (Delhi: Publications Division, Ministry of Information and Broadcasting, 1952), 124, quoted in Nirmala Buch, "State Welfare Policy and Women, 1950–1975," *Economic and Political Weekly* 33, no. 17 (1998): WS19.

6 Durgabai Deshmukh, *Chintaman and I* (New Delhi: Allied Publishers Private, 1980), 60.

7 Deshmukh, *Chintaman and I*, 37.

8 Government of India, Planning Commission, *Second Five Year Plan* (Delhi: Government of India, 1956), 533.

9 Deshmukh, *Chintaman and I*, 38.

10 Address by Durgabai Deshmukh, in "Report of the 23rd Session of the AIWC" (Poona, May 2–5, 1953), 34, Margaret Cousins Library, Sarojini House, New Delhi; Resolutions of Group II on "Future Work of the Conference," in "Report of the 23rd Session of the AIWC" (Poona, May 2–5, 1953), 41, Margaret Cousins Library, Sarojini House, New Delhi.

11 Avabai Wadia, *The Light Is Ours: Memoirs and Movements* (London: International Planned Parenthood Federation, 2001), 520–21.

12 Branch Reports, in "Report of the 23rd Session of the AIWC" (Poona, May 2–5, 1953), 99–124, Margaret Cousins Library, Sarojini House, New Delhi.

13 Avabai Wadia, "Report of the Work of the Family Planning Association of India," in *Report of the Proceedings of the Sixth International Conference on Planned Parenthood* (London: International Planned Parenthood Federation, n.d.,), 359–61.

14 Padmini Sengupta, *Women Workers of India* (New York: Asia Publishing House, 1960), 274. For biographical information about Sengupta, see Barnita Bagchi, "Tracing Two Generations in Twentieth Century Indian Women's Education through Analysis of Literary Sources: Selected Writings by Padmini Sengupta," *Women's History Review* 29, no. 3 (2020): 465–79.

15 Padmini Sengupta, "Report of 8 August 1959," AIWC Papers, subject file 430.

16 K. Meenakshi Amma, "Report for the Month of April 1960," AIWC Papers, subject file 430.

17 P. L. Gupta, "Report for July–September 1959," AIWC Papers, subject file 430.

18 Krishna Agarwal, "Report of Work by Mrs. Krishna Agarwal in the Indore Region," AIWC Papers, reel 43, subject file 146.

19 "Report of the Family Planning Association of India from January 1961 to December 1963," USAID Mission to India/Public Health Division Records, National Archives and Records Administration, College Park, MD (hereafter cited as NARA), RG 286, entry P458: subject files 1961–1967, container 8.

20 Archana Venkatesh, "Women, Medicine and Nation-Building: The 'Lady Doctor' and Development in 20th Century South India," (PhD diss., Ohio State University, 2020).

21 Prem Lata Gupta, "Women's Role in Promotion of Family Planning and in Raising the Status of Women in India," in Bharatiya Grameen Mahila Sangh and Central Institute of Research and Training in Public Co-operation, "Status of Women and Family Planning in India" (unpublished report, n.d.), 2–7.

22 "Role of Voluntary Organizations in Family Planning," AIWC Papers, subject file 989.

23 Aleyamma George, "Speeches Delivered at the 31st Annual Session of the AIWC (December 1961)," AIWC Papers, reel 42, subject file 131.

24 Mrinalini Sinha, *Specters of Mother India: The Global Restructuring of an Empire* (Durham, NC: Duke University Press, 2006), 191–95.

25 Emily Rook-Koepsel, "Constructing Women's Citizenship: The Local, National, and Global Civics Lessons of Rajkumari Amrit Kaur," *Journal of Women's History* 27, no. 3 (2015): 160–61.

26 Rook-Koepsel, "Constructing Women's Citizenship," 156.

27 "Consolidated Report of Family Planning Education Work in the Year 1960 February to 1961 April," AIWC Papers, reel 43, subject file 146.

28 Visakha Dixit, Report, AIWC Papers, reel 43, subject file 146.

29 Aroti Dutt, Report, AIWC Papers, reel 43, subject file 146.

30 K. Meenakshi Amma, "Report for the Month of April 1960," AIWC Papers, subject file 430.

31 "Consolidated Report of Family Planning Education Work in the Year 1960 February to 1961 April," AIWC Papers, reel 43, subject file 146.

32 Hem Sanwal, "Report on the Work of January and February 1960," AIWC Papers, subject file 430. Emphasis mine.

33 Asha Nadkarni, *Eugenic Feminism: Reproductive Nationalism in the United States and India* (Minneapolis: University of Minnesota Press, 2014), 139. This was the case for the state's major development initiative in the 1950s, the Community Development Program. Kim Berry, "Lakshmi and the Scientific Housewife: A Transnational Account of Indian Women's Development and Production of an Indian Modernity," *Economic and Political Weekly* 38, no. 11 (2003): 1055–68.

34 Dhanvanthi Rama Rau, *An Inheritance: The Memoirs of Dhanvanthi Rama Rau* (London: Heinemann, 1977), 278.

35 Betsy Hartmann, *Reproductive Rights and Wrongs: The Global Politics of Population Control*, 3rd ed. (Chicago: Haymarket Books, 2016), 1–11.

36 Rama Rau, *An Inheritance*, 278–79.

37 Visalakshi Narayanswamy, Report of the Family Planning Work, in "All India Women's Conference Report" (Jan–Dec 1966), 57, Margaret Cousins Library, Sarojini House, New Delhi.

38 A. R. Adhav et al., "Methods of Communication in Family Planning in a Labour Area in Bombay City," Fifth All India Conference on Family Planning (Patna, January 17–22, 1964), USAID Mission to India/Public Health Division Records, NARA, RG 286, entry P458: subject files 1961–1967, container 8.

39 K. Meenakshi Amma, "Report for the Month of April 1960," AIWC Papers, subject file 430.

40 P. L. Gupta, "Report for July–September 1959," AIWC Papers, subject file 430.

41 A. R. Adhav et al., "Methods of Communication in Family Planning in a Labour Area in Bombay City," Fifth All India Conference on Family Planning (Patna, January 17–22, 1964), USAID Mission to India/Public Health Division Records, NARA, RG 286, entry P458: subject files 1961–1967, container 8.

42 Hem Sanwal, "Report on the Work of January and February 1960," AIWC Papers, subject file 430.

43 Rebecca Jane Williams, "Revisiting the Khanna Study: Population and Development in India, 1953–1960" (PhD diss., University of Warwick, 2013); Mahmood Mamdani, *The Myth of Population Control: Family, Caste and Class in an Indian Village* (New York: Monthly Review Press, 1972).

44 "Family Planning Seminar," February 28, 1966, AIWC Papers, subject file 842.

45 Sushila Nayar, "Inaugural Address," in *Proceedings of the Seminar on IUCD Nov 29–Dec 1, 1966*, ed. Somnath Roy (New Delhi: Central Family Planning Institute, n.d.), 10.

46 Bharatiya Grameen Mahila Sangh and Central Institute of Research and Training in Public Co-operation, "Status of Women and Family Planning in India" (unpublished report, n.d.).

47 Benjamin R. Siegel, *Hungry Nation: Food, Famine, and the Making of Modern India* (Cambridge: Cambridge University Press, 2018), chaps. 2 and 6.

48 Matthew Connelly, *Fatal Misconception: The Struggle to Control World Population* (Cambridge, MA: Belknap, 2009), 221–22.

49 Nayar, "Inaugural Address," in Roy, *Seminar on IUCD*.

50 *The Population Bomb: Is Voluntary Human Sterilization the Answer?*, Hugh Moore Fund NY (n.d., ca. 1960), Rockefeller Family Archives, Rockefeller Archives Center, Sleepy Hollow, NY (hereafter cited as RAC), record group 5, series 1, subseries 5, box 80, folder 670.

51 Paul R. Ehrlich, *The Population Bomb* (New York: Ballantine Books, 1968), 1.

52 Connelly, *Fatal Misconception*, 258–61.

53 Hartmann, *Reproductive Rights and Wrongs*; Rosalind Pollack Petchesky, "From Population Control to Reproductive Rights: Feminist Fault Lines," *Reproductive Health Matters* 3, no. 6 (November 1995): 152–61; Elena Gutiérrez, *Fertile Matters: The Politics of Mexican-Origin Women's Reproduction* (Austin: University of Texas Press, 2008).

54 Planned Parenthood–World Population Division, Population Council Collection, RAC, record group IV 3 B4. 5, box 107, folder 1997.

55 Edward M. Humberger, "Population Program Management: The Ford Foundation in India, 1951–1970," April 22, 1970, Ford Foundation Archives (hereafter cited as FFA), Ford report 003673; Douglas Ensminger, "The Ford Foundation's Early and Continuous Concern about Population and Family Planning," Oral History, November 1, 1971, FFA, FA744, B.1. All citations of Ford Foundation materials refer to the Ford Foundation Archives, which I consulted at the foundation's headquarters in New York City. These materials have since been deposited with the Rockefeller Archives Center.

56 Mohan Rao, *From Population Control to Reproductive Health: Malthusian Arithmetic* (New Delhi: Sage, 2004), 35.

57 Rao, *From Population Control*, 32–33, 37.

58 Ashwini Tambe, *Defining Girlhood in India: A Transnational History of Sexual Maturity Laws* (Urbana: University of Illinois Press, 2019), 115–17.

59 Michael E. Latham, *The Right Kind of Revolution: Modernization, Development, and U.S. Foreign Policy from the Cold War to the Present* (Ithaca: Cornell University Press, 2011), 115–18.

60 B. Chatterjee and Navrekha Singh, "A Guide to Voluntary Action in Family Planning," April 1971, FFA, Ford report 003679.

61 Chikako Takeshita, *The Global Biopolitics of the IUD: How Science Constructs Contraceptive Users and Women's Bodies* (Cambridge, MA: MIT Press, 2012), 14–15.

62 Takeshita, *Global Biopolitics*, 16.

63 Alan Guttmacher, "Opening Address," in *Intra-uterine Contraceptive Devices: Proceedings of the Conference, April 30–May 1, 1962*, ed. Christopher Tietze and Sarah Lewit (Amsterdam: Excerpta Medica Foundation, n.d.), 7.

64 "Conference Discussion," in Tietze and Lewit, *IUCD*, 123–24.

65 "Conference Discussion," in Tietze and Lewit, *IUCD*, 124.

66 "Conference Discussion," in Tietze and Lewit, *IUCD*, 125.

67 Adaline P. Satterthwaite and Clarence Gamble, "Intra-uterine Contraception with Plastic Devices Inserted without Cervical Dilation," in Tietze and Lewit, *IUCD*, 86, 88.

68   Don Jessen, "The Grafenberg Ring: A Clinical and Histopathologic Study," in Tietze and Lewit, *IUCD*, 43–44.

69   Margaret C. N. Jackson, "The Grafenberg Silver Ring in a Series of Patients Who Had Failed with Other Methods," in Tietze and Lewit, *IUCD*, 37.

70   "Conference Discussion," *IUCD*, 133.

71   "Conference Discussion," *IUCD*, 122.

72   "Conference Discussion," *IUCD*, 128.

73   Bernard Berelson, "Application of Intra-uterine Contraception in Family Planning Programs," in *Intra-uterine Contraception, Proceedings of the 2nd International Conference Oct 2–3, 1964*, ed. A. L. Southam and K. D. Shafer (Amsterdam: Excerpta Medica Foundation, 1965), 13.

74   B. L. Raina and M. W. Freymann, "Intra-uterine Contraception in India," in Southam and Shafer, *Intra-uterine Contraception*, 44.

75   Connelly, *Fatal Misconception*, 215–16.

76   Nayar, "Inaugural Address," in Roy, *Seminar on IUCD*, 7.

77   Connelly, *Fatal Misconception*, 217–20.

78   Will Johnson, "New Technology for Indian Family Planning," FFA, India Program Letter 137, Ford report 001127 (1966), 4–6.

79   Govind Narain, "India: The Family Planning Program since 1965," *Studies in Family Planning*, no. 35 (Nov 1968): 2.

80   Dhanvanthi Rama Rau, "Family Planning in India," *Journal of Sex Research* 3, no. 4 (1967): 273.

81   Connelly, *Fatal Misconception*, 225.

82   Rama Rau, "Family Planning in India," 272–73.

83   Narain, "India," 2.

84   Rama Rau, "Family Planning in India," 272.

85   "Report of the 35th Session of the AIWC" (Balasore, Orissa, 1966), 12, Margaret Cousins Library, Sarojini House, New Delhi.

86   "AIWC Central Skippo Committee Annual Report for Dec 1965–November 1966," in "Report of the 35th Session of the AIWC" (Balasore, Orissa, 1966), 59–62, Margaret Cousins Library, Sarojini House, New Delhi.

87   For example, "Report of the 37th Session of the AIWC" (Chandigarh, 1968), 59–60, Margaret Cousins Library, Sarojini House, New Delhi.

88   Connelly, *Fatal Misconception*, 217–25.

89   Narain, "India," 2.

90   Narain, "India," 4. India's abortion law was liberalized in 1971, as part of the overall push for population control.

91   B. N. Purandare, in Roy, *Seminar on IUCD*, 33, 35.

92   Harry L. Levin to Moye Freymann, October 13, 1965, Population Council Collection, RAC, record group IV3B4.3a, box 65, folder 1148.

93   Matthew Connelly, "Population Control in India: Prologue to the Emergency Period," *Population and Development Review* 32, no. 4 (December 2006), 657.

94   Emma Tarlo, "Body and Space in a Time of Crisis: Sterilization and Resettlement during the Emergency in Delhi," *Violence and Subjectivity*, ed. Veena

Das, Arthur Kleinman, and Mamphela Ramphele (Berkeley: University of California Press, 2000), 242–70.

95 L. C. R. Emmet, "Family Limitation of [*sic*] Tea Estates," in Roy, *Seminar on IUCD*, 66.

96 Dandekar argued that raising the age of marriage might be beneficial in itself but should be delinked from population control motivations. Tambe, *Defining Girlhood in India*, 114–15.

97 Kumudini Dandekar and Surekha Nigam, "What Did Fail? Loop (IUCD) as a Contraceptive? Administrators of Loop Programme? Or, Our Ill-Conceived Expectations?" *Economic and Political Weekly* 6, no. 48 (1971): 2394.

98 R. A. Gopalaswami, "Introduction to the Memorandum on 'Administrative Implementation of Family Planning Policy,'" in *Report of the Proceedings of the Sixth International Conference on Planned Parenthood* (London: International Planned Parenthood Federation, n.d.), 288.

99 Family Planning Board, Government of Madras, *Family Planning Manual* (n.p., n.d., ca. 1956).

100 Everett M. Rogers, "Incentives in the Diffusion of Family Planning Innovations," n.d., FFA, Ford report 06616.

101 Marika Vicziany, "Coercion in a Soft State: The Family Planning Program of India: Part 1: The Myth of Voluntarism," *Pacific Affairs* 55, no. 3 (1982–83): 386.

102 Rao, *From Population Control*, 39–40; Vicziany, "Myth of Voluntarism," 388.

103 Marika Vicziany, "Coercion in a Soft State: The Family Planning Program of India: Part 2: The Sources of Coercion," *Pacific Affairs* 55, no. 4 (1982): 562–67, 580.

104 Sreemanta Banerjee, "Female Sterilization in Population Control Programme," USAID Mission to India/Public Health Division Records, NARA, RG 286, entry P458: subject files 1961–1967, container 5.

105 Berry, "Scientific Housewife." For feminist critiques of this approach to agrarian development, see Ester Boserup's pioneering work, *Woman's Role in Economic Development* (New York: St. Martin's, 1970).

106 "India's Family Planning Program in the Seventies," Part 1, May 1970, FFA, Ford report 001599.

107 Vicziany, "Myth of Voluntarism," 387.

108 Rebecca Jane Williams, "Storming the Citadels: Family Planning under the Emergency in India, 1975–1977," *Journal of Asian Studies* 73, no. 2 (2014): 471–92.

109 Emma Tarlo, *Unsettling Memories: Narratives of the Emergency in Delhi* (Berkeley: University of California Press, 2003), 145.

110 Tambe, *Defining Girlhood in India*, 111.

111 Williams, "Storming the Citadels," 485.

112 Davidson Gwatkin, "Political Will and Family Planning: The Implications of India's Emergency Experience," *Population and Development Review* 5, no. 1 (1979): 38; Williams, "Storming the Citadels," 486.

113 Tarlo, *Unsettling Memories*, 148.

114 Vicziany, "Myth of Voluntarism," 386–87.

115 While the government funded and performed the majority of procedures, the FPAI, with financial support from the IPPF and under the leadership of Avabai Wadia, became a major nongovernmental provider of the procedure, sterilizing over 80,000 people in 1976.

116 Vicziany, "Myth of Voluntarism," 386–87.

117 Connelly, *Fatal Misconception*, 326.

118 Prakash, *Emergency Chronicles*, 303.

119 Williams, "Storming the Citadels," 476–82.

120 Williams, "Storming the Citadels," 476–77.

121 Tarlo, *Unsettling Memories*, 176.

122 Vicziany, "Myth of Voluntarism," 386–87.

123 By 1994, 96 percent of all sterilizations done in India were on women, a ratio that Cecilia Van Hollen ascribes, in part, to the aftermath of the Emergency. *Birth on the Threshold: Childbirth and Modernity in South India* (Berkeley: University of California Press, 2003), 144. Deepa Dhanraj similarly connects high rates of female sterilization to legacies of the Emergency. *Something Like a War* (Women Make Movies, 1991).

124 35.7 percent of married women between ages fifteen and forty-nine use sterilization as their method of family planning; this represents approximately 62.4 percent of contraceptive use among women. Government of India, Ministry of Health and Family Welfare, "National Family Health Survey-4, 2015–2016: India Fact Sheet" (Mumbai: International Institute for Population Sciences), accessed May 22, 2018, http://rchiips.org/nfhs/pdf/NFHS4/India.pdf.

125 Dhanraj, *Something Like a War.*

126 Van Hollen, *Birth on the Threshold*, 159.

127 Tarlo, *Unsettling Memories*, 176.

CHAPTER 5: HETEROSEXUALITY AND THE HAPPY FAMILY

1 Ministry of Information and Broadcasting, Government of India, *Methods of Family Planning* (1964), Field Office Files, Ford Foundation Archives (hereafter cited as FFA), Rockefeller Archives Center, Sleepy Hollow, NY, reel 4026, grant 64-303.

2 Michel Foucault, *The History of Sexuality: An Introduction*, vol. 1, trans. Robert Hurley (New York: Vintage Books, 1990), 104–5.

3 Foucault, *History of Sexuality*, 20.

4 Eunjoo Cho, "Making the 'Modern' Family: The Discourse of Sexuality in the Family Planning Program in South Korea," *Sexualities* 19, no. 7 (2016): 802–18; Susan Greenhalgh, *Cultivating Global Citizens: Population in the Rise of China* (Cambridge, MA: Harvard University Press, 2010).

5 Penelope Deutscher, "Foucault's *History of Sexuality, Volume 1*: Re-reading Its Reproduction," *Theory, Culture & Society* 29, no. 1 (2012): 119–37.

6 Manon Parry, *Broadcasting Birth Control: Mass Media and Family Planning* (New Brunswick, NJ: Rutgers University Press, 2013), 82–86.

7   For example: Gayatri Gopinath, *Impossible Desires: Queer Diasporas and South Asian Public Cultures* (Durham, NC: Duke University Press, 2005); Mary E. John and Janaki Nair, eds., *A Question of Silence: The Sexual Economies of Modern India* (New Delhi: Kali for Women, 1998); Nivedita Menon, *Sexualities* (London: Zed Books, 2007); Sanjay Srivastava, *Passionate Modernity: Sexuality, Class, and Consumption in India* (New Delhi: Routledge, 2007).

8   An important exception is J. Devika, *Individuals, Householders, Citizens: Family Planning in Kerala* (New Delhi: Zubaan, 2008).

9   A. R. Venkatachalapathy, *The Province of the Book: Scholars, Scribes, and Scribblers in Colonial Tamil Nadu* (New Delhi: Permanent Black, 2012).

10 Arvind Rajagopal, ed., *The Indian Public Sphere: Readings in Media History* (Oxford: Oxford University Press, 2009), 324.

11 Benedict Anderson, *Imagined Communities: Reflections on the Origins and Spread of Nationalism*, rev. ed. (London: Verso, 1991), 37–46.

12 Arvind Rajagopal, "Introduction: The Public Sphere in India," in Rajagopal, *Indian Public Sphere*, 3.

13 Sarah Hodges, *Contraception, Colonialism and Commerce: Birth Control in South India, 1920–1940* (New York: Routledge, 2016), chap. 4.

14 J. H. Hutton, *Census of India, 1941*, vol. 1, *Report* (Delhi: Manager of Publications, 1944), 20. Hutton is quoting the census superintendent of Madras.

15 Charu Gupta, "Redefining Obscenity and Aesthetics in Print," in Rajagopal, *Indian Public Sphere*, 108.

16 *Ilvazhkkaiyin irakaciyankal* [Mysteries of wedded life] (Madras: Vanam, 1927), cited in Hodges, *Contraception, Colonialism and Commerce*, 116.

17 Rajagopal, "Introduction," in Rajagopal, *Indian Public Sphere*, 11–12.

18 William Mazzarella, *Shoveling Smoke: Advertising and Globalization in Contemporary India* (Durham, NC: Duke University Press, 2003), 81–82.

19 Parry, *Broadcasting Birth Control*, 85.

20 Ministry of Information and Broadcasting, Government of India, *For a Healthier Tomorrow: Family Planning* (Calcutta: Lalchand Roy, 1968), n.p.

21 Srivastava, *Passionate Modernity*, 2.

22 Douglas Ensminger, "The Ford Foundation's Early and Continuous Concern about Population and Family Planning," Oral History, November 1, 1971, FFA, FA744, B.1.

23 "Signs, Murals Proclaim India's Program," *Population Chronicle* 1 (August 1969), FFA, reel 1995, grant 64-303, section 4.

24 M. K. Gandhi, *Self-Restraint vs. Self-Indulgence*, 3rd ed. (Ahmedabad: Navajivan, 1928), 15.

25 Shrikant Botre and Douglas E. Haynes, "Understanding R. D. Karve: *Brahmacharya*, Modernity, and the Appropriation of Global Sexual Science in Western India, 1927–1953," in *A Global History of Sexual Science, 1880–1960*, ed. Veronika Fuechtner, Douglas E. Haynes, and Ryan M. Jones (Berkeley: University of California Press, 2018), 173.

26 Gandhi, *Self-Restraint vs. Self-Indulgence*, 31.

27 "Gandhi and Mrs. Sanger Debate Birth Control," *Asia* (November 1936), 700, Margaret Sanger Papers, Sophia Smith Collection, Smith College Libraries, Northampton, MA, series III (subseries 5—Family/Miscellany, Transcriptions of Conversations and Interviews).

28 Sanjam Ahluwalia, "'Tyranny of Orgasm': Global Governance of Sexuality from Bombay, 1930s–1950s," in Fuechtner, Haynes, and Jones, *History of Sexual Science*, 353–73.

29 Botre and Haynes, "Understanding R. D. Karve," in Fuechtner, Haynes, and Jones, *History of Sexual Science.*

30 Ishita Pande, "Time for Sex: The Education of Desire and the Conduct of Childhood in Global/Hindu Sexology," in Fuechtner, Haynes, and Jones, *History of Sexual Science*, 291.

31 Advertisement for Contrafant tablets, *Marriage Hygiene* 1, no. 2 (November 1934): 184.

32 *Karppatci, allatu cuvatina karppam* [Contraception, or control over pregnancy], 2nd ed. (Madras: Vasan, 1931 [1st ed. 1929]), 16, 16, 8. Unless otherwise noted, all translations are my own.

33 Devidasan [pseud.], *Karppatatai* [Birth control] (Chennai: Cutan, 1929), 3 (translation by D. Aravindan).

34 Devidasan, *Karppatatai*, 49.

35 Devidasan, *Karppatatai*, 4.

36 Devidasan, *Karppatatai*, 55, 56.

37 Devika, *Individuals, Householders, Citizens*, 47–55.

38 Many texts follow this structure, including Kalaniti, *Katal rakaciyam: Karppattatai vilakkankalaik kontatu* [The secrets of love: Means of birth control explained] (Chennai: Malivu Nulakam, 1960); Citalakshmi Kuyilan, *Karppamum piracavamum* [Pregnancy and childbirth] (Chennai: Tamil Puttakap Pannai, 1955); *Kutumpa kattuppatu, Ovvoru nimitamum 25!* [Family planning: Every minute 25!] (n.p., n.d.).

39 Menon, *Sexualities*, 11.

40 For example: George Mosse, *Nationalism and Sexuality: Respectability and Abnormal Sexuality in Modern Europe* (New York: H. Fertig, 1985); Margot Canaday, *The Straight State: Sexuality and Citizenship in Twentieth-Century America* (Princeton, NJ: Princeton University Press, 2009).

41 Menon, *Sexualities*, 11.

42 Ministry of Information and Broadcasting, Government of India, *Methods of Family Planning* (1964), Field Office Files, FFA, reel 4026, grant 64-303.

43 Kalaniti, *Katal rakaciyam*, 70–71.

44 T. S. Janakakumari, *Kuzhantai ventam enral?* [What if you don't want children?], 2nd ed. (Karaikudi: Selvi, 1963), preface.

45 T. S. Janakakumari, *Kuzhantai ventum* [You want a child], 2nd ed. (Chennai: Star, 1964), 3, 44.

46 Dr. K. Satyavati, *Family Planning (Birth Control)*, 3rd ed. (New Delhi: Satyavati Family Planning Center, 1955).

47 Satyavati, *Family Planning*, 109.

48 *Karppatci, allatu cuvatina karppam*, 7, 10.

49 Ca. Pasyam, *Pale Tankam: Kutumpak kattuppatu virivakkappattatu* [Well done Thangam: Family planning explained] (n.p., 1961), 6.

50 Nilanjana Chatterjee and Nancy E. Riley, "Planning an Indian Modernity: The Gendered Politics of Fertility Control," *Signs* 26, no. 3 (Spring 2001): 831–32.

51 "Planitab," in *Report of the Proceedings of the Fifth All India Conference on Family Planning* (Patna: Family Planning Association of India, 1964), n.p.

52 K. A. Abbas, dir., *Three Families* (Government of India Films Division, 1963); *Enough's Enough* (Prasad Productions, 1973).

53 "Volpar," in *Report of the Proceedings of the Fifth All India Conference on Family Planning*, (Patna: Family Planning Association of India, 1964), n.p.

54 "Protecto," *Journal of Family Welfare* 1, no. 5 (July 1955): n.p.

55 Parry, *Broadcasting Birth Control*, 90.

56 Friends of Vellore, Slides Set 7 (Family Planning, Boxes 1–2, 1965–1975), Friends of Vellore, India Office Records and Private Papers, British Library, MssEur F219/18/44a, 44b.

57 Devika, *Individuals, Householders, Citizens*, 92–95.

58 As I have argued elsewhere, this attention to the conjugal couple was itself the product of legal, economic, and social changes in late colonial India. Mytheli Sreenivas, *Wives, Widows, and Concubines: The Conjugal Family Ideal in Colonial India* (Bloomington: Indiana University Press, 2008).

59 Ashwini Tambe, *Defining Girlhood in India: A Transnational History of Sexual Maturity Laws* (Urbana: University of Illinois Press, 2019).

60 Frank Wilder and D. K. Tyagi, "India's New Departures in Mass Motivation for Fertility Control," *Demography* 5, no. 2 (1968): 776.

61 For example: "National Poets Set the Limit at Two Children," *Centre Calling: A Monthly Newsletter of the Department of Family Planning* 4, no. 4 (April 1969): 3.

62 Family Planning Board, Government of Madras, *Family Planning Manual* (n.p., n.d., ca. 1956), 42 (emphasis mine).

63 A. B. Shetty, "Foreword," in Family Planning Board, *Family Planning Manual*.

64 *Kutumpa kattuppatu titta kaiputtakam* [Family planning instructional handbook] (Chennai: Kutumpa Kattuppatu Tittak Kalakam, 1962), 33. (Translation by D. Aravindan.)

65 *Kutumpa kattuppatu titta kaiputtakam*, 1. (Translation by D. Aravindan.)

66 Pasyam, *Pale Tankam*, 1.

67 Pasyam, *Pale Tankam*, 5.

68 Pasyam, *Pale Tankam*, 16.

69 Pasyam, *Pale Tankam*, 21.

70 Central Board for Workers Education (India), *We Two Our Two* (Nagpur: Shivraj Fine Arts Lith Works, n.d.), n.p.

71 *We Two Our Two*, n.p.

72 *We Two Our Two*, n.p.

73 *We Two Our Two*, n.p.

74 Connelly, *Fatal Misconception*, 264.

75 Les Clark, dir., *Family Planning* (Walt Disney Productions, 1967).

76 "The Population Council: The Disney Film on Family Planning," *Studies in Family Planning* 1, no. 26 (1968): n.p.

77 "Our History: Timeline," Population Council, accessed November 15, 2015, www.popcouncil.org/about/timeline; "The Population Council: The Disney Film on Family Planning," n.p.

78 "The Population Council: The Disney Film on Family Planning," n.p.

79 Robert Eberwein, *Sex Ed: Film, Video, and the Framework of Desire* (New Brunswick, NJ: Rutgers University Press, 1999), 176.

80 B. Chatterjee and Navrekha Singh, "A Guide to Voluntary Action in Family Planning," April 1971, FFA, Ford report 003679, p. 10.

81 Chatterjee and Singh, "A Guide to Voluntary Action in Family Planning," 10.

82 Wilder and Tyagi, "India's New Departures," 775.

83 *Centre Calling: A Newsletter of the Department of Family Planning* 1, no. 3 (December 1966).

84 Wilder and Tyagi, "India's New Departures," 776.

85 Wilder and Tyagi, "India's New Departures," 774.

86 Frank Wilder to James F. Farnham, August 12, 1969, Field Office File, FFA, reel 3847, grant 64-303.

87 For example: Judith Butler, "Is Kinship Always Already Heterosexual?" *Differences* 13, no. 1 (2002): 14–44; Kimberly McKee, "Reproductive Futurity and the Adoptive Family," *Adoption and Culture* 7, no. 2 (2019): 180.

88 Lee Edelman, *No Future: Queer Theory and the Death Drive* (Durham: Duke University Press, 2004), Nook ed., 13.

89 Shannon Winnubst, "Review Essay: *No Future: Queer Theory and the Death Drive*," *Environment and Planning D: Society and Space* 28 (2010): 181–82.

90 Eithne Luibhéid, *Pregnant on Arrival: Making the Illegal Immigrant* (Minneapolis: University of Minnesota Press, 2013), 150, 174.

EPILOGUE

1 IPPF and the Population and Sustainability Network, *Climate Change: Time to "Think Family Planning"; An Advocacy Toolkit for Family Planning Advocates* (2016), www.ippf.org/sites/default/files/2016-11/Climate%20Change%20 Time%20to%20Think%20Family%20Planning%20Advocacy%20Toolkit%20 Final.pdf.

2 NITI Aayog, "NITI Aayog to Draft Roadmap for Achieving Population Stabilization," accessed May 7, 2020, https://pib.gov.in/PressReleasePage.aspx ?PRID=1596946.

3 Devi [pseud.], interview by Archana Venkatesh, June 19, 2014.

4 Jade Sasser, *On Infertile Ground: Population Control and Women's Rights in the Era of Climate Change* (New York: NYU Press, 2018), 89.

5 IPPF, *Climate Change*.

6 "Fighting Climate Change with Family Planning," *Sierra*, May/June 2012, 49.

7 Sasser, *On Infertile Ground*, 50.

8   World Bank, "Fertility Rate," accessed May 6, 2020, https://data.worldbank.org
    /indicator/SP.DYN.TFRT.IN; World Bank, "CO2 emissions," accessed May 6,
    2020, https://data.worldbank.org/indicator/EN.ATM.CO2E.PC.

9   Betsy Hartmann, *Reproductive Rights and Wrongs: The Global Politics of
    Population Control*, 3rd ed. (Chicago: Haymarket Books, 2016), 11.

10 Hartmann, *Reproductive Rights and Wrongs*, 11.

11 IPPF, *Climate Change*.

12 NITI, "NITI Aayog to Draft Roadmap."

13 World Bank, "Fertility Rate"; NITI Aayog, "Total Fertility Rate," accessed
    May 6, 2020, https://niti.gov.in/content/total-fertility-rate-tfr-birth-woman.

14 "International Conference on Population and Development Programme of
    Action," 20th anniv. ed. (New York: UNFPA, 2014), www.unfpa.org
    /publications/international-conference-population-and-development
    -programme-action.

15 Rosalind Pollack Petchesky, "From Population Control to Reproductive
    Rights: Feminist Fault Lines," *Reproductive Health Matters* 3, no. 6 (Novem-
    ber 1995): 152–61.

16 Mohan Rao and Sarah Sexton, eds., *Markets and Malthus: Population, Gender,
    and Health in Neo-liberal Times* (New Delhi: Sage, 2010).

17 Betsy Hartmann and Mohan Rao, "India's Population Programme: Obstacles
    and Opportunities," *Economic and Political Weekly* 44 (October 31, 2015).

18 Sharmila Rudrappa, *Discounted Life: The Price of Global Surrogacy in India*
    (New York: NYU Press, 2015), 172.

19 Vidya Krishnan, "Doctor Freed in Bilaspur Sterilisation Deaths Case," *Hindu*,
    February 21, 2017, www.thehindu.com/news/national/other-states/sterilisation
    -deaths-in-chhattisgarh-doctor-freed/article17336215.ece.

20 "Independence Day: Full Text of PM Modi's Address to Nation," *Business
    Today*, August 15, 2019, www.businesstoday.in/current/economy-politics
    /independence-day-pm-modi-address-nation-full-text-speech-15-august-red
    -fort/story/372903.html.

21 Rajani Bhatia, *Gender before Birth: Sex Selection in a Transnational Context*
    (Seattle: University of Washington Press, 2018), 26. Some scholars use the term
    populationism to underscore the legacies of population control alongside its
    contemporary formations. Anne Hendrixson, Diana Ojeda, Jade S. Sasser,
    Sarojini Madimpally, Ellen E. Foley, and Rajani Bhatia, "Confronting
    Populationism: Feminist Challenges to Population Control in an Era of
    Climate Change," *Gender, Place and Culture* (2019): 1–9.

22 NITI Aayog, "Sex Ratio (Females/1000 Males)," accessed May 11, 2020,
    https://niti.gov.in/content/sex-ratio-females-1000-males.

23 Ashwini Tambe, *Defining Girlhood in India: A Transnational History of Sexual
    Maturity Laws* (Urbana: University of Illinois Press, 2019): 138–40.

24 T. V. Sekher, "Ladlis and Lakshmis: Financial Incentive Schemes for the Girl
    Child," *Economic and Political Weekly* 47, no. 17 (April 28, 2012): 59.

25 The interviews were conducted in June and July 2014 by Archana Venkatesh,
    then a PhD student at Ohio State, who worked collaboratively with me on

designing the research. They took place with women living in two subdivisions, Uthokkottai and Gummidipoondi, of Thiruvallur District. Interviews were conducted in Tamil, and translated to English by me. I use pseudonyms throughout.

26 NITI, "Total Fertility Rate."

27 Devi, interview.

28 Darshini [pseud.], interview by Archana Venkatesh, July 9, 2014.

29 Kasturi [pseud.], interview by Archana Venkatesh, June 16, 2014.

30 Veena [pseud.], interview by Archana Venkatesh, June 16, 2014.

BIBLIOGRAPHY

MANUSCRIPT COLLECTIONS

All India Women's Conference Papers. Margaret Cousins Library, Sarojini House, New Delhi.
All India Women's Conference Papers. Nehru Memorial Library, New Delhi.
Ford Foundation Archives. Rockefeller Archives Center, Sleepy Hollow, NY.
Friends of Vellore. India Office Records and Private Papers. British Library, London.
James Caird Papers, 1878–1881. India Office Records and Private Papers. British Library, London.
Margaret Sanger Papers. Sophia Smith Collection. Smith College Libraries, Northampton, MA.
Marie Stopes Papers. Wellcome Library, London.
Muthulakshmi Reddi Papers. Nehru Memorial Library, New Delhi.
Population Council Collection. Rockefeller Archives Center, Sleepy Hollow, NY.
Richard Temple Papers. India Office Records and Private Papers. British Library, London.
Rockefeller Family Archives. Rockefeller Archives Center, Sleepy Hollow, NY.
Sripati Chandrasekhar Papers. Ward M. Canaday Center for Special Collections, University of Toledo, Toledo, OH.

STATE ARCHIVES

National Archives of India, New Delhi

Proceedings of the Department of Revenue, Agriculture, and Commerce (Famine Branch)

National Archives and Records Administration, College Park, MD

USAID Mission to India/Public Health Division Records

British Library, India Office Records and Private Papers

Report of the Native Papers Published in the Bombay Presidency
Report of the Native Papers Published in the Madras Presidency

MAGAZINES AND JOURNALS

Centre Calling: A Monthly Newsletter of the Department of Family Planning
Journal of Family Welfare
Kuti Aracu
Madras Birth Control Bulletin
Madras Mail
Malthusian
Marriage Hygiene
National Reformer
Quarterly Journal of the Poona Sarvajanik Sabha
Roshni
Studies in Family Planning

BOOKS, REPORTS, ARTICLES, DISSERTATIONS, AND FILMS

Abbas, K. A., dir. *Three Families*. Government of India Films Division, 1963.

Age of Consent Committee. *Report of the Age of Consent Committee, 1928–1929*. Calcutta: Government of India Central Publication Branch, 1929.

Ahluwalia, Sanjam. *Reproductive Restraints: Birth Control in India, 1877–1947*. Urbana: University of Illinois Press, 2008.

Ahluwalia, Sanjam, and Daksha Parmar. "From Gandhi to Gandhi: Contraceptive Technologies and Sexual Politics in Postcolonial India, 1947–1977." In *Reproductive States: Global Perspectives on the Invention and Implementation of Population Policy*, edited by Rickie Solinger and Mie Nakachi, 124–55. Oxford: Oxford University Press, 2016.

Alter, Joseph S. *Gandhi's Body: Sex, Diet, and the Politics of Nationalism*. Philadelphia: University of Pennsylvania Press, 2000.

Ambirajan, S. *Classical Political Economy and British Policy in India*. Cambridge: Cambridge University Press, 1978.

———. "Malthusian Population Theory and Indian Famine Policy in the Nineteenth Century." *Population Studies* 30, no. 1 (1976): 5–14.

Amrith, Sunil. *Decolonizing International Health: India and Southeast Asia, 1930–1965*. London: Palgrave Macmillan, 2006.

———. "Political Culture of Health in India: A Historical Perspective." *Economic and Political Weekly* 42, no. 2 (January 13–19, 2007): 114–21.

Anandhi, S. "Reproductive Bodies and Regulated Sexuality: Birth Control Debates in Early 20th Century Tamil Nadu." In *A Question of Silence? The Sexual Economies of Modern India*, edited by Mary E. John and Janaki Nair, 139–66. New Delhi: Kali for Women, 1998.

———. "The Women's Question in the Dravidian Movement, c. 1925–1948." *Social Scientist* 16, no. 5/6 (1991): 24–41.

Anderson, Benedict. *Imagined Communities: Reflections on the Origins and Spread of Nationalism*. Revised ed. London: Verso, 1991.

Appadurai, Arjun. "Number in the Colonial Imagination." In *Orientalism and the Postcolonial Predicament,* edited by Carol A. Breckinridge and Peter van der Veer, 314–40. Philadelphia: University of Pennsylvania Press, 1993.

Arnold, David. *Famine: Social Crisis and Historical Change.* Oxford: Basil Blackwell, 1988.

Bagchi, Barnita. "Tracing Two Generations in Twentieth Century Indian Women's Education through Analysis of Literary Sources: Selected Writings by Padmini Sengupta." *Women's History Review* 29, no. 3 (2020): 465–79.

Banerjee, Nirmala. "The Unorganized Sector and the Planner." In *Economy, Society and Polity: Essays in the Political Economy of Indian Planning in Honour of Professor Bhabatosh Datta,* edited by Amiya Kumar Bagchi, 71–103. New Delhi: Oxford University Press, 1988.

———. "Whatever Happened to the Dreams of Modernity? The Nehruvian Era and Women's Position." *Economic and Political Weekly* 33, no. 17 (1998): WS2–7.

Banerjee, Sukanya. *Becoming Imperial Citizens: Indians in the Late-Victorian Empire.* Durham, NC: Duke University Press, 2010.

Bashford, Alison. *Global Population: History, Geopolitics, and Life on Earth.* New York: Columbia University Press, 2014.

Bashford, Alison, and Philippa Levine, eds. *The Oxford Handbook of the History of Eugenics.* Oxford: Oxford University Press, 2010.

Bergeron, Suzanne. *Fragments of Development: Nation, Gender, and the Space of Modernity.* Ann Arbor: University of Michigan Press, 2005.

Berry, Kim. "Lakshmi and the Scientific Housewife: A Transnational Account of Indian Women's Development and Production of an Indian Modernity." *Economic and Political Weekly* 38, no. 11 (2003): 1055–68.

Besant, Annie. *Theosophy and the Law of Population.* Benaras: Theosophical Publishing Society, 1896.

Bharatiya Grameen Mahila Sangh and Central Institute of Research and Training in Public Co-operation, "Status of Women and Family Planning in India." Unpublished report, n.d.

Bhatia, Rajani. *Gender before Birth: Sex Selection in a Transnational Context.* Seattle: University of Washington Press, 2018.

Birla, Ritu. *Stages of Capital: Law, Culture, and Market Governance in Late Colonial India.* Durham, NC: Duke University Press, 2009.

Boserup, Ester. *Women's Role in Economic Development.* New York: St. Martin's, 1970.

Briggs, Laura. *Reproducing Empire: Race, Sex, Science, and U.S. Imperialism in Puerto Rico.* Berkeley: University of California Press, 2002.

Buch, Nirmala. "State Welfare Policy and Women, 1950–1975." *Economic and Political Weekly* 33, no. 17 (1998): WS18–WS20.

Buck-Morss, Susan. "Envisioning Capital: Political Economy on Display." *Critical Inquiry* 21, no. 2 (1995): 434–67.

Burton, Antoinette. "From Child Bride to 'Hindoo Lady': Rukhmabai and the Debate on Sexual Respectability in Imperial Britain." *American Historical Review* 103, no. 4 (October 1998): 1119–46.

Butler, Judith. "Is Kinship Always Already Heterosexual?" *Differences* 13, no. 1 (2002): 14–44.

Caldwell, John C. "Malthus and the Less Developed World: The Pivotal Role of India." *Population and Development Review* 24 (1998): 675–96.

Canaday, Margot. *The Straight State: Sexuality and Citizenship in Twentieth-Century America*. Princeton, NJ: Princeton University Press, 2009.

Central Board for Workers Education (India). *We Two Our Two*. Nagpur: Shivraj Fine Arts Lith Works, n.d.

Chandra, Bipan, ed. *Ranade's Economic Writings*. New Delhi: Gian, 1990.

Chandrasekhar, S. *Hungry People and Empty Lands: An Essay on Population Problems and International Tensions*. London: G. Allen & Unwin, 1954.

Chatterjee, Nilanjana, and Nancy E. Riley. "Planning an Indian Modernity: The Gendered Politics of Fertility Control." *Signs* 26, no. 3 (Spring 2001): 811–45.

Chatterjee, Partha. *The Nation and Its Fragments: Colonial and Postcolonial Histories*. Princeton, NJ: Princeton University Press, 1993.

———, ed. *State and Politics in India*. Delhi: Oxford University Press, 1997.

Chattopadhyay, Kamaladevi, and others. *The Awakening of Indian Women*. Madras: Everyman's Press, 1939.

Chaudhuri, Maitrayee. "Citizens, Workers and Emblems of Culture: An Analysis of the First Plan Document on Women." In *Social Reform, Sexuality and the State*, edited by Patricia Uberoi, 211–35. New Delhi: Sage, 1998.

———. *Feminism in India*. London: Zed Books, 2004.

Cho, Eunjoo. "Making the 'Modern' Family: The Discourse of Sexuality in the Family Planning Program in South Korea." *Sexualities* 19, no. 7 (2016): 802–18.

Chokkalingam, T. S. *Piraja urpattiyaik kattuppatuttutal* [Restraining population growth]. Madras: Tamil Nadu Power, 1925.

Clark, Les, dir. *Family Planning*. Walt Disney Productions, 1967.

Connelly, Matthew. *Fatal Misconception: The Struggle to Control World Population*. Cambridge, MA: Belknap, 2009.

———. "Population Control in India: Prologue to the Emergency Period." *Population and Development Review* 32, no. 4 (December 2006): 629–67.

Cornish, W. R. *Report on the Census of Madras Presidency of 1871*. Vol. 1. Madras: Government Gazette Press, 1874.

Currie, Kate. "British Colonial Policy and Famines: Some Effects and Implications of 'Free Trade' in the Bombay, Bengal and Madras Presidencies, 1860–1900." *South Asia: Journal of South Asian Studies* 14, no. 2 (1991): 23–56.

Dandekar, Kumudini, and Surekha Nigam. "What Did Fail? Loop (IUCD) as a Contraceptive? Administrators of Loop Programme? Or, Our Ill-Conceived Expectations?" *Economic and Political Weekly* 6, no. 48 (1971): 2392–94.

Davis, Angela. *Women, Race and Class*. New York: Vintage Books, 1983.

Davis, Mike. *Late Victorian Holocausts: El Niño Famines and the Making of the Third World*. London: Verso, 2002.

Deshmukh, Durgabai. *Chintaman and I*. New Delhi: Allied Publishers Private, 1980.

Deutscher, Penelope. "Foucault's *History of Sexuality, Volume 1*: Re-reading Its Reproduction." *Theory, Culture and Society* 29, no. 1 (2012): 119–37.

Devidasan [pseud.]. *Karppatatai* [Birth control]. Chennai: Cutan, 1929.

Devika, J. *Individuals, Householders, Citizens: Family Planning in Kerala.* New Delhi: Zubaan, 2008.

Dhanraj, Deepa, dir. *Something Like a War.* Women Make Movies, 1991.

Digby, William. *The Famine Campaign in Southern India, 1876–1878.* London: Longmans, Green, 1878.

Directory of the City Health and Baby Week. Compiled by Corporation of Madras. Madras: Current Thought, n.d.

Dirks, Nicholas B., ed. *Colonialism and Culture.* Ann Arbor: University of Michigan Press, 1992.

Eberwein, Robert. *Sex Ed: Film, Video, and the Framework of Desire.* New Brunswick, NJ: Rutgers University Press, 1999.

Edelman, Lee. *No Future: Queer Theory and the Death Drive.* Nook ed. Durham, NC: Duke University Press, 2004.

Ehrlich, Paul R. *The Population Bomb.* New York: Ballantine Books, 1968.

Enough's Enough. Prasad Productions, 1973.

Family Planning Board, Government of Madras. *Family Planning Manual.* N.p., n.d., ca. 1956.

Federici, Silvia. *Caliban and the Witch: Women, the Body and Primitive Accumulation.* New York: Autonomedia, 2004.

"Fighting Climate Change with Family Planning." *Sierra,* May/June, 2012.

Foucault, Michel. *The History of Sexuality: An Introduction. Vol. 1.* Translated by Robert Hurley. New York: Vintage Books, 1990.

———. *Security, Territory, Population: Lectures at the Collège de France, 1977–1978.* Edited by Michel Senellart. Translated by Graham Burchell. New York: Palgrave Macmillan, 2004.

Frankel, Francine R. *India's Political Economy, 1947–2004: The Gradual Revolution.* 2nd ed. New Delhi: Oxford University Press, 2005.

Fuechtner, Veronika, Douglas E. Haynes, and Ryan M. Jones, eds. *A Global History of Sexual Science, 1880–1960.* Berkeley: University of California Press, 2018.

Gallagher, Catherine, and Thomas Laqueur, eds. *The Making of the Modern Body.* Berkeley: University of California Press, 1987.

Gandhi, Mohandas. *The Collected Works of Mahatma Gandhi.* Vol. 12. Delhi: Publication Division, Ministry of Information and Broadcasting, Government of India, 1964.

———. *Self-Restraint vs. Self-Indulgence.* 3rd ed. Ahmedabad: Navajivan, 1928.

Ganesan, Uma. "Gender and Caste: Self Respect Movement in the Madras Presidency, 1925–1950." PhD diss., University of Cincinnati, 2011.

Geetha, V., and S. V. Rajadurai. *Towards a Non-Brahmin Millennium: From Iyothee Thass to Periyar.* 2nd Revised ed. Calcutta: Samya, 2008.

Ginsburg, Faye D., and Rayna Rapp, eds. *Conceiving the New World Order: The Global Politics of Reproduction.* Berkeley: University of California Press, 1995.

Gopal, T. D. *Karppatci, allatu Pillai Perrai Atakki Alutal* [Controlling pregnancy, or preventing the birth of children]. Erode: Kuti Aracu Press, 1936.

Gopalaswami, R. A. *Census of India 1951*. Vol. 1, part 1-A, *Report*. New Delhi: Government of India, 1953.

Gopinath, Gayatri. *Impossible Desires: Queer Diasporas and South Asian Public Cultures*. Durham, NC: Duke University Press, 2005.

Gordon, Linda. *The Moral Property of Women: A History of Birth Control Politics in America*. 3rd ed. Urbana: University of Illinois Press, 2002.

Goswami, Manu. *Producing India: From Colonial Economy to National Space*. Chicago: University of Chicago Press, 2004.

Government of India, Planning Commission. *The First Five Year Plan*. New Delhi: Government of India, 1953.

———. *The Second Five Year Plan*. Delhi: Government of India, 1956.

Greenhalgh, Susan. *Cultivating Global Citizens: Population in the Rise of China*. Cambridge, MA: Harvard University Press, 2010.

Greenhalgh, Susan, and Edwin Winckler. *Governing China's Population: From Leninist to Neoliberal Biopolitics*. Stanford, CA: Stanford University Press, 2005.

Guha, Sumit. *Health and Population in South Asia from Earliest Times to the Present*. New Delhi: Permanent Black, 2001.

———. "The Politics of Identity and Enumeration in India, c. 1600–1900." *Comparative Studies in Society and History* 45, no. 1 (2003): 148–67.

Gupta, Charu. *Sexuality, Obscenity, Community: Women, Muslims and the Hindu Public in Colonial India*. London: Palgrave, 2001.

Gutiérrez, Elena. *Fertile Matters: The Politics of Mexican-Origin Women's Reproduction*. Austin: University of Texas Press, 2008.

Gwatkin, Davidson R. "Political Will and Family Planning: The Implications of India's Emergency Experience." *Population and Development Review* 5, no. 1 (1979): 29–59.

Hacking, Ian. "Biopower and the Avalanche of Printed Numbers." *Humanities in Society* 5, no. 3–4 (1982): 279–95.

Hall-Matthews, David. *Peasants, Famine and the State in Colonial Western India*. London: Palgrave Macmillan, 2005.

Hartmann, Betsy. *Reproductive Rights and Wrongs: The Global Politics of Population Control*. 3rd ed. Chicago: Haymarket Books, 2016.

Hartmann, Betsy, and Mohan Rao. "India's Population Programme: Obstacles and Opportunities." *Economic and Political Weekly* 44 (October 31, 2015).

Hendrixson, Anne, Diana Ojeda, Jade S. Sasser, Sarojini Nadimpally, Ellen E. Foley, and Rajani Bhatia. "Confronting Populationism: Feminist Challenges to Population Control in an Era of Climate Change." *Gender, Place and Culture* (2019): 1–9.

Himes, Norman E. *Medical History of Contraception*. New York: Gamut, 1963.

Hodges, Sarah. *Contraception, Colonialism and Commerce: Birth Control in South India, 1920–1940*. New York: Routledge, 2016.

———, ed. *Reproductive Health in India: History, Politics, Controversies*. Delhi: Orient Longman, 2006.

Hopwood, Nick, Rebecca Flemming, and Lauren Kassell, eds. *Reproduction: Antiquity to the Present Day*. Cambridge: Cambridge University Press, 2018.

Hutton, J. H. *Census of India, 1941.* Vol. 1, *Report.* Delhi: Manager of Publications, 1944.

Indian Famine Commission. *Report of the Indian Famine Commission, Part 1, Famine Relief.* London: G. E. Eyre and W. Spottiswoode, 1880.

Ittmann, Karl. *A Problem of Great Importance: Population, Race, and Power in the British Empire, 1918–1973.* Berkeley: University of California Press, 2013.

Janakakumari, T. S., *Kuzhantai ventam enral?* [What if you don't want children?]. 2nd ed. Karaikudi: Selvi, 1963.

———. *Kuzhantai ventum* [You want a child]. 2nd ed. Chennai: Star, 1964.

Jani, Pranav. *Decentering Rushdie: Cosmopolitanism and the Indian Novel in English.* Columbus: Ohio State University Press, 2010.

Jeffery, Patricia, and Roger Jeffery. *Confronting Saffron Demography: Religion, Fertility, and Women's Status in India.* Gurgaon: Three Essays Collective, 2006.

John, Mary. "Feminist Perspectives on Family and Marriage: A Historical View." *Economic and Political Weekly* 40, no. 8 (2008): 712–15.

———. "Gender, Development and the Women's Movement: Problems for a History of the Present." In *Signposts: Gender Issues in Post-Independence India*, edited by Rajeswari Sunder Rajan, 100–24. New Delhi: Kali/Zubaan, 2000.

John, Mary E., and Janaki Nair, eds. *A Question of Silence: The Sexual Economies of Modern India.* New Delhi: Kali for Women, 1998.

Kalaniti. *Katal rakaciyam: Karppattatai vilakkankalaik kontatu* [The secrets of love: Means of birth control explained]. Chennai: Malivu Nulakam, 1960.

Kalpagam, U. "The Colonial State and Statistical Knowledge." *History of the Human Sciences* 13, no. 2 (2000): 37–55.

———. *Rule by Numbers: Governmentality in Colonial India.* Lanham, MD: Lexington Books, 2014.

Karppatci, allatu cuvatina karppam [Contraception, or control over pregnancy]. 2nd ed. Madras: Vasan, 1931.

Klausen, Susanne M. *Abortion under Apartheid: Nationalism, Sexuality, and Women's Reproductive Rights in South Africa.* Oxford: Oxford University Press, 2015.

Krishnamurthi Ayyar, Murari S. *Population and Birth Control in India.* Madras: People's Printing and Publishing House, n.d.

Kumar, Radha. *The History of Doing: An Illustrated Account of Movements for Women's Rights and Feminism in India, 1800–1990.* New Delhi: Kali for Women, 1993.

Kutumpa kattuppatu, Ovvoru nimitamum 25! [Family planning: Every minute 25!]. n.p., n.d.

Kutumpa kattuppatu titta kaiputtakam [Family planning instructional handbook]. Chennai: Kutumpa Kattuppatu Tittak Kalakam, 1962.

Kuyilan, Citalakshmi. *Karppamum piracavamum* [Pregnancy and childbirth]. Chennai: Tamil Puttakap Pannai, 1955.

Lake, Marilyn, and Henry Reynolds. *Drawing the Global Color Line: White Men's Countries and the International Challenge of Racial Equality.* Cambridge: Cambridge University Press, 2008.

Latham, Michael E. *The Right Kind of Revolution: Modernization, Development, and U.S. Foreign Policy from the Cold War to the Present*. Ithaca: Cornell University Press, 2011.

Ledbetter, Rosanna. *A History of the Malthusian League, 1877–1927*. Columbus: Ohio State University Press, 1976.

Levine, Philippa. *Feminist Lives in Victorian England: Private Roles and Public Commitment*. Oxford: Basil Blackwell, 1990.

———. "Imperial Encounters." In *Reproduction: Antiquity to the Present Day*, edited by Nick Hopwood, Rebecca Flemming and Lauren Kassell, 485–97. Cambridge: Cambridge University Press, 2018.

Luibhéid, Eithne. *Pregnant on Arrival: Making the Illegal Immigrant*. Minneapolis: University of Minnesota Press, 2013.

Madras Neo-Malthusian League. *The Best Birth Control Methods*. Madras: Madras Neo-Malthusian League, 1929.

Malabari, Behramji M. *Infant Marriage and Enforced Widowhood in India*. Bombay: Voice of India, 1887.

Malthus, T. R. *An Essay on the Principle of Population*. Oxford: Oxford University Press, 2004.

Mamdani, Mahmood. *The Myth of Population Control: Family, Caste, and Class in an Indian Village*. New York: Monthly Review Press, 1972.

Mangudkar, M. P. *Dr. Ambedkar and Family Planning*. Pune: Sangam, 1976.

Mayo, Katherine. *Mother India*. New York: Harcourt, Brace, 1927.

Mazzarella, William. *Shoveling Smoke: Advertising and Globalization in Contemporary India*. Durham, NC: Duke University Press, 2003.

Mbembe, Achille. "Necropolitics." Translated by Libby Meintjes. *Public Culture* 15, no. 1 (2003): 11–40.

McCann, Carole. *Figuring the Population Bomb: Gender and Demography in the Mid-Twentieth Century*. Seattle: University of Washington Press, 2017.

———. "Malthusian Men and Demographic Transitions: A Case Study of Hegemonic Masculinity in Mid-Twentieth-Century Population Theory." *Frontiers: A Journal of Women Studies* 30, no. 1 (2009): 142–71.

McClaren, Angus. *A History of Contraception: From Antiquity to the Present Day*. Oxford: Basil Blackwell, 1990.

McIver, Lewis. *Imperial Census of 1881: Operations and Results in the Presidency of Madras, Report*. Vol. 1. Madras: Government Press, 1883.

McKee, Kimberly. "Reproductive Futurity and the Adoptive Family." *Adoption and Culture* 7, no. 2 (2019): 176–91.

Menon, Nivedita. *Sexualities*. London: Zed Books, 2007.

Miller, Ruth. "Rights, Reproduction, Sexuality, and Citizenship in the Ottoman Empire and Turkey." *Signs* 32, no. 2 (2007): 347–73.

Ministry of Information and Broadcasting, Government of India. *For a Healthier Tomorrow: Family Planning*. Calcutta: Lalchand Roy, 1986.

Mitchell, Timothy. "Fixing the Economy." *Cultural Studies* 12, no. 1 (1998): 82–101.

Moreton-Robinson, Aileen. *The White Possessive: Property, Power, and Indigenous Sovereignty*. Minneapolis: University of Minnesota Press, 2015.

Mosse, George. *Nationalism and Sexuality: Respectability and Abnormal Sexuality in Modern Europe*. New York: H. Fertig, 1985.

Mudd, Stuart, ed. *The Population Crisis and the Use of World Resources*. Bloomington: Indiana University Press, 1964.

Mukherjee, Radhakamal. *Food Planning for Four Hundred Millions*. London: Macmillan, 1938.

———. *Migrant Asia*. [Rome?]: Tipografia I. Failly, 1936.

Murphy, Michelle. *The Economization of Life*. Durham, NC: Duke University Press, 2017.

Nadkarni, Asha. *Eugenic Feminism: Reproductive Nationalism in the United States and India*. Minneapolis: University of Minnesota Press, 2014.

Nair, Rahul. "The Construction of a 'Population Problem' in Colonial India 1919–1947." *Journal of Imperial and Commonwealth History* 39, no. 2 (2011): 227–47.

———. "The Discourse on Population in India, 1870–1960." PhD diss., University of Pennsylvania, 2006.

Nand, Brahma, ed. *Famines in Colonial India: Some Unofficial Historical Narratives*. New Delhi: Kanishka, 2007.

Nanda, Reena. *Kamaladevi Chattopadhyay: A Biography*. Oxford: Oxford University Press, 2002.

Naoroji, Dadabhai. *Poverty and Un-British Rule in India*. London: Swan Sonnenschein, 1901.

Narain, Govind. "India: The Family Planning Program since 1965." *Studies in Family Planning* no. 35 (November 1968): 1–12.

National Planning Committee. *National Health*. Edited by K. T. Shah. Bombay: Vora, 1948.

———. *Report of the Sub-committee on Population*. 2nd ed. Edited by K. T. Shah. Bombay: Vora, 1949.

———. *Woman's Role in Planned Economy*. Bombay: Vora, 1947.

Nicholson, Mervyn. "The Eleventh Commandment: Sex and Spirit in Wollstonecraft and Malthus." *Journal of the History of Ideas* 51, no. 3 (July–September 1990): 401–21.

"Over-Population and Marriage Customs." *Quarterly Journal of the Poona Sarvajanik Sabha* 1, no. 7 (1878): 24–32.

Paik, Shailaja. *Dalit Women's Education in Modern India: Double Discrimination*. London: Routledge, 2014.

Parry, Manon. *Broadcasting Birth Control: Mass Media and Family Planning*. New Brunswick, NJ: Rutgers University Press, 2013.

Parvate, T. V. *Mahadev Govind Ranade: A Biography*. New York: Asia Publishing House, 1963.

Pasyam, Ca. *Pale Tankam: Kutumpak kattuppatu virivakkappattatu* [Well done Thangam: Family planning explained]. N.p., 1961.

Peabody, Norbert. "Cents, Sense, Census: Human Inventories in Late Precolonial and Early Colonial India." *Comparative Studies in Society and History* 43, no. 4 (October 2001): 819–50.

Petchesky, Rosalind Pollack. "From Population Control to Reproductive Rights: Feminist Fault Lines." *Reproductive Health Matters* 3, no. 6 (November 1995): 152–61.

Prakash, Gyan. *Emergency Chronicles: Indira Gandhi and Democracy's Turning Point*. Princeton: Princeton University Press, 2019.

The Queen v. Charles Bradlaugh and Annie Besant (Specially Reported). London: Freethought, n.d.

Rajagopal, Arvind, ed. *The Indian Public Sphere: Readings in Media History*. Oxford: Oxford University Press, 2009.

Rama Rau, Dhanvanthi. "Family Planning in India." *Journal of Sex Research* 3, no. 4 (1967): 272–74.

———. *An Inheritance: The Memoirs of Dhanvanthi Rama Rau*. London: Heinemann, 1977.

Ramusack, Barbara. "Bonnie Babes and Modern Mothers: Baby Weeks in Madras." Paper presented at the 36th Annual Conference on South Asia, Madison WI, October 2007.

———. "Embattled Advocates: The Debate over Birth Control in India, 1920–1940." *Journal of Women's History* 1, no. 2 (Fall 1989): 34–64.

Ranade, M. G. *Essays on Indian Economics: A Collection of Essays and Speeches*. Madras: G. A. Natesan, 1906.

Rao, Mohan. *From Population Control to Reproductive Health: Malthusian Arithmetic*. New Delhi: Sage, 2004.

Rao, Mohan, and Sarah Sexton, eds. *Markets and Malthus: Population, Gender, and Health in Neo-liberal Times*. New Delhi: Sage, 2010.

Report of the Proceedings of the Fifth All India Conference on Family Planning. Patna: Family Planning Association of India, 1964.

Report of the Proceedings of the Sixth International Conference on Planned Parenthood. London: International Planned Parenthood Federation, n.d.

Roberts, Dorothy. *Killing the Black Body: Race, Reproduction, and the Meaning of Liberty*. New York: Vintage, 1998.

Rook-Koepsel, Emily. "Constructing Women's Citizenship: The Local, National, and Global Civics Lessons of Rajkumari Amrit Kaur." *Journal of Women's History* 27, no. 3 (2015): 154–75.

Ross, Loretta, and Rickie Solinger. *Reproductive Justice: An Introduction*. Berkeley: University of California Press, 2017.

Roy, Somnath, ed. *Proceedings of the Seminar on IUCD Nov 29–Dec 1, 1966*. New Delhi: Central Family Planning Institute, n.d.

Rudrappa, Sharmila. *Discounted Life: The Price of Global Surrogacy in India*. New York: NYU Press, 2015.

Sarkar, Sumit. *Modern India, 1885–1947*. New York: St. Martin's, 1989.

Sarkar, Sumit, and Tanika Sarkar, eds. *Women and Social Reform in Modern India: A Reader*. Bloomington: Indiana University Press, 2008.

Sarkar, Tanika. *Hindu Wife, Hindu Nation: Community, Religion, and Cultural Nationalism*. Bloomington: Indiana University Press, 2002.

Sasser, Jade. *On Infertile Ground: Population Control and Women's Rights in the Era of Climate Change*. New York: NYU Press, 2018.

Satyavati, K. *Family Planning (Birth Control)*. 3rd ed. New Delhi: Satyavati Family Planning Center, 1955.

Saville, John, ed. *A Selection of the Social and Political Pamphlets of Annie Besant*. New York: Augustus M. Kelley, 1970.

Schoen, Johanna. *Choice and Coercion: Birth Control, Sterilization, and Abortion in Public Health and Welfare*. Chapel Hill: University of North Carolina Press, 2005.

Sekher, T. V. "Ladlis and Lakshmis: Financial Incentive Schemes for the Girl Child." *Economic and Political Weekly* 47, no. 17 (April 28, 2012): 58–65.

Sen, Amartya. *Poverty and Famine: An Essay on Entitlement and Deprivation*. Oxford: Clarendon, 1981.

Sengupta, Padmini. *Women Workers of India*. New York: Asia Publishing House, 1960.

Sherman, Taylor C. "'A New Type of Revolution': Socialist Thought in India, 1940s–1960s." *Postcolonial Studies* 21, no. 4 (2018): 485–504.

Siegel, Benjamin R. *Hungry Nation: Food, Famine, and the Making of Modern India*. Cambridge: Cambridge University Press, 2018.

Sinha, Mrinalini, ed. *Mother India: Selections from the Controversial 1927 Text*. Ann Arbor: University of Michigan Press, 2000.

———. *Specters of Mother India: The Global Restructuring of an Empire*. Durham, NC: Duke University Press, 2006.

Sinha, Subir. "Lineages of the Developmentalist State: Transnationality and Village India, 1900–1965." *Comparative Studies in Society and History* 50, no. 1 (2008): 57–90.

Smith, Andrea. *Conquest: Sexual Violence and American Indian Genocide*. Durham NC: Duke University Press, 2015.

Southam, A. L., and K. D. Shafer, eds. *Intra-uterine Contraception, Proceedings of the 2nd International Conference Oct 2–3, 1964*. Amsterdam: Excerpta Medica Foundation, 1965.

Sreenivas, Mytheli. "Birth Control in the Shadow of Empire: The Trials of Annie Besant, 1877–1878." *Feminist Studies* 41, no. 3 (2015): 509–37.

———. "Sexuality and Modern Imperialism." In *A Global History of Sexuality: The Modern Era*, edited by Robert M. Buffington, Eithne Luibhéid, and Donna J. Guy, 57–88. Hoboken, NJ: Wiley Blackwell, 2014.

———. *Wives, Widows, and Concubines: The Conjugal Family Ideal in Colonial India*. Bloomington: Indiana University Press, 2008.

Srivastava, Sanjay. *Passionate Modernity: Sexuality, Class, and Consumption in India*. New Delhi: Routledge, 2007.

Stein, Burton, ed. *The Making of Agrarian Policy in British India 1770–1900*. Delhi: Oxford University Press, 1992.

Suitters, Beryl. *Be Brave and Angry: Chronicles of the International Planned Parenthood Federation*. London: International Planned Parenthood Federation, 1973.

Takeshita, Chikako. *The Global Biopolitics of the IUD: How Science Constructs Contraceptive Users and Women's Bodies.* Cambridge, MA: MIT Press, 2012.

Takeuchi-Demirci, Aiko. *Contraceptive Diplomacy: Reproductive Politics and Imperial Ambitions in the United States and Japan.* Redwood City, CA: Stanford University Press, 2018.

Tambe, Ashwini. *Defining Girlhood in India: A Transnational History of Sexual Maturity Laws.* Urbana: University of Illinois Press, 2019.

Tarlo, Emma. "Body and Space in a Time of Crisis: Sterilization and Resettlement during the Emergency in Delhi." In *Violence and Subjectivity*, edited by Veena Das, Arthur Kleinman, and Mamphela Ramphele, 242–70. Berkeley: University of California Press, 2000.

———. *Unsettling Memories: Narratives of the Emergency in Delhi.* Berkeley: University of California Press, 2003.

Taylor, Anne. *Annie Besant: A Biography.* Oxford: Oxford University Press, 1992.

Taylor, Barbara. *Eve and the New Jerusalem: Socialism and Feminism in the Nineteenth Century.* New York: Pantheon Books, 1983.

The Third International Conference on Planned Parenthood: Report of the Proceedings. Bombay: Family Planning Association of India, 1952.

Thomas, Lynn. *Politics of the Womb: Women, Reproduction, and the State in Kenya.* Berkeley: University of California Press, 2003.

Tietze, Christopher, and Sarah Lewit, eds. *Intra-uterine Contraceptive Devices: Proceedings of the Conference, April 30–May 1, 1962.* Amsterdam: Excerpta Medica Foundation, n.d.

Tinker, Hugh. *A New System of Slavery: The Export of Indian Labor Overseas, 1830–1920.* London: Oxford University Press, 1974.

Unnithan, Maya. *Fertility, Health and Reproductive Politics: Re-imagining Rights in India.* London: Routledge, 2019.

Van Hollen, Cecilia. *Birth on the Threshold: Childbirth and Modernity in South India.* Berkeley: University of California Press, 2003.

Venkatachalapathy, A. R. *The Province of the Book: Scholars, Scribes, and Scribblers in Colonial Tamil Nadu.* New Delhi: Permanent Black, 2012.

Venkatesh, Archana. "Women, Medicine and Nation-Building: The 'Lady Doctor' and Development in 20th Century South India." PhD diss., Ohio State University, 2020.

Vernon, James. *Hunger: A Modern History.* Cambridge, MA: Harvard University Press, 2007.

Vicziany, Marika. "Coercion in a Soft State: The Family Planning Program of India: Part 1: The Myth of Voluntarism." *Pacific Affairs* 55, no. 3 (1982): 373–402.

———. "Coercion in a Soft State: The Family Planning Program of India: Part 2: The Sources of Coercion." *Pacific Affairs* 55, no. 4 (1982–83): 557–92.

Visvanathan, Nalini, Lynn Duggan, Nan Wiegersma, and Laurie Nisonoff, eds. *The Women, Gender, and Development Reader.* 2nd ed. London: Zed Books, 2001.

Wadia, Avabai. *The Light Is Ours: Memoirs and Movements.* London: International Planned Parenthood Federation, 2001.

Walby, Kevin, and Michael Haan. "Caste Confusion and Census Enumeration in Colonial India, 1872–1921." *Histoire Sociale/Social History* 45, no. 90 (2012): 301–18.

Washbrook, David. "The Commercialization of Agriculture in Colonial India: Production, Subsistence and Reproduction in the 'Dry South,' c. 1870–1930." *Modern Asian Studies* 28, no. 1 (1994): 129–64.

Wattal, P. K. *The Population Problem in India: A Census Study.* Bombay: Bennett, Coleman, 1934.

Watts, Sheldon. *Epidemics and History: Disease, Power and Imperialism.* New Haven, CT: Yale University Press, 1997.

Wilder, Frank, and D. K. Tyagi. "India's New Departures in Mass Motivation for Fertility Control." *Demography* 5, no. 2 (1968): 773–79.

Williams, Rebecca Jane. "Revisiting the Khanna Study: Population and Development in India, 1953–1960." PhD diss., University of Warwick, 2013.

———. "Storming the Citadels: Family Planning under the Emergency in India, 1975–1977." *Journal of Asian Studies* 73, no. 2 (2014): 471–92.

Winnubst, Shannon. "Review Essay: *No Future: Queer Theory and the Death Drive.*" *Environment and Planning D: Society and Space* 28 (2010): 178–83.

Wolpert, Stanley A. *Tilak and Gokhale: Revolution and Reform in the Making of Modern India.* Berkeley: University of California Press, 1962.

INDEX

146–49; impact of, 126; incentives and targets for, 150–52, 153; tail design in, 148; women's responsibility to accept, 141

IPPF. *See* International Planned Parenthood Federation (IPPF)

Ittmann, Karl, 118

IUDs. *See* intrauterine contraceptive devices (IUDs or IUCDs)

Iyer, Sivasami, 84

J

Jackson, Margaret, 148

Janakakumari, T. S., 178–79

Janata Alliance, 161, 162

Jani, Pranav, 115

Jessen, Don, 148

Jhabvala, M. S. H., 102

John, Mary, 229n4

Joshi, Durgabai. *See* Deshmukh, Durgabai

K

Kale, Anasuyabai, 99–100

Karppatci, allatu cuvatina karppam (anon., 1929), 180–81

Karve, R. D., 102, 121, 173

Kasturi (pseud., Tamil Nadu laborer), 210–11

Keynes, John Maynard, 217n56; *Indian Currency and Finance* (1913), 21

Khan, S. K., 124–25, 136

Khanna study (Harvard), 139

Knowlton, Charles, 30, 54; *Fruits of Philosophy*, 55

Krishnakumar, S. S., 156

Kutumpa kattupatu titta kaiputtakam, 187

L

laboring classes. *See* working class

"lady doctors," 62, 131

Lam, Mithan, 102, 109, 231n24

land, politics regarding: empty lands, 112; land rights, 70–71, 111; and poverty, 49; race and, 13; reproduction and, 45–46; unequal distribution, 141. *See also* migration

League of Nations, 66, 71

Levin, Harry, 152–53

Levine, Philippa, 78

life, calibrating the cost of, 6, 25, 40–44, 60

Lippes, Jack, 146

Lippes loops, 149, 150, 152

loop camps, 150, 151

Luibhéid, Eithne, 200

Lytton, Lord, 40–41, 45

M

macroeconomy, 21

Madhavdas, Keshavlal, 52

Madras Birth Control Bulletin, 84

Madras Health and Baby Week, 62–63, 66

Madras Malthusian League, 58, 60, 180

Madras Neo-Malthusian League, 24, 83, 84, 85, 209, 227n66

Madras State. *See* Tamil Nadu

Mahatma Gandhi National Rural Employment Guarantee Act, 208

Mahomedpur village, 124–25, 136

Maiti, Hari Mohan, 53

Malabari, Behramji, 23, 60, 180; "Notes on Infant Marriage and Enforced Widowhood," 50–52

Mallet, Louis, 46–47

Malthus, Thomas: and birth control, 55; critiques of, 17–19; *Essay on the Principle of Population* (1798), 16–17, 44; and large families, 180; and relief to the poor, 29; on sexual continence, 45

Malthusianism: colonial policies during famine, 44–47; critiques of, 49, 53; famine and, 45, 59; and increases in food production, 145; and marriage, 47–54; in Modi's speech, 207; national rereading of, 50; neo-Malthusian thought, 55, 56, 57, 58, 59, 64, 77. *See also* child marriage; climate change; demographic transition theory; heterosexuality; marriage; overpopulation; population control

Malthusian League, 55, 57–58, 223n115. *See also* Madras Malthusian League

Margulies, Lazar, 146

marriage: female desire and heterosexuality in, 179; Indian history of, 6; and Malthusian policies, 47–54; marriage age, 5, 159, 239n96; normative sexual

www.ingramcontent.com/pod-product-compliance
Lightning Source LLC
Chambersburg PA
CBHW030344270326
41926CB00009B/951